On the outskirts of West Belfast in Northern Ireland, and in the shadow of the Black Mountain, is situated the predominantly Catholic community of Andersonstown. Between November 1971 and March 1972 this small area of land, which is just two miles long by one mile deep, became the scene of many gun-battles between the men of 9 (Plassey) Battery, Royal Artillery and 1st Battalion Belfast Brigade, Irish Republican Army.

This book is a record of the violent clashes which took place on an almost daily basis on housing estates which looked no different than those found on mainland Britain. After the events of 'Bloody Sunday' in Londonderry on 30 January 1972 in which 13 civilians were shot dead, the attacks against the soldiers intensified to an unprecedented scale. The whole community of Andersonstown appeared to rise up against the small band of men from 9 Battery.

There are truly terrifying accounts from 20 of the men who took part in the struggle to maintain the peace on the streets of Andersonstown. They describe how it felt to face the rioters, and how it felt to be under attack from the Provo gunmen. Contemporary newspaper reports have been used to illustrate the viewpoints of both sides involved in the conflict. The book contains many recently discovered photographs of the arms and explosives found by the battery in their searches. None of these images have ever been published before. There are also reproduced statements issued by the Provisional IRA which originally appeared in *The Volunteer* news sheet issued around the estates, and these serve to corroborate some of the astonishing tales told by the soldiers.

This is the only book about the Troubles in Northern Ireland which covers just one single tour of duty as seen through the eyes of the men who were there. By the end of the tour in March 1972, the IRA in Andersonstown had been almost completely destroyed as a fighting force. The 110-strong unit of men of 9 Battery were given a task to do, to crack 'The Toughest Nut' – and they gave it their all.

Steve Corbett has had a lifelong interest in military history and the collecting of artefacts from the Great War. At the age of 12 he joined the local Army Cadet unit in Hulme, Manchester and remained a member until he decided to join the Regular Army in 1969.

After serving in Germany for two years – and completing two tours of duty in Northern Ireland – Steve finally left the army in November 1974 and transferred to the Reserves. He moved to Warrington with his wife Pam in 1977 and took up a career in the chemical industry. He retired early in 2001 and in 2008 decided to turn the diaries he kept while serving in Northern Ireland into a book: *Belfast Diaries: A Gunner in Northern Ireland,* which was eventually published in July 2013 by Helion. Steve still lives in Warrington, where he spends much of his free time with his two daughters and two grandchildren.

A TOUGH NUT TO CRACK: ANDERSONSTOWN

VOICES FROM 9 BATTERY ROYAL ARTILLERY IN NORTHERN IRELAND, NOVEMBER 1971–MARCH 1972

Steve Corbett

Helion & Company

Helion & Company Limited
26 Willow Road
Solihull
West Midlands
B91 1UE
England
Tel. 0121 705 3393
Fax 0121 711 4075
Email: info@helion.co.uk
Website: www.helion.co.uk
Twitter: @helionbooks
Visit our blog http://blog.helion.co.uk/

Published by Helion & Company 2015

Designed and typeset by Bookcraft Ltd, Stroud, Gloucestershire
Cover designed by Euan Carter, Leicester (www.euancarter.com)
Printed by Henry Ling Limited, Dorchester, Dorset

Front cover: A mobile patrol from 2 Troop (Courtesy of Steve Corbett).
Rear cover: The flag of 9 (Plassey) Battery (Courtesy of Steve Corbett).

ISBN 978-1-910294-49-9

For details of other military history titles published by Helion & Company Limited
contact the above address, or visit our website: http://www.helion.co.uk.

We always welcome receiving book proposals from prospective authors.

For my two grandchildren, Emily and Tom – an absolute joy to behold.

Contents

List of Photographs and Maps

List of Contributors

Gordon 'Addi' Adamson
Paul Agnello
Renzo Peterson Agnello
Clancy Campbell
Steve Corbett
Brian 'Horace' Corser
Mike Fall
Mick 'Titch' Friel
Phil Gallagher
Keith 'Snowy' H***
Pete Hodkinson
Robert Ian Isherwood
Pete Krasnowski
Mick McHale
'Moira'
James 'Slim' Murray
'Ginger' Robertson
Pete 'Taffy' Roberts
Richard Rothwell
'Davey' S*******
Tony 'Sammy' Symonds
Bob Wilson

Foreword

The history of the British Army has its moments of glory, but there was nothing glorious about the campaign in Northern Ireland in the 1970s. At home it was divisive and generally unpopular. On the ground in cities such as Belfast and Londonderry, it was a thoroughly nasty war fought in backstreets and housing estates. Here the urban scene could suddenly become transformed into a battleground, but one where the soldier could seldom identify his foe – and even when he did, had to conform to restrictive rules in which error could lead to prosecution. It often seemed that every man's – and woman's – hand was against him and that he was surrounded by hostility. It did not even merit the distinction of its own campaign medal.

But the professional soldier cannot choose his campaigns. His duty is simply to get on with the task in hand – in this case to hold the ring and buy enough time, sometimes with his life, for the politicians to find a solution. It is a situation that he has found himself in all too often in recent years.

What did that entail in a Belfast suburb such as Andersonstown, which was a hotbed of Irish Republicanism? The real story can only be told by those who were out on those hostile streets by day and night; who had to face the bombs and bullets; and deal with the violent mobs that would erupt from nowhere. For a few months in the winter of 1971-72 when the IRA campaign was at its height, amid all the chaos one man kept a diary. Over 40 years on, he has combined it with the recollections of some of his comrades, checked the accounts against contemporary records and set them in context of what was happening across the Province at that time. The result is an extraordinarily lively, accurate and detailed picture of what the British soldier did, and thought, and felt in Northern Ireland at that time. It is perhaps unique in that the recollections are entirely those of the 'rank and file'; no contributor wore more than two stripes on his arm at the time. Unsurprisingly, their memoirs pull no punches and their views are forthright.

The account brings out the character of the British soldier under duress, his good humour and his commonsense, but what emerges most strongly is his enduring spirit. I knew these men and I have good reason to be grateful to them, for they did all that was asked of them – and more. It was an honour to have served with them.

Brigadier B.C.M. Harding CBE MC.
March 2014

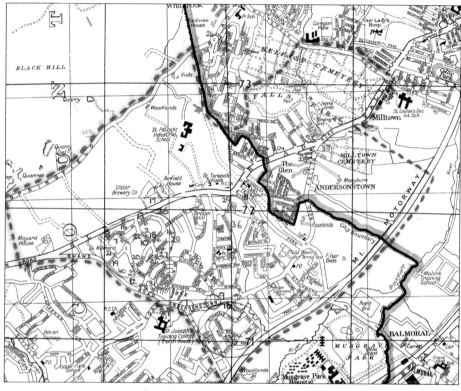

Area map of Andersonstown. (Courtesy of Brian Corser)

Preface

I have had a passion for military history for nearly all my life – and as a very young child in the 1950s, my relatives would often talk to me of their experiences when they served in the last war. As I grew older I became more interested in the Great War and spent hours in the local library reading everything I could on the subject. My first taste of wearing uniform was when I had a spell in the Boy Scouts and went on several camps with them, but all I really wanted to do was join the local unit of the Air Training Corps near where I lived in Wythenshawe, Manchester.

I was now 11 years of age and decided to present myself to the local cadet unit and see about joining up. My first shock was when I was told that I was too young. I would be allowed to join in with the activities at the drill hall, but I couldn't have a uniform. I stuck it out for a few weeks, but not being able to wear the battledress and not being allowed to go on the weekend camps proved too much for me and I left. A few weeks later I found out about an Army Cadet unit in Hulme, Manchester and one Friday night I took myself along to see if they would let me join.

I walked in and presented myself to the Sergeant-Major of 252 Hulme Cadet Battery, Royal Artillery and asked him if I could join. He didn't seem the least bit bothered that I was under the required age limit, and I was soon kitted out with a complete uniform, set of webbing and boots. I couldn't believe it; it seemed to me at the tender age of 11, that I was finally a soldier. The following weekend I was on a training exercise at a military camp in Otterburn. There were regular trips to the ranges with the .303 rifle and Bren gun and courses to learn about map reading and field craft. I was in my element and loved every minute of it.

I had only just celebrated my 17th birthday on 1 January 1969 and had recently been told by the Battery Commander that I was going to be promoted to Sergeant – and then a few days later, I was in Manchester city centre with a friend of mine when we both decided to pop in to the Army Recruiting Office in Fountain Street for a bit of a laugh. I never was sure what happened next, but before I knew it I had accepted the Queen's shilling, took an oath on the Bible and signed on for six years with the Colours and another six with the Reserves. By 24 January I was bound for Woolwich and the start of my training. Because I was only 17, I was in the rather bizarre situation of being too old to be accepted into Boys' service and too young to join the Regulars. I have no recollection of me ever having to seek the permission of my mother to join either, but as far as I know it should have been a legal requirement due to my age; but the understanding I was given at the time was that my first year of service wouldn't count. After training I was posted to 12th Light Air Defence Regiment, Royal Artillery at Napier Barracks, Brackel in Dortmund.

In 1971 the regiment returned back to England to undertake ceremonial duties in London, and then not long after, a tour of duty in Northern Ireland. This was to be the first of my two tours with the regiment. The second tour was to be my last before I left the army for good. I don't know why I did it, but on both of my tours I kept detailed diaries of everything I was personally involved in while over there. On leaving the army the diaries were put away and largely forgotten about until the end of 2007.

By that time I was suffering from a rather debilitating illness, and in 2008 I started a course of treatment which was to last a full year. I decided that it might be a good idea to dig out my original diaries and turn them into a book to give myself something to do, and out of this came my original book, *Belfast Diaries, A Gunner In Northern Ireland*. It was based entirely on my diaries, both my tours in Belfast, and was very much about me and my own experiences – although a few of my former army friends did contribute. The original diaries which I kept at the time proved to be a powerful and important primary source of information from a largely 'forgotten' war. Because of the diaries I was able to put dates and times to many of the incidents in which I was involved. After the book was completed I set about finding a publisher which covered modern conflicts and came across the website of Helion & Company – a specialist military bookseller. I submitted my manuscript to them and not long after, Duncan Rogers got in touch with me and offered me a contract. The book was eventually published in July 2013 and several members of my former regiment purchased a copy.

I was asked by the publisher to do another book on the subject, but this time just purely about my tour in Andersonstown. This was by far the worst of both my tours – and is also the one which former members of the battery remember the most. Fortunately for me, as a result of my original book, I was contacted by an ex-member of 9 Battery who offered to help. It was decided from the start that the next book would be, as far as I could make it, a history of that particular tour in Andersonstown. There would be no references to my diaries; just the testimonies of the men who were there.

At the end of August 2013, I was paid a visit by Brian Corser, who had taken the trouble to travel down all the way from his home in Lincolnshire to see me. With him he had brought his collection of photographs and his much treasured scrapbook which he had so diligently kept while in Andersonstown. It was a wealth of information; there were newspaper cuttings, photographs of all the arms and explosives finds, and much more. Without this material it would have been extremely difficult for me to piece together the events which took place in Andersonstown. Besides the scrapbook he was also instrumental in putting me in touch with many of the people who have contributed to the book. For this I owe him a debt of gratitude.

Because this new book is a record of what we all experienced in Andersonstown, I have included all the stories of incidents which appeared in the original book, but I have been able to include additional information from people who were there at the time. Because I was asked by Duncan Rogers to write a second book, I was able to revisit several incidents featured in the original book and cover them again in more detail and from a different perspective – building a more rounded picture than I could ever have done from my single original account. There are still gaps in the story of what happened during that most frightening four-month period of the tour, and for that I apologise.

As far as possible I have used the correct names of those involved. Certain names have been omitted or changed to protect the identities of people I was unable to contact, or because they chose not to have their full name used. I would like to thank Brigadier Harding CBE MC for his invaluable insight into some of the operations the battery undertook. Indeed I would like to thank everyone who has contributed to the book, and also Duncan Rogers for having faith in me as a writer; and my son-in-law, Christian Ewen, whose amazing skills at proofreading have contributed so much to the book.

The title of the book was derived from a message given to the regiment at the completion of their tour by the General Officer commanding Northern Ireland, Lieutenant-General Sir Harry Tuzo KCB OBE MC in which he stated the following:

> You were certainly confronted with 'the toughest nut' and you have made great progress in cracking it. With any luck we shall get to the kernel very soon indeed thanks to your splendid work.

Although this book is about the men of 9 (Plassey) Battery, we were not the only members of 12th Regiment serving in Northern Ireland. There were also the men of 'T' Battery (Shah Sujah's Troop), 58 (Eyre's) Battery and HQ Battery. They too served in their respective areas in an exemplary manner – and they also deserve credit for their achievements on that most dangerous of tours.

I made a claim in my previous book, *Belfast Diaries*, that at the end of the tour, a serving officer from the regiment had said that 9 Battery had come under the most sustained period of attack that any unit of the British Army had faced since the end of the Second World War. In the light of information recently supplied to me, I would like to put the record straight.

A newspaper report published shortly after the tour in Andersonstown said that 9 Battery had been subjected to the highest concentration of gunfire that any unit in the British Army had faced since the end of the Korean War. The same report went on to say that we had arrested a record-breaking number of 30 officers and 46 volunteers of the IRA. This then is the story of the sometimes ferocious battles which took place between the men of 9 (Plassey) Battery, the 1st Battalion Belfast Brigade, the Provisional IRA, the Official IRA and the local community of Andersonstown.

1

Shock news and ceremonial duties

Around May 1971, the men of 12th Light Air Defence Regiment, Royal Artillery had just been informed that in July they would be returning to Barton Stacey in Hampshire from their present base at Napier Barracks in Dortmund. The regiment at that time was made up of 9 (Plassey) Battery – the senior battery – 'T' (Shah Sujah's Troop) Battery, 58 (Eyre's) Battery and HQ Battery. Prior to returning, they were to immediately start learning the ceremonial duties which the Guards Regiment carried out at the Bank of England, St James's Palace, the Tower of London, and Buckingham Palace. The civil unrest in Northern Ireland, which had started back in 1969, was beginning to spread – and as a result, more British troops were being sent over there to try and bring order back to the streets. The Guards Regiment had been earmarked for a four-month tour of duty in the Province, and so the men of 12th Regiment received orders to take over the public duties of the Guards. After completion of their public duties they too were to immediately start training for their own four months' tour in Northern Ireland.

The news came as a bit of a shock to everyone. It would be fair to say that most of the regiment paid little attention to what was going on back home in England, and even less to the unrest building up in Ulster. The regiment at that time was armed with the Bofors 40mm L70 anti-aircraft gun which was designed to protect against low-level air attacks. It was an extremely accurate and versatile weapons system which could be guided and fired via the FCE7 radar, or completely independent of it. Many former gunners remember it with great fondness. Much of the regiment's time was spent honing their battle skills in the defensive anti-aircraft role with annual trips to the firing camps at Todendorf on the Baltic coast, Den Helder in Holland, and the occasional trip to Mourmelon-le-Grande in France. Exercises were carried out on a regular basis over much of the training grounds of West Germany as part of the NATO commitment to the protection of the borders of Western Europe. The perceived threat came from the might of the Russian Army and its Eastern Bloc allies. If there was going to be a war, it would be here that the regiment would be engaged in battle.

Regular aircraft recognition classes were held so that all personnel were kept up to date with the latest aircraft types used by the Eastern Bloc. Even back then, several of the aircraft types being flown by the Russian allies were of Second World War origin. The emphasis was always on the importance of correct identification of aircraft. Cases of misidentification from the Second World War where Allied aircraft had been shot down by friendly fire were often discussed, and the

On the firing point at Todendorf. (Courtesy of Brian Corser)

reasons for the errors were examined in detail. One of the regular trips for live-firing exercises was to the ranges of Todendorf up on the Baltic coast.

The ranges faced out to sea, and the guns would be spaced out along the firing apron where their target would be a wind-sock towed by a bright red Hawker Sea Fury which would come in from the sea at an angle to the guns. It was rumoured at the time that the aircraft were flown by women pilots. Many years later the author was in conversation with a former member of the post-war *Luftwaffe* who claimed that this was indeed the case, and he told the author that they were owned and flown by Baroness Riebnitz von Thyssen and her small band of women pilots. It was indeed a sight to see, when at the end of the day's shoot, the aircraft would come in over the guns from the right at zero feet and fly the full length of the firing apron before pulling up and giving a 'victory roll' before disappearing into the distance.

It was a considerably long journey from Dortmund to Todendorf, and usually the regiment would park up overnight on the way up to give the drivers a much needed rest. Quite often, the wagons would be laagered near the old concentration camp of Belsen. Very little of the camp remained, but there were huge mass graves containing the remains of thousands who perished at the hands of the Nazis.

The trips to the ranges at Mourmelon-le-Grande in France were to carry out ground shoots with the Bofors at soft-skinned vehicles, and to train with the

The memorial at Belsen. (Courtesy of Brian Corser)

infantry weapons that every regiment held as protection against attack on their gun positions from enemy infantry. One rather novel aspect of this training was for the AA guns to be hitched up and towed around by the Leyland 10-ton wagons while the gun crews fired at wooden cut-outs of tanks which moved along a rail. On one such shoot the fired rounds hit the targets and carried on through for some distance before hitting the ground – bouncing up and carrying on to the range-warden's, hut which ended up being destroyed by fire.

Gnr Steve Corbett, 3 Troop

I remember the last trip I had to Mourmelon. It was a weird place, and it was like stepping back in time. It was just like you saw in these old war films with the drinking establishments near a village square. One of the shops had hung out banners to welcome us, and there was a band playing at some kind of show they had put on for us. The local Mayor was there wearing his sash. To me it really did feel as though we were being treated like some liberating army; everyone was so friendly.

A few days later we went out onto the ranges to have a go with the 3.5-inch Bazooka rocket launcher. I remember being in the back of this wagon going along a wooded country lane, and then we came to a large open patch of land which was full of old First World War trenches and bits of old field guns. I couldn't believe what I was seeing. I was just 17, and I was seeing things that I had only ever read about in library books; I was actually driving through some of the old First World War battlefields. A bit further on we came to a track that turned into some woods and then we reached another clearing. Not many yards ahead was the rusting hulk of an old Sherman tank, and that was to be our target for the rocket launcher. I was put with a lad by the name of 'Jock' H*******, and we were to take it in turns to fire the launcher. He had the first go and I acted as his loader.

The procedure was for the firer to take the prone position and lift the launcher onto his shoulder. The person acting as loader would insert the rocket into the back of the tube and connect the two wires to the terminals. When that was done you tapped the firer on the shoulder to let him know the gun was loaded. So I did all that, lay down next to him and tapped him on the shoulder and he pulls the trigger. I watched in amazement as the rocket sailed right over the top of the tank and took several feet off the top of a tree as it exploded. 'Jock' said it was my fault for tapping him on the shoulder and spoiling his aim! Then it was my turn – and when I fired the rocket I felt a sharp pain between my shoulder blades. I reached up with my hand and found that a coil of wire from the back of the rocket had embedded itself in my back.

Another time I went on the ranges with Pete C**** from London. We were given a Bren with a spare barrel and a full case of magazines each to blast away. If memory serves me correct there were about 12 magazines in the case, and each magazine was designed to hold 30 rounds, but you only ever loaded 28 rounds to prevent jams. We had a great time firing at an old Ferret armoured car which we had covered in tin cans and anything else we could find.

There was a trip laid on to the old battlefields of Verdun as well. This was right up my street, because I was fascinated by the history of the First World War. As a youngster I had read a book written by Alistair Horne, *The Price of Glory: Verdun 1916*. When we got there, a group of us were assembled together in this field not far from Fort Daumont, and it didn't matter where you stood; you were in a shell hole. It was just like the surface of the moon. I remembered the book and the photographs of the battered structure of Daumont, and I never thought that I would actually visit the site. This old French soldier came over and we formed a circle around him. He was a veteran of the fighting and was to be our guide. He started to address us and then just broke down in tears; he couldn't do it and he walked away sobbing.

I found it profoundly moving that even after all those years he still found it so upsetting to talk about his experiences as a soldier. After that I went for a walk through the woods which covered much of the battlefield. They had been planted after the end of the war to try and hide the scars of the battle. When you looked up into the trees you could see bits of leather equipment and helmets hanging in the branches. They had been lifted out of the ground as the trees grew. My last trip there was in 1970.

The ranges at Den Helder in Holland were somewhat different than those used at Todendorf, and instead of aircraft towing the target, there were radio-controlled drones. The instructions were NEVER to fire at the drones and concentrate on the wind-sock which was being towed behind, but the temptation at times was just too great, and at the back of the control room was a collection of wreckage from the drones which had 'accidentally' been shot down as they came over the guns; but the happy times spent at the firing camps, the war games and the trips to old battlefields were now over. The regiment returned to England and settled into their new base at Barton Stacey in Hampshire and continued with

Bombardier Corser with a Corporal from the Guards Regiment outside Buckingham Palace. (Courtesy of Brian Corser)

their training for their duties in London. An instructor was sent down from the Guards Depot to oversee the complex drill which the regiment would be expected to carry out on their deployment. Each building had its own set ceremonies. The Tower of London for instance had the ceremony of the keys when each night the guard would be challenged with the command:

> "Halt, who goes there?"
> The reply was: "The keys."
> The guard would again be challenged: "Whose keys?"
> And the answer would be: "The Queen's keys."

All these different ceremonies had to be learned off by heart, but by the end of August the regiment was ready to take over their allotted duties.

The army made full use of the fact that an artillery regiment was taking over the role of guarding the Sovereign and her heirs; it was something which 12th Regiment had never done before and the publicity generated was tremendous. The regiment earned the nickname of 'The Lancashire and Cumbrian Gunners' because their recruiting drives were mainly carried out in the north-west of England. As a result, the regiment featured heavily in the newspapers from around the area.

2

Training to 'keep the peace' and playing for real

By the end of September the regiment had finished their ceremonial duties in London and were back home in Barton Stacey. They had received much acclaim for the way they conducted themselves in the capital, and also for the standard of their drill and smart turnout. The regiment immediately turned its attention to the training for their tour in Northern Ireland, where they were to be posted towards the end of November. They only had about six weeks to prepare, and there was much to do to transform themselves from being an artillery regiment to taking on the role of the infantry. For one member of B Troop, the very thought of being sent to Northern Ireland filled him with absolute dread. He packed up his belongings a few days before the training started, and disappeared from the base, never to be seen again.

It was decided from the very start that all training for the regiment would be carried out as realistically as possible to prepare everyone for whatever situation they may face in Belfast. The thinking behind this approach was that the harder the training, the better the men would be able to cope with whatever they faced once over there. After settling back into their new surroundings in Hampshire, the battery immediately started their training for their new role as peacekeepers on the streets of Northern Ireland. Back in those days there were none of the establishments which the military had in later years for training troops in the techniques of fighting terrorists in an urban environment. The bases which were in use at the time were largely centered on the needs of the infantryman fighting in open terrain.

The Battery Commander, Major Harding, travelled over to Lenadoon in Belfast – the originally intended deployment for 9 (Plassey) Battery – to spend three days with the unit he was to replace to assess the kind of training which would best suit his men. There were only six weeks to go before deployment, and there was little time to spare if the men were to be ready for the operational tour. Upon the BC's return to Barton Stacey the men were immediately put into a rigorous training regime which he had devised. He wanted the training to concentrate on weapons handling and marksmanship – with particular emphasis on snap shooting from the type of cover usually associated with the built-up urban area of modern housing estates. Every man would be expected to be fit enough to withstand the rigours of a four-month operational tour which would leave little free time for recreational needs. With being an artillery regiment, the infantry skills of the men were wholly inadequate, and they would have to learn from scratch the techniques of both foot and mobile patrols which they would be required to carry out.

The NCOs, who had once been responsible for the running of the Bofors guns of the regiment, now had to learn how to lead their men through some of the most dangerous and toughest areas of Belfast. Urban warfare is hard enough for the seasoned infantryman to carry out, but for the artilleryman it was a case of having to take on board new skills and learn what the foot soldier had spent years perfecting – and the regiment had very little time to prepare themselves for their peacekeeping role in the Province. As the process of transforming from the role of air defence to that of the infantryman began, the regiment moved down to Ogbourne St George, Wiltshire where they practised their anti-riot drills and patrolling techniques. Eventually they moved on to Lydd in Kent to continue with their training where the Commanding Officer of the regiment, Lieutenant-Colonel R.F. Vincent, had devised a regimentally-set test exercise for each battery in turn. Upon arrival, the men were faced by a huge barricade which was blazing away quite fiercely. The barricade was manned by a crew of very willing 'volunteers' from Headquarters Battery, who seemed to take great delight in subjecting the attacking troops to fierce volleys of rocks and petrol bombs.

The exercise planners clearly expected this formidable barricade to hold up the attacking soldiers for some time while they thought of the best way of dealing with it, but when it came to the turn of 9 Battery, they simply charged straight in – scattering the defenders and taking control in a matter of minutes. No doubt it helped that they had recognised their opponents as the men of Headquarters Battery and it gave them added impetus, as the men of 9 Battery had a few scores to settle with them. Once the barricade was out of the way, the men of 9 Battery covered the area with mobile and standing patrols for the rest of the day and night. This frustrated the organisers, who were unable to set up many of the incidents which they had planned, and when the exercise ended, the BC was heard to mutter to the BSM: "I think we may have won."

They had indeed won. As a result, the men of 9 Battery were awarded the rather dubious prize of Andersonstown rather than their original destination of Lenadoon for their operational deployment.

Gnr Steve Corbett, 3 Troop

We were split into two opposing groups. One was supposed to be the rioters and the other the soldiers. We really took things seriously, and we used rocks and all kinds of stuff in the riots. Even proper petrol bombs were used. It was easy to fall into the particular role you were playing, and you really did try to hit the 'soldiers' when you played the part of the rioter.

I remember on one occasion after a particularly nasty 'riot' when we were being forced back through a gate in the compound by the soldiers. Someone in the crowd threw a petrol bomb towards the troops. It hit a concrete gatepost and covered the legs of L/Bdr Les Bradshaw in burning petrol. It was a bit of a shock to see him there with his legs blazing. Several people rushed forward and beat out the flames. Fortunately for Les he came to no harm. I think that brought many of us to our senses, and made us realise that what we were training for was deadly serious and not just some silly game.

The men playing the part of the soldiers were issued with small metal riot shields and a baton. The shield offered very little in the way of protection, and the opposing group who played the part of the rioters took advantage of this and aimed their rocks at the exposed legs of the troops. It stood the men in good stead for the realities of the rioting on the streets of Belfast though, as they soon learned how to avoid the missiles thrown at them. Some of the tactics used at that time caused absolute astonishment to a soldier from 2 Troop.

L/Bdr 'Ginger' Robertson, 2 Troop
I remember the 24 hours I spent at the battle-school at Lydd, Kent. We were to be bloodied – literally! The old square formation we were told to adopt to face the opposition was a disaster, which resulted in numerous injuries. I thought at the time that we had just entered the 1970s – not the 1870s for God's sake! Through trial and error we quickly adopted more modern and individual methods. Train hard and fight easy was the motto, but the real thing turned out to be a lot worse.

As the training continued, the regiment moved to Imber – an old village which had been requisitioned by the army during the last war. It had originally been taken over so that troops could be trained in the art of street-to-street fighting in readiness for the D-Day Landings of 1944. The villagers were assured that at the end of hostilities they would get their village back, but they never did. It was here that the men were taught how to use the night vision equipment, and how to drive around streets in total darkness. Each man was given a new foresight post for his rifle, which had a luminous glass bead in it. All that had to be done was to rotate the post through 90° when on night patrol, and in theory there was a perfectly usable sighting aid, but in practice it was absolutely useless! Some of the infantry tactics being taught at that time defied belief. They really didn't seem to be the kind of methods which would need to be used against the IRA.

Gnr Steve Corbett, 3 Troop

The infantry instructors split us up into sections and had us rushing around these old houses. You would dash up to the window and lob a grenade in before bursting through the door with your rifle at the ready. I thought it was stupid really. I hadn't much idea about what was actually going on in Northern Ireland, but I just couldn't imagine we would have to do anything like that.

Bdr Renzo Peterson Agnello, 2 Troop

Prior to going to Northern Ireland we practised our infantry skills once more, and we had at our disposal a wee village which at that time was being used solely for the training of troops going to Northern Ireland. One troop would play the part of terrorists while another troop would play the part of soldiers.

L/Bdr 'Ginger' Robertson, 2 Troop

I always felt uneasy at Imber. It was like the ghosts of the old residents were following you around and watching what you were doing. I was glad when we moved out of there.

The training at the village finished and the regiment moved back to Lydd, where there were more mock riots to face, and another injury…

Bdr Brian 'Horace' Corser, 2 Troop

We had reached the end of training at Lydd, and we decided to have one last big riot before returning back to Barton Stacey. This huge barricade had been built across the camp road. Some of the regiment was one side of it playing the part of the rioters, and we had to storm it.

The rioters set fire to the barricade just before we stormed it, and all the lads were really wound up and got into the role they were playing. We started running forward and (Sgt) 'Punchy' Wilmot pulled out a Webley riot gun and fired it at the rioters on the other side. The stupid bastard had loaded it with a flare instead of a rubber bullet though, and the burning flare hit someone on the leg and took a piece of his thigh away. We carried on and started jumping over the barricade. I seem to remember we christened it 'The Grand National'.

Gnr Clancy Campbell, 1 Troop

I know it was only coincidence, but when I think back to the training and those that got injured doing it like Johnny Sutton, Renzo and others, it was them that got injured again when we went to Andersonstown and did it for real.

Bdr Renzo Peterson Agnello, 2 Troop

I remember we were playing the part of the troops attempting to move back the guys playing the part of the terrorists, and at times it would become very tense and no holds barred. Well this brick hit me around the eye, cut my face and broke my glasses. I saw the guy who threw the brick and went after him – and it turns out he was a Captain. It's not very often you get the chance to have it out with an officer, and we had a right old ding-dong until Sergeant-Major Don Potter pulled us apart.

The regiment returned to Barton Stacey and carried on honing their battle-skills before their impending deployment to Northern Ireland. Unlike the other two batteries, the men of 9 Battery spent much of the remaining time practising their patrol techniques around the camp at night and resting by day. On one occasion there was a section out doing a night patrol on the derelict land opposite the base. They spotted a car and decided to investigate. Inside were a courting couple, and so the rumour goes, someone saw his wife looking up into the glow of his torch. Searches were also carried out on married quarters to add even more realism to the training. The men were pushed to their limits at times, and for one soldier, the added pressure led to an incident which was to cost him the loss of his embarkation leave – and one last chance to see his relatives before going on active service.

Gnr Dick Rothwell, 2 Troop

I remember once, during the training, when I was designated as the radio operator on one of the foot patrols we practised around the camp … At that time we were using the A42 radio set which was carried in a harness on the back. No-one else wanted the job because of its size and weight, but I was the one picked to do it, and I just had to get on with it. There was this Staff Sergeant in charge of us. We set off patrolling, and after a while I started to get tired through carrying the radio, and I guess I must have slowed up a bit. All of a sudden I was pushed from behind, and the Staff Sergeant is telling me: "*Come on Rothwell, get a move on.*" I muttered something to him under my breath and carried on going – and then I felt another push in the back, and then it happened again.

By now I was pretty fed up with this. I was doing my best to keep up, and the last thing I wanted was for someone to keep pushing me in the back. So I stopped, turned around, and I said something to him. I can't remember what it was, but it was obviously the wrong thing to do – because I ended up being put on a charge. I was taken to the guard room and put under lock and key; and that was where

> I ended up spending my two weeks' embarkation leave. I was only released when we were leaving for Northern Ireland – and I wasn't happy about that at all. What if I had been killed in Ireland and my relatives had been denied the chance of seeing me before I left?

All this extra training which was carried out by the men of 9 Battery would prove its worth when it came to the real thing on the streets of Andersonstown. The men left as little as possible to chance – studying as much as was then known on the weapons and tactics used by the IRA. They practised how to deal with an ambush and worked on their weapon training and marksmanship, although their use seemed to be much restricted by the Rules of Engagement contained in the 'yellow card' which everyone had to be familiar with – but the men still had a lot to learn. Much of their training had been rudimentary compared with what the army provided in later years. In particular, units warned for service in Northern Ireland got to know a great deal more about how the IRA operated. Some of this was taken from a paper that the BC of 9 Battery wrote based on his own experiences after their tour in Andersonstown. The section dealing with 'The Opposition' is worth quoting here to show just what the men were up against:

> Both the Official and the Provisional IRA are organised on similar lines. Within Belfast the Belfast Brigade is organised on an area basis down to battalions and companies; companies are further sub-divided into sections. The rank and file are known as volunteers, and company strength will depend on a number of factors – including our own successes – but seldom exceeded 40 or 50. At the other end of the scale a number of Belfast companies had been reduced earlier this year to two or three members or had been completely eliminated.
>
> There are almost identical staff organisations at brigade, battalion and company level. The Commander is assisted by his Adjutant who, as well as acting as Second-in-Command, is responsible for recruiting and discipline. The next most important appointment is the Quartermaster who is responsible for weapons, explosives and ammunition. Usually only these three officers know the locations of arms dumps.
>
> The Engineering Officer is the explosives expert. The Finance Officer in addition to holding the funds looks after billeting. The Transport Officer runs the fleet of stolen cars and equips them with false number plates. The Intelligence Officer's task is to gather information for all types of operations and in particular to record the movements of members of the Security Forces and to try and establish patterns of behaviour for future ambushes or murders.
>
> All the officers and most of the volunteers will have addresses known to the Security Forces but all will be 'on the run', staying in billets or 'safe houses'

arranged by the Finance Officer, with sympathisers or by intimidation. They may change their billets as often as two or three times each week. Members of the IRA are normally, although not always, unemployed and unless an early morning operation is planned they tend to rise late. Their first commitment is to report to a 'calling house', to register that they have not been arrested during the night and to collect any orders. A further meeting at a 'safe house' will take place in the afternoon or during the evening depending on what operations were due to take place.

Operations generally take three main forms. Armed hold-ups are very much routine and provide the organisation with funds to purchase arms, pay cash retainers to volunteers, and provide billeting money. Bombing operations against targets in the city centre or against Protestant areas call for rather more specialised preparation. The device has to be planned with the particular task in mind, assembled, planted and armed. The Engineering Officer will usually hand-pick his own squad for the actual planting.

The third type of operation is the ambush of Security Forces. This is often very well planned and a number of ingenious ways are used to draw troops into the ambush. Hoax telephone calls, contrived accidents and erection of barricades with burning vehicles to light up our own troops, are all common. One particular ambush in my area involved a dummy containing explosives tied to a railing in a particularly dark area. This was reported to the police network as a tarring and feathering and there was in fact a man tarred and shot in both legs a short distance away. The patrol which investigated the figure was suspicious and remained in their armoured vehicles; a passing civilian was injured when the device was detonated. In this case, as in most ambushes, the explosive device was used in conjunction with automatic fire. Another typical ambush used pistol shots at a passing patrol to attempt to get troops to enter a small area of waste ground in the follow-up. Planted in the waste ground was a large and particularly nasty Claymore type of mine. This also was a failure from the opposition's point of view.

The most successful IRA ambushes used a common technique. The troops' attention was diverted by low-velocity automatic fire from one direction. Then from another direction a sniper in a well-concealed position, such as the back of a darkened room, inflicted the casualties with a high-velocity weapon possibly fitted with telescopic sights. This made it extremely difficult to identify targets, particularly as the initial diversionary firing was un-aimed and the firer did not expose himself.

Subsidiary operations included long-range sniping and the constant harassment of military foot and vehicle patrols; using petrol, acid and gelignite bombs; bottles filled with paint; and lumps of rock and iron. Most of these missiles are thrown by teenaged and even younger children who have become extremely proficient at the game. Such activities are organised through the IRA youth organisation – the Fianna – whilst the Auxiliaries, a part-time force, carry out reconnaissance, scouting and local warning activities in the Roman Catholic estates.*

At the time of their deployment to Andersonstown, the BC had at his disposal approximately 110 men. Around 90 of these were formed into three troops to carry out the actual policing of the area. Every patrol that went out needed at least eight soldiers to man the two vehicles which would usually form the patrol. Besides these duties the men also had to provide guards for the base and also any extra personnel for any special operations which were carried out. In later years the same area would be policed by greater numbers of troops, but 9 Battery had to make do with what they had. If they ever found themselves in need of extra men they would call for assistance from the other two batteries or the brigade reserve. By the end of 1971, it was estimated that the total strength of the Provisional IRA in Belfast was around 1,200 volunteers formed into three battalions: the 1st Battalion covered Andersonstown, Lenadoon and Twinbrook in South-West Belfast; the 2nd Battalion were responsible for the Falls Road, Clonard and the Ballymurphy districts of West Belfast; and the 3rd Battalion were based in Ardoyne, New Lodge and Ligoniel in the north, the Markets and Lower Ormeau in the south, and Short Strand in the east of the city.

The actual strength of the opposition facing 9 Battery was quite large in number. The two terrorist groups within the area consisted of a small number of Official IRA volunteers and in the region of 50 to 70 active Provisional volunteers. Besides this would also be members from the IRA youth wing which carried out such duties as 'spotting' for the gunmen and ferrying arms and ammunition – as well as being heavily involved in the rioting and general harassment of army patrols. The three areas covered by the regiment were predominantly Catholic. Andersonstown covered an area about two miles long by one mile deep. Nearly every one of its residents were implacably opposed to the army presence, and therefore could be classed as a threat to the troops. The IRA nearly always held the advantage. They chose the time and place to ambush the troops, and all they had to do was wait for the soldiers to turn up. This wasn't like previous wars fought against insurgents where the terrorists were few in number. The men of 9 Battery were facing an armed enemy almost equal in number to their own, and in other ways they were completely outnumbered; they had just 110 men against the whole community of Andersonstown. This was going to be guerilla warfare at its most savage, and it was carried out on the streets of housing estates which looked no different than any other estate in mainland UK.

---

*   Taken from 'Hindsight on Belfast' by Major B.C.M. Harding, RA (with kind permission of the Royal Artillery Institution).

Final preparations were made before deployment to the Province and advice was given from soldiers who had already done a tour over there. The men were told to buy 'Granny books' – small photo albums which would fit in the top pockets of the flak jackets. In these were stored pictures of the IRA suspects. The men were also advised to take women's tights to wear under their combat trousers. It would be winter-time when the regiment was going, and the tights would keep the cold out of their legs when on patrol. Finally, the training was complete. Everyone had to make a will. Some wrote letters to be left with their relatives 'just in case' anything happened. As with all soldiers though, they never thought it would be 'them' that got injured. It was always somebody else.

Bdr Renzo Peterson Agnello, 2 Troop

Filling in the will forms didn't really mean much to me, as it would not be me that came to any harm. It would of course be some other guy. I suspect that was the same thought for most of the troops. I was excited at the prospect of going to Northern Ireland, and like most of the lads I was looking forward to it.

Gnr Steve Corbett, 3 Troop

I was given my will form to fill in, and I remember thinking how morbid it seemed. I was excited at the prospect of going, but I didn't think of Northern Ireland as being a war – and so it never entered my head that I could end up dead. I didn't have anything to leave to anyone anyway, so I just put my mum's name on the form to receive anything I had if I was killed. I got a bit of a taste of what was in store for me over there while I had my embarkation leave though. There were a few Irish families who lived just opposite my mum's house, and while I was on my leave I called to see my friend. His father answered the door and he gave me a right old telling-off for being in the army and getting posted to Northern Ireland. I got another bollocking off him when I came home for my four days' R&R leave too – and these were people I had grown up with. It just shows how deep the hatred of the British soldier ran for some Irish families.

Gnr Pete Hodkinson, HQ Battery

The will form for me was the first time I had serious thoughts about going over there, and the possibility of what could happen to me. At the end of my embarkation leave I just wanted to get back and get the tour over with. I remember leaving home, the bus journey to the station and boarding the train. I looked out of the carriage window and watched Blackburn disappear into the distance as I headed back to camp. I wondered if I would ever see it again, and I just wanted to get the four months over and done with.

L/Bdr 'Ginger' Robertson, 2 Troop

I never really gave much thought about going to Northern Ireland. After all it was what I was paid for. I suppose it was a bit stupid really to think like that, but as long as I never dropped my mates in it and did what I was supposed to, I was happy. I had a couple of girlfriends at the time, but nothing serious. I don't suppose they were that bothered about me going as long as I didn't come back with a DSO (dick shot off).

For one member of the battery, the thought of going to Belfast filled him with dread. Prior to being told about deployment to the Province, he had been thinking about how he would spend his last few years as a soldier...

Gnr Mick McHale, 3 Troop

When I found out we were going to Ulster I was pretty pissed off. In fact I had secured a posting to Woolwich to see out my last few years in the army before demob – and when I was on the boat going over to Northern Ireland I was thinking about that, and I wasn't very happy at all.

3

NOVEMBER
Deployment in Andersonstown

Finally the day came to move out to Belfast. The regiment was transported to Euston Station in London where they boarded troop-trains bound for Liverpool. The men were crammed in like sardines – kitbags and weapons blocking the aisles of the carriages. Eventually the regiment reached its destination and made their way down to the ferry terminal. It was a wet, dreary day – the weather adding to the sense of foreboding for what lay ahead. Weapons were taken off the men and placed in the Pursers cage for security during the voyage.

Gnr Steve Corbett, 3 Troop

I was stood at the stern of the ship and looking over the side as we waited to leave, and I always remember the raw sewage and toilet paper floating about in the water next to the ship. I stayed there for a while as the boat pulled out. I remember seeing the mast of a ship that had sunk in the last war sticking out of the water, and I carried on watching as Liverpool disappeared in the distance. I was thinking of my home back in Manchester and my mum. She was a widow, and I was a bit upset at not being able to see her before I left. Some of the passengers were singing rebel songs, and I wondered what lay in store for us. Even now when I go down to Liverpool Docks I remember that day on the ferry.

THURSDAY 25th...

The ship finally docked in Belfast Harbour. The regiment disembarked and mounted up on the trucks waiting to take them to their various bases which were to be their homes for the next four months. This was it now: it wasn't some training exercise back at camp; this was the real thing. For the men of 9 Battery their new home was a bus depot situated on the Falls Road directly opposite Milltown Cemetery. At the top end of the depot were situated the billets of 1 and 3 Troop. Down at the bottom end, tucked inside the main entrance to the depot, stood the old house which was to be the home of 2 Troop.

L/Bdr 'Ginger' Robertson, 2 Troop

We boarded 3-tonners and were transported to our new accommodation at the top of Falls Road; "*welcome to hell,*" I thought. We debussed and were ushered into, basically, a house in the grounds of the bus depot. I still remember the caption scrawled above the door by a previous resident: '*Abandon hope all ye that enter here*'. I thought that was bloody charming.

The exterior walls were decorated with bullet-holes caused by loaded weapons being cleared in the weapons clearing area … Still, they added to the ambience of the building, which looked like something out of a Hammer House horror film. Inside was worst; downstairs was furnished with the ubiquitous army issue six-foot table and some chairs – and the ceiling leading to the stairs was also pock-marked with bullet-holes; more evidence of dodgy unloading procedures.

Upstairs, and our sleeping arrangements were three-tier bunks arranged around a normal-sized bedroom. Wardrobes were a square box two feet by 18 inches square situated on the floor. Still, we did not have a need for civvy clothes.

The accommodation block of 2 Troop. (Courtesy of Brian Corser)

Gnr Pete 'Taffy' Roberts, 2 Troop

I remember the bunks we had. Three beds high they were, and I had the top one. After 'Ginger' Robertson left us in December we got Dick Rothwell as a replacement. He ended up in the middle bunk below me. Whenever we got called out I seemed to be out of my bunk quicker than him, and I always seemed to land on top of his head when I jumped down.

The accommodation at the top end was little better – and probably had far fewer comforts. The men of 1 Troop were billeted in a small brick building just inside the entrance to the bus yard on Divis Drive. The same building also served as the cookhouse for both 1 and 3 Troop. Just opposite, and by the entrance to the workshops, stood a wooden cabin surrounded by a wall of sandbags. This was to be the home of 3 Troop.

Gnr Steve Corbett, 3 Troop

I remember pulling into the bus depot at the top end. There was a wooden building sandwiched between the workshops and a storage facility. The front of it was surrounded by a wall of sandbags almost up to the gutters. When I went inside the first thing I noticed was there were no toilets and nowhere to get a wash. There was hardly any room for anything; the room was just crammed with bunk beds in every available bit of space. All the washing facilities were situated at the back of the brick building near the sangar at the entrance. So when you wanted to use this block, you had to walk or run in the open to it. For the first week or so I found this a bit worrying, and every time I went out I expected to be shot at. In the end you just got used to it.

The defensive arrangements at the top end of the depot consisted of a solitary sangar just by the entrance to the compound. In the right-hand corner by the chain-link fence stood a wrecked double-decker bus which was also used as an observation point. On two sides of the compound was the open space of Falls Park.

At the bottom end of the depot, the defences were much more elaborate. There were several observation posts by the Falls Road built into the walls which fronted the depot. Another was on the roof of the old house. The RUC Station was situated at the fork in the road where the Falls Road split into two. The right fork was the start of Glen Road, while the left fork was the continuation of the Falls Road before it changed to Andersonstown Road at the Kennedy Way roundabout.

The RUC Station was a rather imposing structure which was surrounded by scaffolding and wire netting to the height of the building. This was the defensive

3 Troop accommodation block. (Courtesy of Richard Rothwell)

perimeter to protect the structure from rocket-propelled grenades and other explosive devices. On the Glen Road side of the building, just by the speed ramps, stood a concrete observation post. On the opposite side of the building, and overlooking the entrance to the cemetery, stood another observation post which was raised off the ground. This was a rather flimsy affair fitted with large Perspex windows, and the only protection it appeared to offer was against the chill of the winter wind that used to blow in from around the park and the cemetery. Up in the roof was the final observation post situated right over the interview room.

L/Bdr 'Ginger' Robertson, 2 Troop
After settling in, and an intelligence brief and a 'get to know the locals', it was, by then, night-time. The locals had arranged a welcome party which went on all night. We had to be tested after all; they wanted to see how good we were. I cannot remember how many contacts were recorded that first night, but it must have been in the hundreds.

The opening skirmishes between 1st Battalion PIRA and 9 (Plassey) Battery were small-scale affairs, each side just testing and probing to see how the other side would react. A couple of mobile patrols ventured out and moved into Rossnareen to learn the layout of the roads they would be expected to patrol on foot over the next four months. The previous regiment had never dared enter this area on foot; it was always considered far too dangerous. Later that evening, the first foot patrol from 3 Troop moved out of the safety of their base and entered Milltown Cemetery. It was a dark, foreboding place even in daylight. On occasions, when there was a full moon, the headstones seemed to be illuminated by shafts of light streaking down from the sky. Many of the towering monuments dated back to the Victorian era, with carvings of religious figures and angels everywhere. In the dark they sometimes appeared to come to life, and it looked as though they were moving towards you as you made your way around the narrow pathways which cut through their ranks.

Gnr Steve Corbett, 3 Troop

I always remember that first patrol we did through the cemetery. I was issued with the night sight to carry around on my rifle; the bloody thing weighed almost as much as the gun. You never got chance to zero it in for your rifle though; it was just a case of slapping it on. We were told to look out for any graves that looked as though they had been disturbed in any way. The Provos (we were told) used to hide weapons and even their own dead in recently-dug graves. Apparently, they did this to hide their casualties from the army.

We were making our way through, and heading in the direction of the Felons Club, and just ahead was a row of shrubs which lined an access road. The RUC officer signalled us to stop. He moved forward with our Sergeant and the pair of them were peering through the shrubs with the other night sight. The Sergeant signalled the other three of us to move forward. We spread out and peered through the bushes. A few yards in front was a courting couple. This bloke was lying there between his girlfriend's legs with his trousers around his ankles. The RUC officer passed the night sight along for everyone to have a look. I was trying my hardest not to laugh. The sight of that naked arse bathed in the green of the scope was so funny to see.

The patrol continued on its way and came out on the Falls Road, where they crossed over and moved on to a house to do a 'P' (person) check. These 'P' checks were the cause of much resentment within the Catholic communities. Wherever they went, whatever they were doing, they were constantly being stopped and asked for proof of their identity by the army. For their part, the soldiers had no choice but to carry out these checks. The enemy they were fighting didn't wear a uniform; they looked just the same as anyone else. One day they would be talking to you in the street, and then the next day they might be hiding in a bedroom with a rifle – waiting for an army patrol to pass by. It would usually just be a single shot fired at a receding target, and then they would make their escape.

Gnr Steve Corbett, 3 Troop

We crossed Falls Road and went to this house that stood at the end of a short street; it was right on the edge of our battery area. The Sergeant hammered on the door, which was eventually opened by a rather sheepish-looking individual, and we trooped inside. The first thing I noticed was a dartboard with a picture of a British soldier pinned to it, and right in his face were the three arrows. I found it hilarious for some reason and had to put my hand to my mouth to stop myself laughing.

The men of 2 Troop also engaged in these first foot patrols conducted by the battery into the depths of Milltown Cemetery:

L/Bdr 'Ginger' Robertson, 2 Troop

Like every other member of the battery in Andersonstown, I suffered the privations of trying to placate a community that openly hated us. I remember why I had originally joined the Armed Forces. I was working in the local coal mines and, at the time, getting into trouble hanging around on street corners getting into fights – and guess what? I joined the army and ended up on street corners in another part of the country getting into fights – and worst, people were actually shooting at me as well!

Military discipline kicked in and we all got on with our required roles. Foot patrols were a welcome relief to sedentary sangar duties. We conducted various patrols throughout our patch, obviously varying the routes and times for security purposes. Those patrols served to advertise our presence, allow us to enhance our local knowledge and, most importantly, gather intelligence. A different vehicle parked outside a residence or an unfamiliar face – or even an increase in a doorstep order of milk – could indicate a rise in household numbers. This would all be passed on to intelligence in debrief. We generally adopted an 'offensive' attitude in this area; anything and everything was a possible threat.

I remember being part of a section undertaking a patrol through Milltown Cemetery situated in front of our main operating base. We used to patrol this area on a regular basis, and it was only this place that the residents wouldn't give us any hassle. We used to check the graves of recent burials for any signs of being disturbed, as it was not unknown for the IRA to use a bona fide funeral to inter some of their fallen comrades.

Operational procedures for their gunmen would involve a blanket of some sort. They would spread it on the ground and lie on it when

The entrance to Milltown Cemetery. (Courtesy of 'Snowy' H***)

they were engaging the army in gun-battles. This would catch any spent rounds – and in the event of their demise, it would allow the body to be spirited away by their comrades. It was just a matter of picking up each end of the blanket and everything was gone. Anyway, on this particular patrol I had noticed that the flowers and wreaths on one grave seemed a bit askew and related this information to our officer in charge. I think it was Lieutenant Dick Burland. He asked me to get the aerial off the radio and push it into the grave. This I did to a depth of about four feet. The aerial exited the grave clean; we continued on our way.

Gnr Tony 'Sammy' Symonds, 2 Troop

I remember those early patrols through the cemetery. I always seemed to have the night sight. I ended up lumbered with it for several weeks. It was a big heavy thing, and nobody else seemed interested in carrying it around. It was at its best in the cemetery though, with it being such a dark place. Sometimes we went up to the quarries at the back of Andersonstown to keep watch as well.

Bdr Renzo Peterson Agnello, 2 Troop

The only patrol that I did not like was the one through Milltown Cemetery. I used to read a lot of Dennis Wheatley books at this time, and they were all on the occult, evil spirits and that kind of thing. I was tail-end Charlie on this particular patrol, and as we were short-handed, a couple of REME lads joined us. As we proceeded through the cemetery, the guy in front of me did not move for what seemed like an age. I moved up beside him and asked what was going on. He said to me: *"I appear to have lost the man in front of me. Which way should we go?"*

I gave it a few minutes' thought. There was a patrol out there armed to the teeth, and we were out there armed and with our usual war paint on. So I decided that we would stop crawling about and go straight to the rendezvous point – making as much noise as possible on the way. Once within range of the rendezvous, I shouted out: "Bdr Agnello and sad-sack coming in."

Luckily they had expected us, as someone had realised after a while that we were missing. After that, the Dennis Wheatley books went straight in the bin – and I've never picked one up since.

Another duty that took up a great amount of time were the house searches. These would be planned, co-ordinated and executed with inner and outer cordons in situ. The searches were generally intelligence led and were usually carried out in the early morning hours. One aspect of these searches that never ceased to amaze those taking part was the sudden arrival of Rent-a-Mob. No sooner would you arrive at the target address, and the women from the surrounding streets would be out with their whistles and dustbin lids making as much racket as they could. One anomaly that had to be overcome was the required presence of an attending RUC officer. At that time it was a lawful requirement that entry to an address could only be gained after the production of a police officer's warrant card.

Bdr Renzo Peterson Agnello, 2 Troop

I remember once when we were carrying out house-searches, and I was with the RUC inside a house. I started the search, and on pulling open a drawer I was confronted by what appeared to be a woman's used sanitary towel. I rammed the drawer shut in absolute disgust, but the RUC officer told me to open it again and tip out the contents. This I did, and much to my surprise, out fell all these rolls of bank-notes. I looked at the RUC man and he shook his head. The sanitary towel just had sauce on it, and the ruse had very nearly worked. It was later revealed that the house owner was Brigade Paymaster for the Provisional IRA.

SATURDAY 27th...

It was just two days since the battery had arrived in Andersonstown, and already they were caught up in a massive bombing and shooting blitz launched by the Provisional IRA the previous evening. At first the bombings were thought to be the work of a new splinter group, the *Saor Éire*. In a 20-hour period there were 30 explosions across the Province. The attacks began with two bomb explosions at 9:00 a.m. – the first at Queen's Quay Railway Station, and the second at a car showroom in Adelaide Street. A customs post in Fermanagh was also set on fire, and then the bombings and shootings started to escalate at an alarming rate:

9:05 a.m. – A bomb was placed in Killeen customs post. In another attack, Tullydonnell customs post was set on fire.

9:11 a.m. – Two bomb explosions at concrete plants. The first at Ready-Mix Concrete, Suffolk and the second at Colinwell Concrete, Glen Road, Belfast.

9:15 a.m. – Clontivrin customs post, Fermanagh and Amasco Tarmac, Stonyford – both bombed.

9:20 a.m. – Garrison youth hostel blown up in bomb attack.

10:00 a.m. – Fathom customs post set ablaze. Bomb found in empty building in Donegal Street, Belfast.

10:15 a.m. – Bomb explodes in McClunes glass dealers, York Street, Belfast.

10:20 a.m. – Watson's furniture showroom in Donegal Street, Belfast attacked with incendiary devices. Middletown telephone exchange damaged in bomb explosion.

11:05 a.m. – Bomb discovered in the old RUC barracks at Ligoniel.

11:22 a.m. – Reports came through to Andersonstown RUC Station of a bomb being planted at the Green Briars Club, Glen Road, Andersonstown.

11:27 a.m. – Two customs officers shot dead by the Provisional IRA at Killeen. The post had been badly damaged in a bomb attack two hours earlier.

11:30 a.m. – A second call was made to Andersonstown RUC Station claiming another bomb had been planted in the Ulster Brewery, Glen Road.

11:34 a.m. – Bomb destroys shop in North Queen Street, Belfast.

11:37 a.m. – Halls book shop damaged by incendiary device in Smithfield Market, Belfast.

11:48 a.m. – Heinz factory at Springfield Road, Belfast damaged in bomb explosion.

12:10 p.m. – Guardsman Paul Nichols (18) shot dead by Provisional IRA sniper in the Falls area of Belfast.

12:15 p.m. – Slight damage caused to premises in Ann Street, Belfast by incendiary device.

12:35 p.m. – Fane Vale Creamery in Newtonhamilton damaged in bomb explosion.

12:40 p.m. – Shots fired at army patrol in Andersonstown.

12:42 p.m. – Army patrol in Londonderry come under machine gun fire in an attack launched by the IRA.

2:10 p.m. – Fire bombs explode at Supermac shopping centre, Belfast.

2:45 p.m. – The Balmoral Inn, Lisburn Road, Belfast damaged in bomb attack.*

The men of 9 Battery had been in the Province for barely more than 48 hours and already they were at full stretch as volunteers from 1st Battalion, PIRA launched attacks on their patrols. At around 11:30 a.m. a patrol from 1 Troop was in the area of Rossnareen Avenue when they came under fire from gunmen as they headed towards the Ulster Brewery after reports that a bomb had been left inside the main building. Elsewhere, another patrol from 3 Troop were heading towards the high ground which overlooked the Green Briars Golf Club after another call claiming a bomb had been left there too.

Gnr Steve Corbett, 3 Troop

We made our way up a track in our Pigs, and after we pulled up and dismounted I was told to take up position behind a mound of earth. There was a track to the left of me, and just in front and to the right stood a wooden hut. Every now and then there would be a 'crack' above my head as someone started taking pot-shots at me. It was the first time I had ever experienced being under fire, and I wasn't really sure where the shooting was coming from.

Just beyond the building, the ground sloped upwards towards my left. It was carpeted in tufts of long grass. Suddenly, I caught sight of two figures crawling upwards several yards in front of me. I could see the grass moving, and just now and then I caught a glimpse of them. I looked around wondering what the hell I should do, but I couldn't see anyone else near me, and this was totally different to the training I had done at Imber. I had never been faced with this kind of situation before. I wanted to shout out and challenge them to see who they were, but I hesitated and wondered what to do. It could have only been a matter of seconds, but by then I just completely lost sight of them.

Even later in the tour I seemed to hold back from using my rifle when I came under fire. I was never bothered when I had to use the riot gun though. In my eyes I was just giving the bastards what they

---

*   Source taken from *The Troubles* Magazine (Glenravel Publications).

deserved if they were rioting, but somehow, when I was being shot at, I almost always held back from returning fire until I was absolutely sure that they were armed. I don't think it was the thought of having to possibly kill someone though. After all, that was what I had been trained to do, but I guess I was just frightened to death of making a grave error and killing a totally innocent person. It wasn't as though you could look at someone and know for sure that he or she was the enemy, unless you actually saw a weapon in their hands either. The gunmen didn't run around in uniforms, and what if it was only a pole they were holding? It could easily be mistaken for a gun in the heat of the moment. You get people who have never had to face situations like that, and they have been critical of the actions taken by soldiers, but it's different when you are there and you are the one that has to make that split-second decision which could result in someone being killed. Once you take someone's life, it is impossible to give it back.

As Mick Burton's patrol came under fire from the Provo gunmen on the hill, another patrol – also from 3 Troop – were making their way up Finaghy Road North towards the junction with Andersonstown Road. This road junction would become the scene of many ambushes over the coming months, and became known to the men of 9 Battery as 'snipers' corner'. Every time a mobile patrol approached this spot, the men expected to hear gunshots. The Humber 'Pigs' which the men relied upon so heavily for their protection on these patrols were always in demand. Qualified drivers were in short supply during those first few days, and the drivers they had were already feeling the strain of too many hours at the wheel and not enough rest.

Gordon 'Addi' Adamson was one of the regular drivers – and in the short time he had been in Andersonstown, he was always being told to take out yet another patrol. Already he was worn out through the lack of sleep. Shortly after lunch, 'Addi' set off on another mobile around the estates. The Provos were lying in wait for their first opportunity to engage in battle with 9 Battery, determined to show 'the Brits' they meant business. The patrol had been touring around Riverdale Estate when they too heard the call from 1 Troop who had come under fire in Rossnareen. There had also been reports of a bomb being left at the petrol station situated on the corner of Finaghy Road North and Andersonstown Road. 'Punchy' Wilmot was urging 'Addi' to get his foot down to go to the aid of the patrol.

SOLDIER WOUNDED BY A SNIPER

Another soldier was shot and wounded in Belfast after an army vehicle collided with a bus. The soldier, a member of the 12th Light Air Defence Regiment, Royal Artillery was hit as he stood near a recovery vehicle at the scene of the accident. One bullet grazed his skull and he was rushed to the Royal Victoria Hospital, but his condition was said to be 'not serious'.

The accident between the bus and the 1-ton armoured personnel carrier happened at the junction of Finaghy Road North and the Stewartstown Road in the Andersonstown area. The army vehicle went into a ditch, but it is believed no-one was injured. Troops did not return fire, but they were later carrying out a search for the sniper.

Meanwhile, two masked gunmen got away with less than £200 after a raid on a Post Office in the Andersonstown area.

The raiders, according to a Post Office spokesman, held staff at gunpoint in Upper Falls PO shortly before 11:30 a.m.

One gunman rifled the till and both made off before the alarm was raised. No-one was injured in the raid.*

* Source taken from The Belfast Telegraph.

Gnr 'Addi' Adamson, 3 Troop

The only thing I can remember before the crash is that our section was responding to a call about 1 Troop being ambushed and a bomb at a petrol station at the junction of Andersonstown Road and Finaghy Road North. I was driving the lead Pig with Sgt 'Punchy' Wilmot alongside me. We were going up Finaghy Road North, heading for the junction with Andersonstown Road. As we got near the junction, 'Punchy' told me to put my foot down and get around the corner. I started turning, but I have no recollection of what happened next.

The next thing I remember was coming to, and hearing 'Punchy' shouting for someone to help him get me out of the Pig. I vaguely remember being pulled out and carried to the back of the other Pig, where they lay me down on the bench seat. He was telling me that I had driven into the side of a bus and the vehicle had ended up stuck in the embankment next to St Joseph's Training College.

The radio operator called through to the bus depot to let them know what had happened, and arrangements were immediately made for two more Pigs to go out to try and recover 'Addi' Adamson's stranded Humber. Sergeant-Major Tom McShane took charge of the lead Pig, and following up the rear were Bombardier Bob Wilson with his driver, Jock Scott. A short time later the two vehicles arrived at the scene. Bob Wilson jumped out and guided Jock forward while they tried to get a tow bar on the stranded vehicle to pull it clear. He walked around to the back of the Pig and got on the radio to BSM Don Potter to keep him informed of the situation. Shots were heard, and then Bob was seen clutching the side of his head.

Gnr Mick McHale, 3 Troop

The first time I returned fire was the day that Bob Wilson got shot, and I think we were at the junction in front of St Joseph's College. I was over on the bend at Tullymore Gardens where it meets up with Glassmullin Gardens. I took cover behind a wall about three feet high, did a quick scan of the area, and noticed movement behind a frosted bathroom window which was slightly open. I fired a couple of rounds and saw my bullets hitting the bricks around the window – and as I fired, two Paratroopers got behind the wall and let off a few rounds as well.

Mick McHale.
(Courtesy of Mick McHale)

Luckily, our marksmanship wasn't that good because on reflection, I don't think the person in the bathroom had anything to do with the shooting. It's just that in the heat of the moment, I heard the shooting and saw movement behind the window – and I suppose I must have convinced myself it was the gunman. While we were behind the wall, Albert Manners ran across the grass verge to join us. He stumbled and fell forward, digging his rifle barrel into the earth. When he reached us he cocked his rifle and was going to fire, but one of the Paratroopers saw what he had done to his rifle and grabbed it off him before he could fire.

Back at the hill overlooking the Green Briars Club, the patrol of S/Sgt Burton was almost ready to move out. The gunmen engaging Mick's men had, by now, disappeared and so the patrol watched the recovery efforts with the stranded Pig down below on Andersonstown Road. The soldiers around the vehicles were seen to scatter as a couple of shots rang out. Mick ordered his patrol to mount up and they rushed towards the scene of the shooting. Meanwhile, 'Addi' Adamson had fully regained consciousness.

Gnr 'Addi' Adamson, 3 Troop

They told me that my head hit the steering wheel and I was knocked out cold for a bit. I felt a right pillock for hitting the bus. I mean, the colour and the size of the bloody things, you can hardly miss them can you? I was that knackered I couldn't concentrate properly – and it didn't help much when 'Punchy' told me to get a move on. I remember lying there in the back of the Pig; then hearing gunshots, and everyone was running around and taking cover – and then someone told me that Bob had just been shot in the head.

The bullet which struck Bob had hit the side of the Pig and ricocheted off – hitting him on the side of the head. When he was eventually taken to hospital it took 12 stitches to close the wound. As soon as the shooting started, the radio operator sent a message to base requesting backup, and it is probably this call that S/Sgt Burton had answered. The Pigs finally arrived and the men dismounted and took up firing positions, but by then the gunmen had probably fled.

Gnr Steve Corbett, 3 Troop

As we got up there I saw a line of Paratroopers dressed in Dennison smocks and wearing helmets – and they were heading towards the Stewartstown Road. I didn't have a clue what they were doing in our area, but from time to time they did seem to appear on our patch – and it seemed to me that every time they came, trouble was sure to follow. Our Pigs pulled up near the petrol station, and I saw Tom McShane holding a shell dressing to Bob Wilson's head, so I walked over to see how he was. Although he was obviously in a great deal of pain, he was grinning and pointing to his head. He said to me: "*I'll get a new car out of this.*"

This was a reference to the criminal injury compensation which we were all entitled to at that time. The government didn't look on the Troubles in Northern Ireland as a war. Well they wouldn't, would they? They weren't the poor bastards stuck over there getting shot and bombed nearly every day.

A few minutes after the author spoke to Bob, he was taken away in the Pig to Musgrave Park Hospital to have his wound dressed. By then he was beginning to lose consciousness. When they arrived, Bob was immediately rushed into surgery while the injury was examined. They shaved his head and put 12 stitches in the gaping wound. 'Punchy' Wilmot and Tom McShane went to visit him a few days later to see if there was anything he needed…

Bdr Bob Wilson, 3 Troop
I asked them to bring my shaving gear so that I could smarten myself up a bit – and the next day they returned with my bag. After they left I opened it up. I couldn't find my shaving gear, but inside were four cans of beer.

Eventually 'Addi' Adamson had to go before the Commanding Officer after he had been charged with dangerous driving. He was told that the BC wasn't allowed to deal with the case due to the fact that civilians had been involved in the crash.

Gnr 'Addi' Adamson, 3 Troop
I told him (the CO) that I couldn't remember anything about the accident. I didn't want to get 'Punchy' in trouble for telling me to get a move on, so I just told him how knackered I was through the constant driving, but it made no difference. He just said that we were all tired and I should have watched what I was doing. I got fined £20 by him. That was around two weeks' pay back then. It could have been worse though. I was told that there was talk of it going to a civil court because of the civilian passengers on the bus being involved, but then it was said that if the CO dealt with it, that would do.

This was the first major incident which 9 Battery were involved in – just two days after their arrival at the bus depot, and already they had a man injured.

There was no sign of a bomb at the petrol station. It had just been a ruse to lure the patrol into an ambush, and it was the same at the Ulster Brewery and the golf club as well. Bob Wilson was a very lucky man. If the bullet had hit him at a slightly different angle, there is every possibility that it would have been fatal.

VICTIMS OF THE TROUBLES WHO DIED THIS DAY...

Guardsman Paul Nichols (18) – The Scots Guards. Died of wounds after being shot by an IRA sniper while on foot patrol in St James Crescent, West Belfast.

Jimmy O'Neill (45) – Customs Officer. Shot dead at a customs post in Killeen which had been bombed a few hours previously. The IRA lay in wait for the army to respond to the bombing, and opened fire as they arrived. Jimmy O'Neill was killed as he stood inside his office.

Ian Hankin (26) – Customs Officer. Killed in the same incident. Shot dead as he was about to step inside a caravan.

* List compiled from *The Troubles Magazine* (Glenravel Publications).

SUNDAY 28th...

Most of the mobile patrols undertaken by 9 Battery were carried out with the Humber 'Pig' armoured personnel carrier. Around that time it was considered far too dangerous to use Land Rovers for patrol, and the Macralon armoured version was still some months off. On each side of the Pig were two observation slits, just a little larger than a letterbox. The rear doors were also equipped with observation slits, but the standard procedure was to drive around with the doors wide open. Having the doors open gave a much better view and also allowed the occupants to do a rapid dismount when events called for it. It did carry its risks though, and on several occasions there were shooting incidents where bullets entered the Pig through the open doors.

The inside furnishing was very basic: a wooden bench ran up each side in the back. Depending on available manpower, it was usual to travel with driver and co-driver and two men in the back, but on some of the patrols when extra men were needed, there would be a third or fourth man. They would squeeze in where they could, and quite often someone would sit on top of the A42 man-pack radio which was used at that time. Each man carried his personal weapon, either the SLR or the Sterling SMG. There would also be a couple of riot guns and boxes of rubber bullets and CS gas canisters.

L/Bdr 'Ginger' Robertson, 2 Troop

Pigs were our mode of transport, and I happened to be the nominated driver on a day when the locals were unduly restive. We always used to travel in pairs but I cannot remember if I was in the first or the second Pig. Anyway, we proceeded out of the bus station, turned right and were immediately faced with Rent-a-Mob. They were bearing gifts – bottles, bricks and various other missiles not conducive to a healthy body.

The Pig I was driving had not been fitted with a metal windscreen protector; these could be raised or lowered from inside the cab. We proceeded up the road and the missiles started to rain down. The Pigs had a split windscreen, and my driver's windscreen was smashed on the first pass, but still remained intact, although I could hardly see through it. On the way back down the road the window was actually breached and debris from it entered my eye. I then had to drive the vehicle with my head sticking out of the side-window in the door. Fortunately for me we were, by then, out of range of the missiles. The locals did not care for our drab-coloured vehicles and were most imaginative in designing new colour schemes. Lilac and other pastel shades were well favoured. However, application by hurling bottles as we drove past was not conducive to an even finish.

'Ginger' Robertson and 'Snowy' H***.
(Courtesy of 'Ginger' Robertson)

Gnr Steve Corbett, 3 Troop

We felt safe in the Pigs, even though we drove around with the doors wide open. I was usually in the back with either 'Scouse' Coulson or Mick Krasnowski, and I used to take two riot guns with me as well as my SLR. The back of the

Pig had a hinged metal plate just below the bumper, and when we were on patrol in the early hours we would just cruise around to make as little noise as possible. Then the Pig would hit a bump or something, and this bloody plate would swing and go 'clang-clang-clang' and announce our presence to all and sundry.

Gnr 'Sammy' Symonds, 2 Troop

I often carried the riot gun when I was in the Pig and I fired it on several occasions. I remember one incident when I fired at some youths charging up to the back of our Pig. One of them reeled back after the rubber bullet hit the ground in front of him and then bounced up and hit him – sending him to the ground.

When we returned to the UK after the tour I was told to report to the Commanding Officer of our regiment. The youth I hit had reported the incident and the CO wanted to know if I wanted to go back to Belfast to be questioned about it. I didn't go, but I did fill out a report.

L/Bdr 'Ginger' Robertson, 2 Troop

As already mentioned, Pigs were the designated mode of transport. We had been called out to a road barricade which had been constructed on the estate. This consisted of burned-out vehicles which had been placed across the road – something which was an almost daily affair. You had to be careful in these situations, as it could be a decoy to draw you in with snipers or bombs being positioned ready to ambush you.

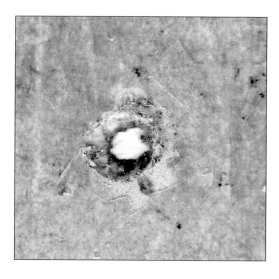

The card covering off one of the batteries pierced by a bullet. (Courtesy of Brian Corser)

We checked the area, put out a perimeter guard and cleared the barricade with the Pig. We then made our way back to our lines, and en route three high-velocity rounds were fired. I was sitting at the rear of the vehicle passenger's side with the back rear doors open. This wasn't an act of bravado; it was just that any contacts could be identified and dealt with more effectively, but driving with all the doors closed severely restricted your view. On our return to our lines I checked the spare batteries that were placed under the seat which I had previously occupied. There were two bullet-holes through them. The bullets had missed my legs by less than an inch.

Gnr Pete Roberts, 2 Troop

One of our drivers was an Irish lad by the name of Paddy Keane. On one occasion he was out on patrol at about 2:00 a.m. He was driving our Pig along the road when he suddenly swerved and hit three parked cars. Lt Burland said to him: *"What did you do that for?"* Paddy kept a straight face and said: *"Sorry Sir, I was hit by a stone and I momentarily lost control of the vehicle."*

Foot patrols were again out in force probing the area close to the RUC Station. During those first few days the battery still hadn't ventured out on foot to the outlying estates of Riverdale and Rossnareen. They spent much of their time around Fruithill and Glenhill learning how to properly conduct these patrols in relative safety. The men were still learning the skills of doing 'footsies' and it was considered wiser to stick closer to home until they became more familiar with their new surroundings. Just across the road from the base, a patrol from 3 Troop made its way through the depths of Milltown Cemetery and came out near the Felons Club.

Gnr Steve Corbett, 3 Troop

We came out of the graveyard and were passing the Felons Club as this crowd of people came out. There was about 100 of them and only six or eight of us. They looked over and started jeering at us, and I think we all expected something to happen, but much to our relief they didn't start any bother and they went on their way.

MONDAY 29th…

The bombings which took place on the previous Saturday had been presumed to be the work of the *Saor Éire*, but it later turned out to be the Provisionals who had orchestrated the multiple attacks.

PROVISIONALS BEHIND WEEKEND ATTACKS

Security Forces are certain that the Provisional IRA are behind the bombing offensive which was mounted at the weekend and not the crack unit being formed by the Saor Éire. They have been left in no doubt either that it was one of the most carefully planned series of explosions of the current campaign.

As senior RUC and army officers studied reports of the weekend's upsurge in activity, they were trying to determine what made the IRA choose this weekend. It is believed that security chiefs knew from intelligence reports that a major offensive was to be launched, but even some of them were taken by surprise when the true picture of the intensification of the operation began to unfold. It was hardly coincidence that the IRA went on the offensive a few days after Mr Wilson's speech and the decision by the Parliamentary Labour Party to end by-partisan policy. It is certain that the operations were planned over a number of weeks. Having done that, it was only merely the question of choosing the right psychological moment to put it into operation. In view of the events of the past week, the IRA chose the best possible time to attack.[*]

VICTIMS OF THE TROUBLES WHO DIED THIS DAY...

Pte Robert Benner (25) – The Queens Regiment. Abducted while off duty and unarmed. He was murdered by the IRA while visiting his girlfriend in Dundalk. His body was found near Crossmaglen.[†]

[*] Source taken from *The Troubles* Magazine (Glenravel Publications).
[†] List compiled from *The Troubles* Magazine (Glenravel Publications).

TUESDAY 30th...

At around 2:00 a.m. a mobile patrol moved out of camp and up to the flats near Tullymore Gardens to conduct a search. The procedure for these operations would usually entail one unit carrying out the actual search, while another provided the cover for protection against rioting mobs or gunmen. The larger searches were normally carried out in the early hours while everybody was in bed to try and avoid much of the trouble normally associated with these operations. The defensive cordon was put around the chosen streets and the search teams would then move in and work their way through the properties. Every outbuilding had to be checked for weapons or other terrorist-related material, but on this particular search, the only items recovered were a few rounds of ammunition and paper wrappers off sticks of explosives.

At around 10:00 p.m. that evening, a unit from 3 Troop left the base and made its way up the Andersonstown Road on a routine patrol. As the two vehicles reached the Busy Bee shops near the corner of Slievegallion Drive, they came under attack from a small group of youths who had congregated outside the complex. A volley of rocks and bottles came cascading down on them from both sides of the road as the two Pigs slowed down.

Gnr Steve Corbett, 3 Troop

I was in the rear Pig with S/Sgt Burton from the sniper patrol. We were just going up Andersonstown Road with the intention of going around the estates to see if anything was going on, and as we got near the shops, Mick noticed a fire blazing away in a passage between the buildings. He told the driver to slow down while we had a look to see what was going on, and then this crowd of youths started having a go at us with bricks and bottles.

The rioters were silhouetted against the glow of the fire, and Mick told me to use the riot gun against them. I dropped a round into the breech and stuck the barrel through the observation slit. I took aim and squeezed the trigger, and to my amazement this lad fell backwards into the fire. A pile of sparks flew up into the air where he landed, and then his mates rushed over and pulled him clear. This was the very first time I had ever used this weapon, and I was quite pleased to have actually hit someone with it. Mick congratulated me on my success, and we carried on our way.

When we finished the patrol I had to go over to the RUC Station to be interviewed by the BC about the firing of the riot gun. He wanted to know why I fired it and that kind of thing. As far as I remember, I was the first person in the battery to actually use one.

As the tour progressed, these weapons were used far more frequently to such an extent that questions were never asked again as to why they had been used. The answer to that was rather obvious: the rioting on the streets of Andersonstown had become an almost everyday occurrence. The Busy Bee shops was like a magnet to the local youths. They would gather outside there and wait for the army patrols to drive past and then subject them to a barrage of bricks and bottles.

Bdr Renzo Peterson Agnello, 2 Troop

Our Battery Commander (BC) was a Major Harding, and we used to call him 'Pebbles' due to his posh accent. We were a bit apprehensive about him being our leader at first, but he turned out to be absolutely brilliant. He used to plan wee sorties which gave us a chance to get our own back on the mobs that had been stoning us and battling us during the day. One such sortie included the patrols from two troops. One patrol would go up Andersonstown Road and drive slowly past the shops at the Busy Bee and take all the bottling and stoning, and another patrol would move in on foot from the rear of the café and shops. Then we would have them between us. It was a very successful ploy, and many a thug got a good hiding.

4

DECEMBER
More injuries and the first successes

WEDNESDAY 1st...

At about 7:00 p.m. a suspicious parcel was found on the back seat of one of the buses which had returned to the depot. Both accommodation blocks had to be evacuated and a safety cordon set up around the depot as Felix (bomb disposal) made their way to the incident. Around that time the use of the remotely controlled 'Wheelbarrow' by the bomb disposal teams was still some way off, and it was up to the explosives expert to make the walk and inspect the bomb visually. For their part, the IRA bomb makers were busy trying to devise new methods to catch out and kill Felix.

It took a special kind of person to be able to face such a situation as a suspicious package – knowing full well that the object they were dealing with could turn out to be the last thing they ever saw, but on this occasion the bomb turned out to be nothing more than a house brick wrapped in brown paper – but the threat it posed and disruption it caused was very real. There was once an incident where a package was left on a bus outside the RUC Station. Bdr 'Horace' of 2 Troop rather recklessly took it upon himself to remove the package and then he proceeded to carry it over to the roundabout in front of the RUC Station. Situated on the roundabout was a grid set about one foot below the surface, and into this hole 'Horace' placed the bomb for safety. When bomb disposal turned up they were none too pleased at 'Horace's' handiwork. The lack of room made it almost impossible for them to work on the 'bomb'. Fortunately for them, it turned out to be another hoax.

Incidents such as this caused enormous problems throughout the Province. Every suspected package had to be treated as though it was a bomb until it had been properly checked out. They often caused as much chaos as an actual explosion through the disruption to transport and evacuation of shops and public buildings.

The RUC Station. The grid where 'Horace' placed the bomb can clearly be seen on the roundabout. (Courtesy of Richard Rothwell)

VICTIMS OF THE TROUBLES WHO DIED THIS DAY...

Vivienne Gibney (17) – Died of wounds received four days earlier. She was stood outside a chemist when an IRA gunman fired at an RUC patrol at Cliftonville Circus, Belfast. Four other people were injured in the same incident.

Pte Denis Wilson (31) – 8th Battalion, The Ulster Defence Regiment. Shot dead when IRA gunmen forced their way into his bedroom at the family farm in Curlough.*

* List compiled from *The Troubles* Magazine (Glenravel Publications).

THURSDAY 2nd...

On 9 November a unit from the Green Howards raided a club in the Ardoyne district of Belfast after receiving a tip-off that they would find one of the army's most wanted suspects, Martin Meehan, hiding there. He was the Provisional IRA terrorist considered by them to be responsible for the brutal slaying of five members of their regiment and, quite understandably, feelings amongst the men were running high at the capture of this man. He was taken to Flax Street Mill, where he met up with another wanted gunman who had also been detained,

Tony 'Dutch' Doherty. Both of them were later to give graphic accounts of their treatment at the hands of the soldiers, although this was always flatly denied by the army. They were both taken to Palace Barracks for questioning before being transferred to Crumlin Road Gaol towards the end of November. On 2 December the press contacted the prison authorities and told them that they had noticed bonfires over much of the Ardoyne, and they had asked the local residents what the celebrations were for. The residents replied that it was because Martin Meehan had escaped from prison. The press asked the authorities whether they could confirm this to be true.

After a quick search of the prison it was soon discovered that Meehan was indeed missing. In fact there were three men who had escaped: Martin Meehan, Tony 'Dutch' Doherty and Hugh McCann. While all the Republican prisoners were enjoying a break in the exercise yard of the prison, the three men managed to remove a manhole cover and hide themselves inside the drain. They spent five hours stood in freezing water while they waited for the right moment to make their bid for freedom. Under cover of darkness and thick fog, they climbed out of the drain and used several blankets as a makeshift ladder to scale the outer wall and disappear into the surrounding streets. As news of the escape spread, the whole of Belfast was put on high alert as the authorities searched for the escapees. Back in Andersonstown, men from 1 Troop were taking part in the hunt for the prisoners and 3 Troop were providing the cover for the search teams as they moved in on various addresses around the estates.

Gnr Steve Corbett, 3 Troop

After the search for the wanted men had been completed by C11, our section headed back to base – but further down the road the local youths were lying in wait. As we neared, we were met by a hail of bottles and rocks aimed at both our Pigs. A gang of 20 or 30 of them came charging up to the open doors at the back of the Pig. I picked up one of the riot guns, took aim, and let off one shot which hit a lad who was bowled over by the impact. Mick Krasnowski handed me the other gun and I fired again. I got off about four shots in total, and hit at least two of the rioters.

The Catholics always claimed that these weapons were deliberately used against children – some of whom had been quite badly injured and even killed during rioting – but the truth was that these weapons were the only line of defence the soldiers dare use against rioters; and they were far less lethal than the 7.62mm SLR rifle. Wherever the soldiers went in the Nationalist estates, there were usually crowds of people waiting to have a go at them. Young children were often encouraged by their parents to join in the rioting, and it was hardly surprising that some of the youths would be hit and, in some cases, injured by the rubber bullets. A brick thrown by a child hurt just as much as one thrown by an adult if it happens to hit you.

FRIDAY 3rd...

All over Belfast, the searches continued throughout the night in the hunt for the escaped Provos. In the early hours of the morning of 3 December the whole battery was involved in a big house search being carried out by 58 Battery near the power station on the Lenadoon Estate as the hunt continued for Meehan and Doherty. As 3 Troop arrived on the scene they were met by the sound of dustbin lids being rattled on the walls of the houses. All the women were out in force, blowing whistles and banging the lids as the patrol made its way through to where the search was to take place.

Gnr Steve Corbett, 3 Troop

We went up to Lenadoon to help out 58 Battery with a big search they were doing. As we got nearer I could hear this terrific din, and I didn't have a clue what it was at first. Then we all climbed out of the back of the Pigs, and I saw all these women outside their houses with metal dustbin lids in their hands. They were rattling them on the walls of the houses and the footpaths. They were blowing whistles as well – and those that weren't blowing whistles were cursing us. I'd never seen anything like it in my life. The best way I can describe it is that it was like that scene from the film 'Zulu' when all the Impi warriors were lined up in their hundreds, and they were banging the backs of their shields with their spears. Whenever I see that film I always think back to that incident in Lenadoon. It makes the hairs on the back of my neck stand on end.

Not all the women were willing participants in this though. The Provisional IRA took a dim view of any family that didn't get involved.

'Moira' – Belfast resident

When I went in work the next day after the rioting it was easy to spot the women who had been taking part. They were all tired after being awake all night. They had to join in though. The boys would come and pay a visit to those who didn't get involved. Many of us really didn't want to be part of it, but we were too scared not to.

The search drew to a close and the teams returned to base. It was by now 8:00 a.m. but other patrols were still out in force – still trying to track down the escaped prisoners. Just beyond the RUC Station and near the Post Office on the

Falls Road, a section from 2 Troop were manning a road block. VCPs (vehicle check points) were a good way of introducing yourself to the local population – especially in an urban location like Andersonstown – but usually they caused aggravation and impatience.

L/Bdr 'Ginger' Robertson, 2 Troop

I remember the first check point I ever conducted. It was a snap affair carried out just past the Post Office from the Police Station. A prison break had occurred the day before, and I was told to conduct a VCP. The morning was the start of a typical Belfast December day, and the time was around 7:00 a.m. but it was unusually foggy, and it was probably the reason the escape had taken place earlier.

We began to process vehicles through and conduct searches; it was still early and we weren't overwhelmed with customers. Through the shadows cast by the street lights and down towards the Police Station, my eye was drawn to a group of cyclists emerging from the fog. They looked like crows riding bikes, and they turned out to be priests – around six of them clad in black cassocks flapping in the breeze. I bid the leading cyclist *"Good day"* and he replied: *"Good day – a good day for dying, son."* I thought: *"Bloody charming"* – and me being a good Catholic boy as well! I was hoping it wasn't the escaped prisoners I was talking to.

At the same VCP, we checked a vehicle and the chap indicated he was a member of the Security Forces: Special Branch I think. I asked him for his identification, which he begrudgingly passed. I scrutinised the picture, and it was nothing like him at all. The driver had more hair than Kate Bush, but the picture on the pass showed a bald head. I asked him about the discrepancy and he pulled his thatch back. It was him alright – a member of the hairy branch. I sent him on his way.

Over the next couple of weeks everyone got on with the tasks in hand: sangar duties, patrols, VCPs, contacts or house searches. However, things were about to change. In the early days of the tour, contacts involving small arms fire were experienced by the patrols with no critical injuries being suffered, but within a few weeks two men would be badly injured in an ambush.

SATURDAY 4th...

The searches for the three escapees continued around the whole of Northern Ireland. Back in Andersonstown, patrols from 3 Troop spent most of the day setting up vehicle check points on the Andersonstown Road and Glen Road. The check points would usually just consist of a coil of barbed wire strung across the road, and vehicles would be directed to one side while the identities of the occupants were checked and cars searched for weapons or explosives, but as with everything in Northern Ireland, even these tasks had their dangers. Several years later, in September 1990 – and at the scene of a similar road block – a car failed to stop and was driven through at speed. The four-man squad all opened fire on the car as it accelerated towards them. Two soldiers eventually went on trial for the murder of Martin Peake and Karen Reilley. Pte Aindow claimed he was hit by the car as it passed by. Pte Clegg fired three shots at the car as it approached and one *after* it had passed by.

The final shot that Clegg fired was adjudged to have killed Karen Reilly and he was later charged and found guilty with her murder. The reasoning behind the judgment was that he had fired his last shot *after* the danger had passed by. The two who were killed had no terrorist connections, and were simply joyriders who failed to stop when requested to do so. Clegg was eventually released after an appeal to the sentence – to the obvious distress of the relatives of the dead – but the reaction of the soldiers that day were entirely understandable. For all they knew the two occupants of the car may well have been terrorists. When you are facing what may well be a life or death situation you have to make an instant decision on how to react to it.

Gnr Steve Corbett, 3 Troop

I hated doing the road blocks. You spent much of the time stood in the open while you flagged the cars down and pulled them over, but you could never be sure if the driver heading towards you was going to make a break for it and drive through – and then other times you could be checking someone and they would tell you they were carrying a pistol for personal protection, as many Protestants did who had to pass through Republican areas. They would show you their driving licence and permit for the gun, but for all we knew they could still have been members of a Protestant paramilitary organisation.

On one occasion I pulled over a car which was occupied by soldiers from Intelligence working in plain-clothes. The driver whispered to me that he was army, flashed his ID card at me and asked me to give his car a search just in case anyone was watching, but the biggest worry was always the fear of a car forcing its way through and the occupants shooting at you.

Later in the evening a patrol from 2 Troop was sent down to the Felons Club near the cemetery to conduct a search after Bdr K**** from Battery Headquarters had gone missing while on foot patrol. There was some concern that he may have been captured and was being held inside the club.

L/Bdr 'Ginger' Robertson, 2 Troop

The Felons Club was situated to the left of Milltown Cemetery and membership was apparently subject to how many stints individuals had spent at Her Majesty's pleasure, although this was probably an urban myth! We had occasion to enter the Felons Club – but not in a social context… We had been conducting a patrol around the area of the club and it was reported that one of the patrol was missing. I think it was Bdr K**** from BHQ.

The powers that be thought that the club was somehow involved in the missing Bdr's non-appearance, so we entered the club and made our way into the main function room, which being a Saturday night was full to bursting with patrons anticipating the start of the evening's entertainment. We burst in – armed to the teeth and with our faces blacked-up with camo-paint. However, after an initial stunned silence, the audience soon guessed that we were not the 'Black & White Minstrels' assembled for their entertainment.

At this moment, one of the patrol suffered an unauthorised discharge from his SLR. I actually saw the bullet bury itself three inches from a seated female's thigh. Talk about silence! You could hear people breathing, and then one of the locals jumped up and screamed out: *"This means war!"* The place erupted, and Battle Royal commenced. Eventually we made a tactical withdrawal in the best of military traditions. The missing Bdr was later found safe and well at the back of the building. As for us, club membership seemed out of the question.

'Ginger' Robertson and 'Snowy' H***. (Courtesy of 'Snowy' H***)

Bdr Renzo Peterson Agnello, 2 Troop

That raid on the Felons Club came back to haunt me when I was back in civvy street after leaving the army. I came home from work one night, and my wife told me that two well-dressed guys called and asked for me. She mentioned that they seemed to avoid her questions like: *"Who are you, and where are you from?"* They said that they would return the next evening when I would be at home. This set alarm bells ringing in my head, and so I had a couple of heavies – from a friend of mine who was controlling club doormen – arrive at the house before the appointed time.

The two suspects duly arrived and I invited them in. The two heavies positioned themselves behind them, and left them in no doubt why they were there. One of the visitors said: *"Bdr Agnello, you have got it wrong. We are from the Special Investigation Branch Military. We have orders to investigate a criminal accusation brought against you by a Mr O'Brien, in that while in the Felons Club, he was hit over the head with a rifle butt by you during a disturbance."*

I checked out their ID, which appeared to be in order, and then I informed them that I had been shot in Northern Ireland by the IRA and, as a result, I could not remember any incidents prior to and after the incident due to my medical condition. They were satisfied with that and went on to inform me that there were thousands of claims made against the British forces. The IRA used this method to tie up the legal system with tons of paperwork. We all relaxed, had a cup of tea and then told a few yarns – and then they said the matter was closed 'due to my impaired memory'.

After the bombings in Belfast the previous Saturday, the authorities were determined that there would be no repetition the following weekend. The hunt for the three IRA men who escaped on 2 December was still in progress and extra troops were also on the streets to try and deter the bombers from carrying out any more attacks. Despite all this extra security around Belfast, one of the worst atrocities of the Troubles was about to take place. A three-man unit from the Ulster Volunteer Force had been instructed to carry out a bomb attack on a pub in North Queen Street which was known to be used by the Official IRA. At around 7:30 p.m. a car with the three terrorists drew up outside the 'Gem' pub, but they were apparently unable to gain access to the building. They waited for the best part of an hour before giving up, and they finally drove off in search of another target.

Just a short distance away was McGurk's Bar, and at around 8:45 p.m. the bomb was placed inside the St George's Street entrance to the pub. The three occupants of the car immediately fled the scene and the bomb exploded moments later with devastating results. The whole building collapsed, 15 Catholics were killed and another 17 were badly injured. British troops, police, and doctors were immediately on the scene and joined in with civilians in the desperate attempts to free the injured. Many years later, in December 2011, Pat Irvine recalled the day her mum Kathleen Irvine was killed in the bombing. She told the *North Belfast News* how she was playing in the streets of New Lodge with her friend Catherine. She told how the streets were unusually clear of patrolling soldiers that night and how everywhere was silent. She said that after the bomb went off she saw a 'hill of people' clawing at the remains of the pub, not realising that her own mother and father were under the wreckage.

Pat also remembered running down one of the 'long' streets in New Lodge, and how, when she turned on to North Queen Street, she saw a crowd of people at the Protestant Tiger's Bay – cheering and singing the pop song 'Bits and Pieces'. It seems beyond belief that people could so cruelly taunt another section of the community simply because they were of a different religion, but this was the stark reality of the absolute hatred both sides of the divide had for each other. A few hours after the bombing, there was an outbreak of violence between the Protestant and Catholic communities at the New Lodge – Tiger's Bay divide. The police and army moved in to try and quell the trouble and a gun battle broke out between the Provisional IRA and the soldiers. Major Jeremy Snow of the Royal Regiment of Fusiliers ended up being fatally injured and he died of his wounds four days later on 8 December. Two RUC officers and five civilians were also injured in the exchange of gunfire. The violence became so bad that five companies of soldiers were eventually brought in to strengthen the patrols attending the incident, and almost 50 houses were searched in the hunt for the Provo gunmen.

Many Catholics thought at the time that the army and RUC were somehow involved in the bombing. They claimed that despite the extra security measures taken to prevent a repetition of the previous Saturday, the bombers seemed to have no trouble getting through the security cordon. They also cited the lack of patrols on the streets of New Lodge as further evidence that the bombers were allowed a clear run to their target. Even Pat Irvine had mentioned how the streets were unusually empty of the army patrols that night. For their part, the army and RUC had their own ideas as to the likely identity of those responsible. They were working on the assumption that the most likely cause was an 'own goal' by an IRA unit transporting the bomb intended for another target. In the RUC report dated 5 December 1971, they claimed:

> Just before the explosion a man entered the licensed premises and left down a suitcase, presumably to be picked up by a known member of the IRA. The bomb was intended for use on other premises. Before the 'pick-up' was made the bomb exploded...*

---

*   Police Ombudsman's report pp. 20–21.

There was never any evidence to support this theory, and all it served to do was strengthen the belief that the army and RUC were in some way involved. This was the largest loss of life in a single incident which had ever occurred since the Troubles started, and it was to be the catalyst for further bombing outrages carried out on innocent civilians in the years to come.

VICTIMS OF THE TROUBLES WHO DIED THIS DAY...

Philomena McGurk (46) – Died in a bomb attack on her husband's pub. Other victims of the explosion were…

Maria McGurk (14)
James Cromie (13)
Edward Keenan (69)
Sarah Keenan (58)
John Colton (49)
Thomas McLaughlin (55)

David Milligan (52)
James Smyth (55)
Francis Bradley (61)
Thomas Kane (45)
Phillip Garry (73)
Kathleen Irvine (45)
Edward Kane (25)
Robert Spotswood (38)*

* List compiled from *The Troubles Magazine* (Glenravel Publications).

SUNDAY 5th…

At around 5:00 a.m. and under cover of darkness a section of men made their way down the Falls Road to a track which ran alongside the fencing of Milltown Cemetery. A short distance in from the track was a long ditch about five feet deep. Their instructions were to take cover in the ditch and watch the IRA burial plot to see who came to visit. The weather was absolutely freezing and the ground was carpeted by a very heavy ground frost.

Gnr Steve Corbett, 3 Troop
We moved into the ditch and waited for daylight. I was frozen to the bone. Five hours we spent there, and not one person came near the memorial. Even if they had, they would have spotted us anyway because our breath was rising up like clouds from where we were in the ditch.

These small-scale patrols must have seemed pointless to the men carrying them out, but they were all part of the constant intelligence gathering operations which helped to build up the information required to launch successful raids on the homes of Provisional IRA suspects. In the coming months they would prove their worth. In the evening, a patrol headed out to Riverdale Estate to carry out a house search, and as soon as the vehicles pulled up, the crowds appeared almost immediately. A couple of men from the section entered the building and the rest surrounded the area to form the cordon to keep out the rioters. The youths started to congregate in front of the soldiers, and then the fun began. First the abuse, and then the bricks and bottles started to come over. It was always worst at night; the missiles were harder to spot with all the street lighting being broken. The men of the search teams would just take whatever cover they could find and hope for the best. Once the suspect had been detained, the men broke cover and made for the Pigs.

As the patrol drew away, both vehicles were pelted by a barrage of paint bombs. They were no more than a bottle filled with bright paint – and sometimes acid too – but they had a deadly purpose. Street lighting was the enemy of the mobile patrol and foot patrol. At night it provided the sniper with a clear shot of any mobile patrol or unwary soldier on foot who was foolish enough to pass through its glare – and every opportunity the soldiers got, they would put the lights out of action. These paint bombs were also used to blind the driver of the vehicle by covering the windscreen with paint. The vehicle would have no alternative but to stop while the windscreen was cleaned off. Someone would then have to get outside the vehicle to wipe the paint away, and then they would become a target for rock-throwing youths or a hidden sniper.

MONDAY 6th...

VICTIMS OF THE TROUBLES WHO DIED THIS DAY...

Mary Thompson (61) – A member of the Salvation Army. Killed when a wall collapsed on her at the Salvation Army Citadel shortly after an IRA bomb attack in Dublin Road, Belfast.[*]

[*] List compiled from *The Troubles* Magazine (Glenravel Publications).

TUESDAY 7th...

In the early hours of the morning, another patrol was sent out to monitor the IRA burial plot in Milltown Cemetery. Six victims of the bombing at McGurk's Bar were due to be interred, and it was expected that many prominent Republicans would be in attendance.

VICTIMS OF PUB BOMB BURIED

Six victims of the explosion at McGurk's public house have been buried, including one of the two children killed in the blast. Six schoolboys walked beside the hearse of their 13 year-old classmate James Cromie. Many other pupils from St Malachy's College walked in the boy's funeral procession as it made its way from his home in New Lodge to Milltown Cemetery. About 600 people walked silently behind the coffin as it made its way up North Queen Street. The funeral paused briefly as it passed the tangled wreckage of the public house where 15 people died when a bomb exploded on Saturday night. James Cromie was playing table football in an upstairs room with the proprietor's son and friends when the bomb went off. He died instantly.

Earlier, Requiem Mass was celebrated in St Patrick's Chapel, Donegal Street for 25-year-old Edward Kane of Ashton Street. Black flags fluttered from many houses in North Queen Street and Unity Flats. Several shops in the area closed as the funeral passed. The funerals of Mrs Kathleen Irvine of Victoria Parade and Mr James Smyth of Alexander House left the New Lodge Road together. At the junction of Clifton Street they joined up with the funerals of Mr and Mrs Keenan.*

* Source taken from *The Troubles* Magazine (Glenravel Publications).

As the funerals had made their way past the Protestant enclaves in the city, there were groups of Loyalists waiting to taunt the mourners. Pat Irvine told the *North Belfast News*:

I remember the funeral procession walking along and there was a crowd gathered at the bottom of the Shankill and they threw stones at the coffins. I was hit in the back of my head and it was split open.*

The funeral procession eventually reached the gates of Milltown Cemetery, where the six coffins were carried through in absolute silence. In the ditch just outside the cemetery, the section of soldiers watched on as the victims of the bombing were carried to their final resting place.

* Source taken from the *North Belfast News*, 5 December 2011.

Later that day, several members from 9 Battery were treated to a concert at Holywood Barracks, laid on by the British comedian Frankie Howerd. These shows helped to boost the morale of the soldiers serving in Northern Ireland and gave them a bit of respite from the everyday dangers they faced on the streets of Belfast. It was also rather ironic that while one group of people were laying to rest the victims of a Loyalist bombing outrage, another group – British soldiers – were being taken out to have a break from the violence shown towards them by the Nationalists (the very people they were trying to protect).

The show was held in a large room inside the barracks. All the officers were sat on the floor at the front while the other ranks either had chairs (if they were lucky) or stood where they could. Frankie entered the room and looked around. Immediately he spotted all the officers sat at the front and insisted they moved to the back before he would start the show. He gave them a terrible time – much to the amusement of the other ranks. The show finally got under way and Frankie started with his routine of jokes before introducing a strong-woman act. The lady came on stage, and amongst cheers from the onlookers began to bend steel bars around her neck and hammer 6-inch nails into planks of wood with her bare fists. A touch of glamour was added to the occasion by Miss World 1969. The show drew to a close and the men were ferried back to their bases in a fleet of Bedford 3-tonners.

WEDNESDAY 8th…

Eight more victims of the McGurk's Bar bombing were laid to rest, and again the soldiers of 9 Battery had to monitor the funerals from the ditch running alongside the fencing.

EIGHT MORE BOMB VICTIMS BURIED

Thousands of mourners lined the streets for the funeral of the remaining eight victims of the bomb at McGurk's Bar. Buried today were Mrs Philomena McGurk, her 13-year-old daughter, and Mr John Colton, a cousin of Mrs McGurk, Mr Francis Bradley, Mr Philip Garry, Mr David Milligan and Mr Thomas McLaughlin. A death notice for Mr McLaughlin appeared in a morning newspaper from a Long Kesh internee, a woman in Armagh Prison and a man on remand in Crumlin Road Prison.*

* Source taken from *The Troubles* Magazine (Glenravel Publications).

It was when confronted by these sad occasions that the full horrors of the Troubles were brought home to the watching soldiers. To see the hundreds of mourners following the coffins raised high on shoulders to their last resting place was very moving, but it has to be said that terrorists and their supporters from both sides of the religious divide seemed indifferent to the suffering they were causing to the innocents of this terrible conflict. The bombing campaign in and around Belfast continued, and another five devices exploded within hours of each other. It was rather ironic that at the same time as the funeral procession of one of the victims of the McGurk's Bar bombing passed close by, an army bomb disposal team were trying to defuse one of the devices.

VICTIMS OF THE TROUBLES WHO DIED THIS DAY...

Major Jeremy Snow (36) – The Royal Regiment of Fusiliers. He died of wounds received during a gun battle with the IRA in New Lodge shortly after the bombing at McGurk's Bar.

Pte Sean Russell (30) – 10th Battalion The Ulster Defence Regiment. He was shot dead by the IRA at his home on the Republican New Barnsley Estate while watching television. He was the first Catholic member of the UDR to be killed by the IRA.

Anthony Nolan (20) – Provisional IRA. Accidentally shot in a house in the Markets area of Belfast.[*]

[*] List compiled from *The Troubles* Magazine (Glenravel Publications).

THURSDAY 9th...

The final victim of the McGurk's Bar bombing was laid to rest on this day. Mr Robert Spotswood was the last person to be identified, and about 200 people attended his funeral. Black flags were hung from the Unity Flats and soldiers sealed off all side streets to prevent any stoning of the cortege by the Protestants. Back at the bus depot, the soldiers carried on with their task of keeping the peace. The everyday essentials that the soldiers needed for their welfare were impossible to purchase in Andersonstown. The men couldn't just walk into a Catholic-owned shop and expect to be able to buy goods. For them to serve a soldier would be seen by the Provisionals as an act of fraternisation, and the punishment for such an offence could lead to the destruction of their premises, or even their execution. Every so often a patrol would travel up to the Cash and Carry at Lisburn and purchase goods to restock the Battery Quartermaster's shop.

Gnr Steve Corbett, 3 Troop

I remember one trip we made up to Lisburn, and we bought some balloons as well. We inflated them all and tied them to the aerial of our Pig. When we got to the outskirts of Andersonstown, people were stopping and staring at us as we drove past. I bet they wondered what the hell was going on.

Besides doing their own restocking, there would also be supplies brought down by the men of HQ Battery based in Palace Barracks, Lisburn.

Gnr Pete Hodkinson, HQ Bty

I remember once, I only did it the once, but I went to Lenadoon where 58 Battery were based. There were two council houses with the adjoining wall knocked out to make it one big building. I was with 'Addi' Adamson, and if I remember rightly, this building was at the bottom of a hill and 'Addi' took me inside while we resupplied the men with bread, confectionary and that kind of stuff. Anyway, I had a look around with 'Addi', and it was bloody horrendous in there. The bunks were three high, so the poor sod that had the top bunk was almost touching the ceiling. It wasn't a very nice place at all, and I remember 'Addi' telling me they got attacked quite a bit at that period.

We used to resupply 9 Battery as well – down at the bus depot at Andersonstown. We got the bread from a bakery at Dunmurry, and then we would get the rest of the provisions and go down there. When we passed under the M1 motorway we would drive flat-out in the Bedford 3-tonners to get through Andersonstown as fast as we could. It was a pretty scary place, and we knew the reputation it had. We really didn't want to be hanging around any longer than we had to.

FRIDAY 10th…

The funeral of Anthony Nolan, a member of the Provisional IRA, was due to take place later in the day. The Provo gunman had accidentally shot himself on 8 December while presumably undertaking weapons training. A section from 9 Battery again had to undertake the task of manning the ditch close to the IRA burial plot and monitoring who attended. At Nolan's home in Staunton Street, Belfast the procession set off with a gathering of around 150 men walking behind the coffin. Large groups of women lined the street as it made its way to Cromac Square. As the procession approached, a snatch-squad of Paratroopers moved in to try and cut off a section of the men following the coffin. Scuffles broke out as the women tried to protect their men, and it was some minutes before the cortege was able to continue its journey to Milltown Cemetery.

The procession finally reached the gates opposite the bus depot and the mortal remains of the Provo gunman were carried through – his coffin draped in the Irish tricolor; beret and gloves placed on top. A Guard of Honour stood either side as he was slowly lowered into the ground. *The Belfast Telegraph* claimed that a volley of shots was fired over his grave in a final salute, but this was not the case. Troops from 9 Battery were on standby to prevent such displays of Republican defiance from happening, and the service at the graveside went off without any further incident. It was around this time that the BC started to take an interest in the Green Briars Club which was situated just off the Glen Road past the Ulster Brewery. There were strong suspicions that the IRA were holding meetings there, and he decided that in future it would be kept under observation to see who was using it.

Bdr 'Horace', 2 Troop

The BC got information that top IRA people were holding meetings in the Green Briars Club, and he decided to keep a watch on it. Myself and my little group and Mick Burton and his group used to take turns in watching it. Sometimes we used to watch it from the rear, and other times the front. I was once watching from the rear, I think it was with Pete Roberts, and we tried to move a bit closer; then this huge security light came on. You couldn't get anywhere near the place without being seen. Even though there was a big field surrounded by trees and plenty of other cover, you just couldn't get any closer to the building.

On another occasion I went out with Bob C*****, an RUC policeman who was an old veteran of the police and he knew just about everybody in Andersonstown. Bob and I were lying in a ditch at the front of the Green Briars. We were watching who came in and out, and then Bob said to me: "*That's Malachy M****** going in there.*" He was one of the top IRA officials who was in charge of stirring up the people against us and that kind of thing, and I said to Bob: "*Are you sure it's him?*" and he replied: "*Oh yes, it's him alright. I used to go to school with him.*" I got a bit excited, and I jokingly said to him: "*Should I shoot him?*" I knew that I couldn't, but it was probably just the excitement of the moment and seeing him there in front of me. Bob said to me: "*I don't think the Battery Commander would like that 'Horace'*," and I saw the sense in that, but I knew I couldn't just shoot him anyway.

Eventually a raid was planned for the Green Briars, but it never took place for quite a while. Word got out to the IRA that the army had the club under surveillance, and from then on they were on their guard. It wouldn't be until the following March that Operation *Cotton-Wool* would finally be put into action.

Bdr 'Horace', 2 Troop

I have to put my hand on my heart and say that it is possible that I had something to do with that. One night I met up with Mick Burton and his section on the street, and I just got chatting to him and said to him: *"Have you been up to the Green Briars lately Mick?"* and he said to me: *"For fuck's sake, 'Horace'. I've got prisoners in the back of the Pig."* I looked around and saw these men in the back of the vehicle, and I realised what I had done. Whether they actually heard what I said I will never know, but it is likely that they were far more concerned about what was going to happen to them rather than my conversation with Mick.

VICTIMS OF THE TROUBLES WHO DIED THIS DAY...

Sgt Kenneth Smyth (28) – 6th Battalion, The Ulster Defence Regiment. Shot dead while off duty by the IRA.

Daniel McCormick (29) – A former member of the Ulster Defence Regiment. Shot dead in the same incident.

Joseph Parker (25) – Shot dead after an argument broke out with members of an army patrol in Butler Street, Ardoyne, Belfast.[*]

[*] List compiled from *The Troubles* Magazine (Glenravel Publications).

SATURDAY 11th...

At approximately 12:25 p.m. a green saloon car stopped outside the Balmoral Furnishing Company on the Protestant Shankill Road. The area was packed with Saturday shoppers going about their business, and nobody paid much attention to the man who got out of the car and left a package in the doorway of the shop. He calmly placed it down, got back into the car and was driven away. Moments later there was a huge explosion which destroyed much of the building. Two young children were sitting in a pram outside the shop at the time. The bomber must have seen the pram; there is no way he could have missed seeing it – and he would have been fully aware of the two young children sat in it when he planted the bomb – but it was of no concern to him; they were Protestant and his sworn enemy. Both children were killed instantly when one of the walls of the building came crashing down. Two adults inside the building were also killed and 14 injured. The explosion was so powerful it was heard in Andersonstown.

Billy McQuiston, a 15-year old Protestant, was walking down the Shankill Road with a friend when he heard the explosion. The two of them immediately rushed to the scene to see if they could help and he later gave a chilling account of what he saw:

> Women were crying. Men were trying to dig out the rubble. Other men were hitting the walls. One person was crying beside you and the next person was shouting: *"Bastards"* and things like that. I didn't actually see the babies' bodies as they had them wrapped in sheets, but the blood was just coming right through them. They were just like lumps of meat, you know; small lumps of meat. All these emotions were going through you and you wanted to help. There were people shouting at the back: *"Let's get something done about this."*
>
> To be perfectly honest with you, I just stood there and cried – just totally and utterly numb. It wasn't until I got back home I realised, this isn't a game. There's a war going on here. These people are trying to do us all in. They're trying to kill us all and they don't care who we are or what age we are. Because we're Protestants, they are going to kill us so we're going to have to do something here.[*]

Large crowds gathered at the scene and the bombing was immediately assumed to be the work of the IRA. The Protestants swore they would have their revenge on the Catholics for what they had done. One of the onlookers in the gathering made a comment to someone about the bombing and his remark was misunderstood. The cry immediately went out: "He's a Catholic!" A furious mob surrounded him and gave him a savage beating, and it took the joint efforts of the army and RUC to rescue the totally innocent Protestant from his attackers. The bombing was later believed to have been a revenge attack for the explosion at McGurk's Bar the previous Saturday.

Billy McQuiston and several of his friends went on to join the UDA and the UVF as a direct result of this bombing because they were so appalled and traumatised by what they had seen that day. The comments that Billy made about the Catholics after the bombing were just the same thoughts that many Catholics had about the Protestants after the McGurk's Bar atrocity. Both sides hated each other so much they were blind to the suffering they were causing to each other.

---

[*]   Source taken from Taylor, Peter, *Loyalists* (London: Bloomsbury Publishing Plc, 1999) p. 90.

THE HERO

I struck a blow for liberty
And killed a child or two;
But I'm an Irish patriot –
What would you have me do?

I threw a bomb for Ireland,
And maimed a girl for life.
(Such side-effects one can't avoid
In a patriotic strife.)

I blew a local factory
Sky-high in sheets of flame;
Some jobs were lost, undoubtedly,
But all in freedom's name.

By bullet, bomb and booby-trap,
By stocking-mask and gun,
I use my most persuasive powers
To make our people one.

And every homeless family,
And every building less,
And every installation wrecked,
I count as a success.

Then rally round, true Irishmen,
That you may shortly see,
Your country 'liberated' –
And ruled by men like me!*

* JACRON.

VICTIMS OF THE TROUBLES WHO DIED THIS DAY...

Harold King (29) – Killed in a bomb attack on a furniture shop on the Shankill Road. A youth placed a bomb at the entrance to the shop and sped off in a waiting car. Moments later the bomb exploded.

Hugh Bruce (70) – Killed in the same incident.

Tracy Munn (2) – Killed in the same incident.

Colin Nicholl (17 months) – Killed in the same incident.

Both children were in a pram outside the building when the bomb exploded.*

* List compiled from *The Troubles* Magazine (Glenravel Publications).

SUNDAY 12th…

Shortly after midnight, a foot patrol left the base at the bus depot and ventured up Glen Road. At this early phase of the tour, the patrols were still sticking very close to the immediate area around the RUC Station. It was generally considered to be reasonably 'safe' to patrol this part on foot, although Andersonstown wasn't the kind of place where you could ever afford to drop your guard. It did, however, prove to be an ideal place to perfect patrol techniques before moving on to the more dangerous areas of the Stockmans, Riverdale, and Rossnareen Estates. The previous unit who had been in Andersonstown didn't carry out foot patrols around these other areas – it was always considered to be far too dangerous – but with 9 Battery, they viewed it entirely differently. The armoured Humber Pigs used so frequently by the patrols were quite easy to spot at night, and often they would be heard by the terrorists long before they were actually seen. It was considered that it would be far better to go in on foot and maintain a certain element of surprise.

The most dangerous estates were too far away from the base to risk doing a foot patrol all the way. and so it became standard procedure to go up in the Pigs and get dropped off in the area to be patrolled. The vehicles would then continue on their mobile operations, and the soldiers on foot would feel safe in the knowledge that backup was never that far away if it was needed. One particular incident serves to illustrate how well this form of patrolling could work.

Gnr Clancy Campbell, 1 Troop

I remember one time when we had gone out in the Pigs and we were dropped off somewhere up Rossnareen. Me and 'Scouse' A***** were leading the foot patrol along this street. It was pitch-black because all the lights had been put out, and then we saw these two lads walking down the street towards us. Anyway, they didn't spot us and we caught them – and we found they had nail bombs in their pockets – and 'Scouse' says to them: *"Ah, bloody hell, go on lads, and get yourselves away"* and he left them with the bombs in their pockets, and this lad says: *"Can we go then?"* and 'Scouse' says: *"Aye, you can go… But you won't get further than 10 yards, because I'll light you up like a Roman fucking candle."*

The two youths stayed where they were and took the bombs out of their pockets, and a few minutes later the Pigs came back and they were taken away. Communications between the patrols and base were usually maintained with the A42 man pack radio. This was carried in a metal frame on the back and had an aerial about four feet in length. Pye pocket radios were also issued to some of the patrols conducting undercover work where the more bulky items of equipment would have been more of a hindrance, but at that time they weren't very reliable and the batteries soon ran down. The standard issue rifle – the SLR – would be carried, and perhaps a few riot guns and ammunition. The problem with being on foot was when the patrols were eventually spotted by marauding gangs of youths; it was then that the dangers of being on foot became apparent. There was nothing more terrifying than being caught out in the open and being subjected to a barrage of bricks and bottles. The rioters were fully aware of the soldier's Rules of Engagement, and they knew that they wouldn't use their rifles to defend themselves unless they were either being shot at or petrol-bombed.

The housing estates where these early patrols were conducted seemed a million miles away from the more grim surroundings of Rossnareen. It was almost like being back in England and walking around some leafy suburb where grand Victorian houses lined the streets. In the whole of the tour there were only about three serious incidents that happened in this area. For the soldiers, to patrol these streets was a welcome break from the violence usually dished out to them just a mile or so away, but at times, even these quiet backwaters could become a source of danger. There was always the constant worry that despite the best made plans, something might go wrong. In a place like Andersonstown, plans were constantly being overtaken by the unexpected. One dark night, the BC had ordered the area to be flooded with patrols in an attempt to bring a halt to the increasing violence which was occurring around the estates. At around the same time there was also a unit of the Blues and Royals out in the same vicinity going along the streets in their Ferret scout cars, shooting out street lights. It would seem that probably, through lack of communication, the Blues and Royals were unaware of the patrols from 9 Battery being out in the same area. This simple lack of communication almost cost one soldier his life.

Bdr 'Horace', 2 Troop

I can't remember exactly when this happened, but the BC decided he wanted to swamp the area to search certain buildings. I'm not exactly sure what was behind it, but everybody in the unit was out, and we even brought in units from the Province Reserve Troops. I'm not sure who they were, but I think it was a Scots unit. As usual, the Blues and Royals were there as well.

I had a bad feeling as soon as I got in my position. I was on the east side of the area nearer towards the bus depot on one of the 'nice' estates near to where I had the explosives find. I had a bad feeling because there were so many people around, and everywhere you looked there were soldiers on the street corners, but anyway, I deployed – we were part of a large cordon – and I deployed my men along the street, whichever one it was that we were on. Suddenly there were shots flying over the top of us from the west end of the estate.

I later found out that these shots had been fired by the Blues and Royals as they went along one of the main roads shooting out the street lights. Unfortunately we had no idea who had fired them at the time and I put Gnr Donaldson forward to a wall so he could look over into the next street to see if he could see where the shooting was coming from. All of a sudden there was a shot fired very close from where we were, and I almost instinctively knew it was from an SLR. I had feared something like this happening, and I got all my section off the street and back in the Pig to see what would materialise.

Unbeknown to Bdr 'Horace', there was another patrol in the area that night. Mick Burton and his 'sniper patrol' were out and hunting for Provo gunmen…

Gnr Mike Fall, 3 Troop

I was out with Mick Burton, and I had the night sight, and I looked through it and said to Mick: "*There's a guy with a rifle here who hasn't got a beret on.*" My immediate thought was that he was a gunman, and I said to Mick: "*It's no good me shooting because the sight isn't zeroed in for me,*" so he said to me: "*Well give it to me then,*" and then Mick took it; he took the rifle and fired the shot. It could have only been seconds later, and the BC came over and started shouting that we were shooting at each other.

Bdr 'Horace', 2 Troop

About a minute later, Mick Burton came walking around the corner onto our street. He came swaggering along with the night sight on his rifle and he addressed me. He said: "*Who the bloody hell was that just then standing on the wall? I nearly got him. If he hadn't stumbled when he did, he would have been dead.*" He obviously knew it was almost a blue on blue after he fired the shot. Somebody did mention that Gnr Donaldson didn't have his beret on and was mistaken for a gunman. I can't remember that, but it is possible, but Mick Burton had obviously realised by this time that it was one of our own battery as I had done. According to Mick, Gnr Donaldson had stumbled as he fired at him, and that's what probably saved his life.

VICTIMS OF THE TROUBLES WHO DIED THIS DAY…

John Barnhill (65) – Shot dead by the Official IRA at his home near Strabane. This was the first political assassination carried out by the Official IRA since 1922.[*]

[*] List compiled from *The Troubles* Magazine (Glenravel Publications).

MONDAY 13th...

At around 8:00 p.m. a mobile patrol from 3 Troop was passing Musgrave Park Hospital when they came under fire from a hidden gunman. Approximately four low-velocity shots were directed at the vehicle, but no fire was returned and the patrol continued on its journey. In all probability it was a ruse to get the vehicles to halt, and then there would have been other gunmen lying in wait to engage the soldiers, but the Patrol Commander didn't fall for the trap. This was just another incident of many that didn't even warrant a mention in the newspapers. Such incidents were almost an everyday occurrence.

TUESDAY 14th...

At around 3:00 p.m. a call came through that the two Pigs of C11 were caught up in a riot in Rossnareen. Most of the rioting seemed to coincide with either when the youths were going to school, or when they were on their way home. It was a kind of game to the youths, but equally, it was also at times orchestrated by the Provisionals when they wished to launch an attack on the army patrols. The rioting would provide the distraction to the troops and draw them into the area while the gunmen targeted the soldiers. On this particular occasion, a patrol had been passing a local school when they came under attack. Two Pigs from 3 Troop raced to the scene, and as they turned in off Glen Road they were met by the sight of the stranded Pigs being battered by a ferocious barrage from the rioters. The air was full of the sound of baton rounds being fired and the screams from the rampaging mob.

Gnr Steve Corbett, 3 Troop
We got up there to help out 1 Troop, who were having a hard time of it. The Pigs were completely surrounded by the rioters, and they were getting an absolute pasting. We pulled up and we all bailed out of the back. Some of us had these big long Perspex riot shields we used to use, and others were just armed with a riot gun. Sentries stayed with the Pigs and kept guard with their SLRs in case we got shot at. We made a charge at the youths, firing the riot guns as we went.

Suddenly a gap appeared within the ranks of the howling mob and a burst of gunfire was heard above the sound of the rioting. Shots had been fired in the direction of the advancing soldiers, and everyone – including the rioters – scattered as the sound of the shooting filled the air. It was impossible to tell where the gunfire had come from though. The soldiers took cover and scanned the buildings for any sign of the gunmen. Each side paused at the sound of the shooting. The rioters were looking behind, fearing for their own safety from the indiscriminate shooting. It stayed like this for a few moments as everyone tried to locate the gunmen, but they had fled. The rioters gradually moved out into the open, and once more the rocks and bottles came raining down on the two patrols, but the combined efforts of both units finally cleared the mob and the vehicles withdrew.

VICTIMS OF THE TROUBLES WHO DIED THIS DAY...

Martin McShane (16) – Shot dead by British soldiers when they opened fire with a sub-machine gun in Coalisland. The soldiers opened fire when they thought he was pointing a gun at them.*

* List compiled from *The Troubles* Magazine (Glenravel Publications).

WEDNESDAY 15th...

A mobile from 1 Troop was preparing to go out on yet another patrol around the streets of Andersonstown. The four-man crew checked their equipment, put on their flak jackets and loaded their weapons. 'Brummie' Morrison was the first to finish and walked on ahead to the waiting Pig. He climbed in the back and settled himself down on the wooden bench by the open back door. A few moments later he was joined by the rest of the crew. Brian Kingsnorth – the Bombardier in charge of the patrol – climbed into his position in the front, and

Gnr Fred Jeffreys.
(Taken from the *Lancashire Evening Post*)

Clancy Campbell – the driver – took his place behind the wheel. Young Fred Jeffreys had volunteered to go on this patrol. The man who should have gone was waiting for a booked phone call from a relative back in England, and Fred had volunteered to take his place so that he wouldn't miss it. Fred walked to the rear of the vehicle to take up his usual position and stopped dead in his tracks... Brummie was in HIS seat! Fred was horrified. This was HIS seat, and he always sat there when he went out on patrol.

He asked Brummie to move, but Brummie was having none of it. He told him it was only a bloody seat and Fred should stop moaning and get in the Pig. Bdr Kingsnorth told them both to stop arguing and ordered Fred to mount up, which he reluctantly did. Fred was still grumbling as the Pig turned out into Divis Drive and up Falls Road towards Andersonstown Road. They drove on to the estates up at the top end of Andersonstown

Road, turned in to Slievegallion Drive and onwards to Ramoan Gardens. Everything seemed strangely quiet; there were no rioters out on the streets and people were just going about their everyday business. The Pig proceeded up to the top end of Ramoan Gardens and slowed down to negotiate the corner onto the Glen Road. Suddenly, there was a burst of automatic gunfire.

TWO SOLDIERS WOUNDED IN AMBUSH

Two soldiers were shot and seriously wounded when a gunman ambushed an army patrol on the outskirts of Belfast this afternoon. The gunman fired from a position near the junction of Ramoan Gardens and the Glen Road at Andersonstown. It is believed at least two of the seven shots fired by the terrorist hit the soldiers who were travelling in an army Land Rover.

Both men were rushed to Musgrave Park Hospital, but the army was unable to give their conditions. Police, however, said both men were reported to be 'seriously hurt'.

They were members of a patrol of the 12th Light Air Defence Regiment, Royal Artillery. One was hit in the neck by a ricochet, and the other was hit twice in the back. According to an army spokesman, fire was not returned.[*]

[*] Source taken from *The Belfast Telegraph*.

Gnr Clancy Campbell, 1 Troop

I was just approaching the junction of Glen Road when some shots rang out and Brian slumped forward over the dashboard after being shot in the back of the head. Fred Jeffreys turned around and looked to the front to see what was happening and took two shots in his lower back. I looked around to see what was going on and Brummie was holding onto Fred to stop him falling out of the back of the Pig. Brian was slumped in his seat with blood pouring from the back of his head and poor old Fred was screaming out in pain. I put my foot down and drove as fast as I could towards Musgrave Park Hospital – swerving from side to side as I went.

The Pig drew up outside the hospital and Clancy dashed inside to get help while Brummie stayed with the injured…

I dashed inside and the Army Medical Orderly was sat there with his chair tilted back and his beret pushed to the back of his head. I

Clancy Campbell and 'Brummie' Morrison.
(Courtesy of Clancy Campbell)

told him I had two injured men outside who were in urgent need of help. I can't remember his exact words, but it was something on the line of: "*Well, what do you expect me to do about it?*" I saw red when he said that. I cocked my rifle and aimed it at his head and said to him: "*I've got a man out there with two bullets in his back and another with a hole in the back of his head. Get off your bloody arse and give me a hand before I put a hole in YOUR head.*" I can tell you, he soon moved then!

Fred was only 19, and he had been in the army for just six months. The previous October, his family were at Woolwich Barracks, where they watched with pride as he and his troop of fellow recruits held their Passing Out Parade at the completion of their training – and now here he lay, gravely injured in a bed at Royal Victoria Hospital* after being shot in the back by a Provo gunman. Back at home in Morecambe, his mother was busy icing a Christmas cake at her mother's house as the police frantically tried to find her to let her know about poor Fred. In the end they took to touring the streets with loudspeakers in an attempt to locate her. Mrs Jeffreys later told her local newspaper in Morecambe how she found out about her son:

---

*   Fred Jeffreys was transferred to this hospital after initial treatment at Musgrave Park Hospital.

I had just finished icing a Christmas cake at my mother's house in Christie Avenue when we heard the tannoy. It was about quarter to four in the afternoon by the time they found me. They drove me to my own flat to grab some things and then took me by police car with an escort to Liverpool Airport to catch the plane. I was met in Belfast and was at the hospital before eight o'clock the same night. At that time, because of the state of the wounds, they didn't hold out much hope.

I don't feel bitter towards the Irish or the army. If anyone should feel bitter it is Fred, but he doesn't. He said it was just bad luck and if it hadn't been him, it would have been someone else. These lads pick their own careers. Fred liked the army. He wasn't in it long – we only went to his Passing Out Parade in October – but he said it was a grand life; but what happened to him could have happened to the most hardened veteran. It isn't like a normal war; you just don't know who you are fighting.

The newspaper article explained how the incident occurred…

Fred was hit twice in a surprise attack as his mobile patrol moved down the city's Ramoan Gardens. He was a member of 12th Light Air Defence Regiment's 9 Battery, given the task of patrolling the troubled Andersonstown area of the city, and had hardly had time to get into the routine of six hours on patrol, 12 hours off eating and sleeping, and six on standby when he was shot.

"The soldiers were sitting in the back of a Pig – a 1-ton armoured vehicle – when three rounds were fired into the back of it," said Major Ian MacKenzie.

"The Pig usually goes about with its doors open so the men can get out quickly and they were not expecting an attack in this area."

One round whistled around the inside of the truck – hitting Bdr Kingsnorth in the side of the head. He is now recovering. The other two rounds hit Gnr Jeffreys in the back.

The injured soldiers were immediately rushed to hospital and Gnr Jeffreys had an operation. One bullet had damaged nerves at the base of his spine and he was unable to move his legs.

It was a short 'war' for Gnr Fred Jeffreys, but the fighting wasn't over. The real battle – back to complete fitness so he can have a second go at the life he loves – is just beginning.

Last year in Northern Ireland, 43 soldiers never had that second chance.[*]

[*] Source taken from the *Lancashire Evening Post*.

Feelings within the battery were running high after this latest incident, and many of the men were looking for revenge.

L/Bdr 'Ginger' Robertson, 2 Troop

I remember that shooting of Fred and Brian quite clearly. We knew where the gunman had fired from and we wanted to go in and sort the bastards out, but we required the OK from London as I remember it. We waited all day and word came back that we could not, so we went in and gave them a hard time anyway.

Brian Kingsnorth went on to make a full recovery, but Fred wasn't so lucky. He ended up paralysed from the waist down. Such was the hands of fate for poor Fred. Volunteering for the patrol – and being in the wrong seat – cost him the use of his legs.

THURSDAY 16th...

The death rate amongst the British troops was rising, and by 16 December there had been 42 British Army regular soldiers killed since the start of 1971. The RUC lost 11 men and the UDR lost five. Civilian casualties were 107 dead. The previous year there had been 20 deaths, and in 1969 there were only 13 deaths. The killing spree was now rising at an alarming rate, as the attacks on the Security Forces became more frequent and savage in their execution. If more proof of the brutality and callous indifference of the Provisional IRA were needed, the killing of Pte Anthony Aspinwall of the Gloucester Regiment provided it. Pte Aspinwall was part of a patrol that was providing cover for another section which was conducting a house search in Milan Street, Belfast. Pte Aspinwall's patrol was in nearby Alma Street when they became engaged in a gun battle with the Provisionals. Pte Aspinwall was fatally injured and rushed to hospital. The civilian ambulance that picked up the wounded soldier was ambushed by Provo gunmen as it sped towards the Royal Victoria Hospital, and at least two bullets hit the vehicle as it passed through the Lower Falls area. It was a callous attempt to finish off a gravely injured soldier, and even the presence of the civilian crew of medics in the vehicle didn't deter the gunmen. Pte Aspinwall died with his family at his bedside. He had been in the Province for just one week. It was such outrages as this that made so many soldiers feel so bitter towards the people they had been sent to protect. Although it was wrong to retaliate, it sometimes happened.

That evening, a large search was mounted in the area around Shaw's Road and Tullymore Gardens by the men of 9 Battery. Two patrols from 3 Troop provided the cordon while 1 Troop carried out the search.

Gnr Steve Corbett, 3 Troop

I was positioned in the front garden of a house in a cul-de-sac as the search got under way. All went well – although nothing was found – and then a Ferret scout car turned into the cul-de-sac. He drove forward just past me and slammed into reverse. He went straight through the hedges of the garden where I was stood and made a right mess of it. I didn't see the need for that. He could have just reversed back around the corner rather than plough up the garden and the hedges. It was stupid acts like this that turned many people against us. Although I could understand why some soldiers did this kind of thing, it didn't make it right.

The whole operation lasted until 5:30 a.m. and yet again, nothing was found. The crews mounted up and were just about to drive off when someone noticed that 'Addi' Adamson was missing.

Gnr Steve Corbett, 3 Troop

We got back out of the Pigs and immediately started searching the area for 'Addi'. I found him hiding under a privet hedge where he had been left to keep guard. I asked him what the hell he was playing at, but he just said that he hadn't heard the call to mount up. I suppose the outcome could have been a lot worst though. If the locals had found him before us, they would have just handed him over to the IRA, and that would have been the end of 'Addi'.

Gnr Gordon 'Addi' Adamson, 3 Troop

I honestly didn't hear the call to mount up. I heard the Pigs start up and wondered what the hell was going on, and then I spotted 'Harry' [the author] running towards me, and then I realised how lucky I had been not to be left behind.

Back in Dublin, the Provisional IRA issued a statement claiming responsibility for the killing of three UDR soldiers and a British Army officer over the past few days. They went on to say that they had also shot and wounded 22 soldiers. Over the same period, they claimed that their own losses were one volunteer, who was accidentally shot dead, and two others who were wounded.

VICTIMS OF THE TROUBLES WHO DIED THIS DAY...

Pte Anthony Aspinwall (22) – The Gloucestershire Regiment. Died of wounds after a gun battle with the IRA in Alma Street, Belfast.*

* List compiled from The Troubles Magazine (Glenravel Publications).

FRIDAY 17th...

Sporadic attacks continued on the mobile patrols as they continued to probe deep into the estates. Sometimes it would be just a single shot fired at a patrol as they slowed down to negotiate a corner. On other occasions the gunman might chance his luck against a stationary target.

Gnr Clancy Campbell, 1 Troop

I don't remember where or when it actually happened, but I seem to remember it was up Andersonstown Road, and we were up there on a roundabout. We got sent up there for some reason I don't recall now, and BSM Don Potter and all them were there. I was leaning on the bonnet of the Pig, and then all of a sudden I fell backwards, and I couldn't see anything. A bullet hit the bonnet of the Pig and I ended up with chips of paint and stuff in my eyes. Don Potter turned around and said to me: *"Ah, Clancy. I knew it hadn't got you, because if it had, it would have gone straight through you and into me."*

That evening, the patrols were out again in the Rossnareen area conducting searches for arms and explosives.

Bdr Renzo Peterson Agnello, 2 Troop

I remember on one occasion when we were searching houses, and this time I was on the outside cordon. It was around 11:00 p.m. on a Friday night, and not a good time to carry out these house searches. Within minutes of us reaching the house we were to search, a mob fueled by alcohol appeared and started to get very aggressive. I thought to myself: *"Here we go again"* when suddenly there was a loud bang and what appeared to be a cloud of smoke hanging over the mob. I looked at our vehicle and noticed that our driver, Paddy Keane, was grinning to himself. I went over and asked him if he had fired a CS (gas) canister. *"Oh"* he says, *"in the excitement I must have grabbed it from the wrong box. I was sure it was a rubber bullet."* Now I couldn't be sure if Paddy's mistake was genuine or not, but it worked a treat and the crowd soon dispersed. I was able to truthfully explain to the officer in charge that the mistake could easily be done, as both the rubber bullets and CS canisters were stored close together – and both were fired from the same gun.

I remember on another occasion when as soon as we pulled off the Glen Road into the housing estates, there was always this same large female waiting to sound the alarm. She would be there blowing her whistle, rattling her dustbin lid and really giving it the works. Well, this time she came over to the vehicle screaming and spitting, and with her very large bosom hanging down to her waist. She reached through and tried to punch the driver in the face, and the next moment I heard an almighty smack. Yes… the driver was at it again. Paddy Keane had picked up his Fed riot gun and gave her a clout with it into that ample bosom. I don't remember ever seeing her again after that.

Paddy Keane was a well-known character of the battery who was immensely liked by everyone who knew him. When his R&R leave came up, he borrowed an old car off someone to drive down to Southern Ireland to visit his mother. The day came for his return back to base, but the car refused to start, and so he set off on foot. About an hour after he left, his mother received a visit from some men asking for Paddy. It was only a small village where she lived, and it wasn't the kind of place where a secret stays that way for long. The probability was that they were from the IRA and they had heard of Paddy being home on leave. It had been a narrow escape for him, but his luck lasted even longer and became almost comical.

Paddy had got some distance between himself and his mother's house and decided to start thumbing a lift. Eventually a car with a couple of occupants drew alongside him, and the front passenger asked Paddy where he was going. He told them he was returning to work in Andersonstown after visiting his mother and so they offered him a lift. Paddy got in the car and they went on their way. The conversation soon turned around to 'the Troubles' and the two men told Paddy that they were members of the Provisional IRA. Eventually they reached Andersonstown and Paddy was asked where he wanted dropping off. He directed them to the bus depot after telling them he worked there. As Paddy got out of the car one of them is reputed to have asked him if he was a bus conductor. Paddy told him: "No, I'm a British soldier."

Paddy's late return back to base did cause some concern, with him being from Southern Ireland. The body of a man was found on the border around the time of Paddy's disappearance, and the unfortunate victim had been shot through the head. Many of the men in 9 Battery were worried that it might have been Paddy.

SATURDAY 18th…

At around 4:30 p.m. a patrol from 3 Troop set off to Cavanmore Gardens to conduct an arms search at a house. The cordon was set up around the immediate area as the search team moved in. After so many failures, they finally hit the jackpot:

MACHINE GUN AMONG BIG ARMS HAUL

Troops recovered a Bren light machine gun in one of several raids in Belfast yesterday.

The weapon was discovered in a search by soldiers of the 12th Light Air Defence Regiment, Royal Artillery at a house in Cavanmore Gardens, Andersonstown at 5:05 p.m.

Also found in the search were a bipod for the Bren, six Bren magazines – two of them loaded – a .303 rifle with telescopic sight, a .22 rifle with telescopic sight, one bayonet, 69 .303 rounds, a .303 magazine with 10 rounds in it, four 12 bore shotgun cartridges, and 13 .303 cartridge clips.[*]

[*] Sourced from Brian Corser's private collection of newspaper cuttings.

The Bren gun and rifles. (Courtesy of Brian Corser)

Upstairs, hidden in a wardrobe, they found a small arsenal of deadly weapons. The woman who lived there swore that she knew nothing about the guns, but how you could have such a haul of weapons under your roof and know nothing about them really took some believing. The search team came out and started loading all the guns into the back of a Pig before taking them back to the RUC Station to be photographed and examined. It was one hell of a boost to everyone's morale to make such a large find. A weapon such as the Bren machine gun, or a sniping rifle in capable hands, was a formidable weapon to face.

Gnr Steve Corbett, 3 Troop

I was on the cordon of that particular search. I thought it would turn out just the same as all the others we had done. I watched as the search team moved into the house – and it wasn't long before they came out with the weapons wrapped up in blankets and put them in the back of one of the Pigs. We were all over the moon when we saw the Bren gun; then they brought the woman out. She was mouthing off at us all, and claiming she knew nothing about the stuff found in the wardrobe. It wasn't exactly the kind of thing you wouldn't notice though. There were the two rifles as well, and all the magazines for the Bren. It certainly made us feel a bit safer knowing that lot wasn't available for use anymore. It was also rumoured that the Bren may have been the gun used on Clancy Campbell's Pig a few days before.

VICTIMS OF THE TROUBLES WHO DIED THIS DAY...

John Bateson (18) – Provisional IRA. Killed when the bomb he was transporting in a vehicle exploded prematurely in King Street, Magherafelt, County Derry.

Martin Lee (18) – Provisional IRA. Killed in the same incident.

James Sheridan (19) – Provisional IRA. Killed in the same incident.

James McCallum (16) – Killed in a bomb explosion at the Star Bar on Springfield Road. The bomb was planted by the Protestant UVF and no warning was given.*

* List compiled from *The Troubles* Magazine (Glenravel Publications).

MONDAY 20th...

The IRA issued a statement to the newspapers which made it quite clear that their struggle was to continue, and over the next few weeks the attacks against 9 Battery were to become far more frequent...

FIGHT WILL GO ON SAY IRA

The Provisional IRA has warned that it will not accept passively internment without trial or any 'new style repressive measures' against Republicans in the South. In a statement replying to Mr Jack Lynch, who warned that he would not allow the IRA to usurp the functions of his government, the Provisionals said that such actions by him, in response to British and right-wing pressure, could only serve the interests of British Imperialists and would be a dastardly betrayal of the Nationalist people of the North. The Provisionals claimed that their 'struggle against British Occupation Forces would continue'.*

* Source taken from *The Troubles* Magazine (Glenravel Publications).

Republican News, 19 December 1971. (Courtesy of Brian Corser)

Later that evening, two patrols were sent out from the bus depot on a routine mission to conduct car checks and 'P' checks. While 3 Troop were detailed to set up the road block, the vehicles of 2 Troop were to go up the Glen Road at the junction with Shaw's Road and check anyone going into or leaving the Green Briars Club. Most of the Humber Pigs at that time were, by then, being painted in whatever dark colours were available. The vehicles were subjected to attacks with paint bombs virtually every time they went on patrol, and the usual army olive green was in short supply. Some of the Pigs of 2 Troop ended up with a liberal coating of matte black – used as a last resort to cover up the brilliant white

How the Pigs looked after a few paint bombs. (Courtesy of Brian Corser)

paint which regularly covered the bodywork and made the patrolling vehicles so easy to pick out on the darkened streets.

TEENAGE GIRL DIES IN CRASH

A teenage girl was killed when the ice-cream van in which she was travelling was involved in a collision with an army vehicle at a check point. The 16-year-old who died was one of three passengers in the vehicle, which collided with a stationary 1-ton army armoured car at the junction of Glen Road and Shaw's Road. She was named as Anne Marie Caldwell, of Ramoan Drive, Andersonstown. Another girl was seriously injured.[*]

[*] Source taken from *The Troubles* Magazine (Glenravel Publications).

Bdr 'Horace', 2 Troop

We got orders to do a person check outside the Green Briars Club in the evening. We had done one previously, which turned out to be a bit of a flop, so they decided to have another crack at it and see who exactly was using the club. I was in charge of the lead Pig and Renzo took command of the other. We parked up at the entrance to the drive which led to the Green Briars Club and waited to see who went in or came out. It was pitch-black on Glen Road, as nearly all the street lights were smashed. Our Pigs were painted black at that time, and we had no lights on.

As people started leaving the club, I walked forward with some other lads from the patrol and started 'P' checking them to see who they were. All of a sudden there was an almighty crash. I turned around and saw a sight I will never forget. An ice-cream van had come tearing down the hill and had not seen the Pigs parked up in the dark.

The crew inside the vehicle had seen the van coming and had the presence of mind to pull the doors shut just before the van slammed into them. The force of the collision was so great that it knocked the rear Pig several feet forward.

Bdr 'Horace', 2 Troop
When I turned around, the van was actually two or three feet in the air and there were thousands of shards of glass flying around everywhere. The serving hatch was open, and there was a young girl hanging out. I could see the upper part of her body and her arms were flying about like a rag-doll. It was a dreadful sight. The van came crashing down to the ground and we all rushed forward to help – including some of those who had come out of the club.

Some of the younger lads from the patrol were quite shocked by what they saw, and I was fairly stunned myself by what had happened. I went over to see what I could do, and the girl who had been in the serving hatch was lying on the road with her knees pulled up. I later found out she had a badly broken pelvis. I tried to offer her some help; I had some morphine, but she refused it. The other girl had been dragged out of the wreckage, and she was in a really serious condition. The driver was a young lad, who we later found out was a 'stickie', and they had been out spotting for the Provos.

It was common practice for these ice-cream vans to be used as a type of 'early warning' system by the Provos. They would drive around the estates, and when an army patrol was spotted they would start playing their chimes to warn any local Provo units of the army presence. The vans were also used to ferry arms and money around the estates.

Bdr 'Horace', 2 Troop
By now the crowd around the crash scene was growing quite large, and we were being subjected to an awful lot of abuse – being called "*British bastards*" and that kind of thing. Some of them were trying to wrestle the rifles from the grip of my men, and it was really beginning

'Horace'. (Courtesy of Brian Corser)

to turn ugly. Renzo got on the radio to the RUC Station to call for help as I tried to calm things down and see to the other girl – and then all of a sudden a BBC film crew came up the road, set up some floodlights and started filming the scene.

This was the last thing we needed. The floodlights made us all sitting ducks to anyone who may have been hanging around with a gun, so I quickly grabbed hold of the person who appeared to be in charge and tried to get him to turn off the lights. He either didn't care, or he didn't seem to understand the danger he was putting my men in, and he refused to turn them out – so I just walked over to the other injured girl and tried to help. An Irishman grabbed hold of me and dragged me off – telling me: *"Get your filthy English hands off her."* He got down and started massaging her heart and giving her mouth-to-mouth. I stood and watched as he tried to save her.

Eventually, another patrol from 3 Troop arrived at the scene – commanded by an officer known to the men of 9 Battery as 'Sydney Slug'. He approached the BBC crew and forced them to turn off the lights and stop filming. A cordon was set up around the scene and Slug ordered 2 Troop to return to base while they dealt with the incident.

Gnr Steve Corbett, 3 Troop
We had been doing a Glen trap when our section was sent up to assist 2 Troop after a traffic accident. When we arrived, I didn't really see much of what had happened, but I was later told it was quite serious and that a young girl had died in the collision.

Eventually, 2 Troop arrived back at the bus depot and 'Horace' had time to reflect on what he had witnessed…

Bdr 'Horace', 2 Troop

I was very upset by the whole experience because I really thought that I could have saved the young girl's life, but I was later told that there was nothing I would have been able to do for her, as her head had gone through the windscreen and her throat had been cut wide open on the shards of glass. The other girl made a good recovery, but I often think of the young girl who lost her life. It was all so sad. The driver of the ice-cream van was arrested and taken back to the RUC Station to be interviewed. He later admitted that he had been out 'spotting' for the IRA.

The reaction of the civilian when 'Horace' tried to help the girl showed the depth of hatred felt by the people of Andersonstown towards the soldiers of 9 Battery. There had been claims of beatings at the hands of soldiers, and also claims of the killing of unarmed volunteers by British troops since the Troubles began but, for their part, the army always denied such things happened. The IRA and Protestant paramilitary groups were also guilty of 'punishment' beatings and summary execution of anyone they captured or who crossed them. They didn't take prisoners – and if they did, they wouldn't live for very long. Terrorists would often kill someone for the most trivial of reasons.

'Moira' – Belfast resident

I once knew a young boy who lived a few doors away from me. I think he was about 19 and he had got himself a job in a bar. He really enjoyed that job, and then the IRA started calling on him and asking him to join… but he wouldn't – and then one night someone called to his house and asked for him; and when he came to the door they shot him dead. It was the IRA.

On the night of 23 October 1971, two volunteers of the *Cumann na mBan* were shot dead by British troops in the Lower Falls area of Belfast. The two sisters, Maura Meehan and Dorothy Maguire, were driving around in a car with their horn blaring to warn of approaching army patrols and RUC policemen. A soldier from one of the patrols opened fire on the car – killing the two women. The army claimed that they were fired at first by the occupants of the car, but no weapons were ever found in the vehicle. The two women were the first casualties suffered by the *Cumann na mBan* during the Troubles, and the IRA made sure that they exploited this incident to the full. There were always claims and counter-claims with such controversial incidents, but whatever the truth about the shooting, the two women became martyrs for their cause. Not long after their deaths, the Republican propaganda machine had another poem published in the papers sympathetic to their cause in an attempt to capitalise on the incident and to recruit more volunteers to the women's wing of the IRA. It was controversial shootings such as this which stoked up the hatred of the British Army within the Catholic community.

'MAGUIRE AND MEEHAN – MARTYRS FOR A CAUSE'
Two sisters born to fight a cause
Have died a tragic death.
Mowed down by British justice
In a part of Belfast West.
They travelled in the early hours
To give a warning clear,
Of the infiltrating soldiers
Who were drawing near.

But then some crazy soldier
Somewhere up behind,
With an automatic weapon
Lost control and fired it blind.
The car sped on, but all at once
A salvo from the dark;
The rear windscreen was shattered
British soldiers found their mark.

No doubt there'll be enquiries
So all the facts are known,
And we the people of the land
Demand the truth be shown.
But like everything that's happened
In Ireland's freedom fight,
Foul deeds like this one now being told
Will be white-washed out of sight.

Their car turned into Cape Street,
And they noticed right away
Much soldiery activity
For the British were at play.
They travelled on that darkened way,
As if it was their main intent
To waken every household
Everywhere they went.

Very soon the British
Spread the story near and far,
That girls in men's attire
Were engaging them in war.
They said a gun was fired at them
But this was never found.
It's amazing all the stories
The army put around.

Two martyrs more are added to
A never-ending list.
Their deaths won't make us falter
But will help us to resist.
The force of Britain's army
And Stormont's evil men
Won't break the cause within our hearts
'A NATION ONCE AGAIN"

Another young woman died on the same day that Anne Marie Caldwell was killed in the collision with the army patrol on the Glen Road. Margaret McCorry was just another innocent victim of the many indiscriminate shootings carried out by trigger-happy terrorist gunmen from both sides of the religious divide, but unlike the killing of the two IRA volunteers – Maguire and Meehan back in October – for Margaret McCorry there would be no poems, and neither would she become a martyr for any terrorist cause. She left behind a devastated family who had good reason to hate the so-called 'freedom fighters' who didn't give a damn about the safety of innocent civilians when they carried out their random attacks on those trying to keep the peace.

Two Provo gunmen – one armed with a Thompson sub-machine gun, and the other an M1 carbine – forced their way into a house on the Crumlin Road and waited. On the opposite side of the road, 20-year-old Margaret McCorry was waiting to catch a bus into the city centre. A short while later, a military patrol drove past the house and came under attack from the two gunmen. Margaret was hit in the head and died as she was being taken to hospital. She was yet another victim of the terrorists who were fighting for their 'cause'. Even when incidents such as this happened the IRA would try to shift the blame onto the army, or they might issue an 'apology' to the bereaved family and give some lame excuse as to why the innocent person was killed.

---

*   Sourced from Brian Corser's private collection of newspaper cuttings.

VICTIMS OF THE TROUBLES WHO DIED THIS DAY...

Margaret McCorry (20) – Shot dead by the IRA when they ambushed an army mobile patrol in Crumlin Road, Belfast.

Anne Marie Caldwell (16) – Killed in a collision with a Humber armoured car whilst travelling as a passenger in an ice-cream van which was out spotting for the IRA.*

* List compiled from *The Troubles* Magazine (Glenravel Publications).

TUESDAY 21st...

As the build-up to Christmas continued, so too did the bombings and shootings. On the Lisburn Road, the owner of a pub tried to save his premises after a bomb had been left on the bar. Despite pleas from his staff to get out of the building, Mr Lavery was blown to pieces when the bomb exploded as he tried to remove it. A suspicious package was also found at the entrance to Great Victoria Street Railway Station, but after the bomb disposal team dismantled it, they found it contained nothing more than clothing. Troops came under attack when gunmen fired around 25 shots at them near McKenna's Bar on the Oldpark Road after a bomb had also been thrown. The RUC Station on the same road also came under fire and shots were fired at Crumlin Road Prison.

In the Markets area of Belfast during the early hours, an 18-year-old man carrying a package was shot in the arm by the army when he failed to stop after being challenged by the patrol. The man was challenged twice, and it was only when he was challenged the second time (and still failed to stop) that he was shot. His package contained a turkey he had purchased for Christmas.

The Provisional IRA Commander, *Seán Mac Stíofáin*, claimed to be

Republican Christmas card.
(Courtesy of Brian Corser)

holding talks with 'Protestants of good standing'. He said the meeting was held on the request of Protestants in the Republic, but refused to go into too much detail. He also claimed that the recent bombings of Protestant pubs were not the work of the IRA: 'It is not the IRA's policy to attack or kill Protestants. If Protestants were killed, it was because they were members of the UDR or RUC'. The relatives of the young children killed in the recent bombing of the Balmoral furniture shop, and indeed the relatives of all the innocent victims killed in the shootings and bombings carried out since the start of the Troubles, must surely have been astonished by the Provo Commander's callous remarks.

There seemed little point in holding these discussions at all, as just days earlier the Provisionals had issued a statement claiming that the struggle would continue – and so, it was quite apparent that these meetings were no more than displays of political propaganda for the newspapers. In the Ardoyne, a Staff Captain of the Provisionals was shot dead by an army foot patrol. Gerard McDade was amongst a group of men who were asked to line up while their identities were checked by the patrol. He must have known that he would be recognised, and so he decided to try and escape. A soldier shouted several warnings for him to halt, but he carried on and was shot and injured. He died shortly afterwards. This was yet another Provo killer off the streets.

VICTIMS OF THE TROUBLES WHO DIED THIS DAY...

John Lavery (60) – Killed by an IRA bomb which exploded as he carried it out of his bar on Lisburn Road, Belfast.

Gerald McDade (23) – Provisional IRA. Shot dead while trying to escape after being detained by an army patrol in Kerrera Street, Ardoyne, Belfast.[*]

[*] List compiled from *The Troubles* Magazine (Glenravel Publications).

WEDNESDAY 22nd...

The battery continued with their duties around Andersonstown as Christmas approached. Patrols were out on the Springfield Road carrying out spot checks on vehicles in an attempt to intercept the bombs which were being transported into the city centre by the IRA.

Later in the afternoon, gangs of youths started to gather in Falls Park and move towards the fencing which surrounded the bus depot. As the returning patrols entered the compound, they were targeted by the youths and came under

[*]   Source taken from *The Troubles* Magazine (Glenravel Publications).

a heavy barrage of rocks and bottles. Some of the men of 1 Troop came out of their quarters and brought the riot guns into action, but the rubber bullets just bounced off the fence. In desperation they started picking up the rubble which now littered the compound and began to throw it back. The exchange lasted for around 30 minutes before the youths grew tired of their 'game' and moved on. In the distance there came the sound of shooting, as yet another mobile patrol came under fire at the top of the Andersonstown Road, but fortunately there were no casualties. Gunners Mike Fall and Mick McHale recall the time they were involved in a similar ambush…

Gnr Mike Fall, 3 Troop

I was out on mobile patrol with our section. Bob Wilson was in command of our truck and Mick McHale was the driver. We were just doing the usual rounds and came down Slievegallion Drive at the bottom and followed the lead Pig around to the right onto Andersonstown Road. We were intending to do the big loop back to base by turning right onto Shaw's Road and right again at the top to come back down Glen Road and back to the depot. I think we had travelled about 100 yards and the lead Pig was just passing the hill where St Joseph's College was – and there was this burst of automatic fire which hit the bonnet of our Pig. The bullets went ding-ding-ding off the bonnet and hit the metal strut between the wind-screens. Bob dropped the visors over the windscreen and Mick sort of lost it a bit and dropped to the floor when the bullets hit. I mean, he was looking directly at where the bullets hit the glass when they went ding-ding-ding, and I think it would have put the shits up me as well if I had been sat there. Bob grabbed hold of him and pulled him back up.

I looked out of the back slit in the door, and there was a woman sprawled out on the path with all her shopping bags around her. She hadn't been hit; she was just trying to keep out of the way of the bullets. 'Hercules' [Kenny S*****] got on the radio to call for help. I'll never forget it; he was as cool as a cucumber, even though they were firing at us. He was sat there with his back against the bulkhead of the Pig talking to the ops room on the radio, and I'll always remember how calm he was while we were firing back at the gunman. Danny Coulton was sat behind me nearer the door, and Bob Wilson was sat there all exposed in the front seat. He was trying to cover himself up from the gunfire because he couldn't get his rifle out to return fire. We couldn't really see the gunmen properly; they were just lay there on the top of the hill pouring all this fire at us.

The windscreen of Mick McHale's Pig photographed shortly after the ambush. (Courtesy of Mick McHale)

Gnr Mick McHale, 3 Troop

The day we were fired on, one of the fellas that shot us up had a machine gun – possibly a Thompson. We saw him open up, and four or five bullets hit the road and a few raked across the bonnet of the Pig. Luckily for me, they hit the armoured strip that separated the two sections of the windscreen. They got deflected onto the glass and shattered it without coming through. On getting back to the bus station, I was really shook up. We de-briefed and Don Potter told me to clear off and get some rest.

A minute or so later, the shooting died down. The woman picked herself up, gathered her shopping and went on her way. The two Pigs left the scene and completed the patrol without further incident. The reaction of Mick McHale was entirely understandable. To have bullets striking the windscreen of a vehicle while you are sitting there driving it would be enough to unnerve anyone. While Mick was busy risking his life on the streets of Andersonstown, back in England his wife had a taste of the anti-Irish feeling which was much in evidence at that time.

Gnr Mick McHale, 3 Troop

What really pissed me off more than anything about my time in Andersonstown was something my wife Freda told me when I was home on R&R leave. While I was over in Ireland, she went to live with her mother. We had two young kids at the time; one three years old and the other nine months. She told me she was out shopping one day, and was almost set upon and verbally vilified for buying Irish cheese. People were ranting at her about what was happening 'over there'. It didn't take long before she ironed them out... It was just a case of people jumping in before they know how deep it is.

THURSDAY 23rd...

Back in New Lodge, there was still tension between the soldiers and the residents after the events of the McGurk's Bar bombing on 4 December. The army were still convinced that the IRA were somehow responsible for the deaths, and in an attempt to try and win the residents over, the Commanding Officer of the Royal Regiment of Fusiliers (RRF) decided to distribute a letter to every household explaining why they had to carry out searches of their properties and carry out identity checks – but the letter only served to cause further distress to the still grieving relatives of the victims of the bombing outrage.

From: Lieutenant Colonel J.C. Reilly
Commanding Officer
2nd Battalion
The Royal Regiment of Fusiliers
Glenravel St RUC Station
Belfast

23rd December 1971

Dear Householder,
I have asked my patrols to deliver this message to your house in the hope that it will help you to understand the purpose behind my operations in your area, which I realise must be both embarrassing and annoying to you on occasion.

My immediate aim and first priority is to remove the presence of B Coy 1st Bn Official IRA and C Coy 3rd Bn Provisional IRA as active terrorist organisations. When this is done we can look forward jointly to the banishment of fear and terror and to a peace in which civil and political development can take place. To a period in which you will not lose your friends in a repetition of the 'Provo' accident in the McGurk's Bar and in which I am not left to console the widow and young children of other soldiers shot down by the IRA whilst protecting your community from interference from others. To times when policemen replace soldiers and when street lights are turned on, bus services operating, public telephones installed, glass windows safe, children disciplined and the degrading slogans removed from your walls.

In order to achieve my aim I must seek out the small number of men who are active members of these organisations and who exercise intimidation by fear in many of the households to which this letter will be delivered. In order to hunt them down I must screen people and search houses, cars and pedestrians. I must patrol your streets and peer at you from observation posts. I sincerely ask you to understand that these actions are designed to assist in the arrest of individual gangsters who live or operate in your area and that they are not intended to be penal afflictions upon your community.

My Fusiliers have firm instructions to be polite and quite impartial and the impression which I have obtained in conversations is that they have observed these instructions despite the provocation of recent casualties. Despite, too, the provocation of knowing that many of these men live on the run with the conivence and knowledge of a few members of your community. But their disciplined forbearance is also due to an understanding that this area has suffered much and contains many decent folk and only very few individuals who are responsible for the shootings, bombings and stone throwing which has taken place.

It is very distressing and a great sadness to have to write on such matters at Christmas time. May God bless those that merit it and bring peace to your City in 1972.[*]

Although the intentions of the letter were well meant, it was ill-advised and there can be little doubt that it would have infuriated the relatives of those who died in the bombing and the residents of New Lodge as a whole. The British Army always seemed to be held responsible in some way or another for these attacks launched on their community by the Protestant terror groups, but the willingness of the military to hold the IRA responsible for the McGurk's Bar bombing was seen by some as proof of a cover-up by the authorities. It wouldn't be until March 1976 that the RUC eventually started to receive intelligence reports which finally pointed the finger of blame at the Protestant terrorist group the UVF for the bombing – but even at the time of writing, there are still those within the Catholic community who still believe that the police and military were somehow involved in the atrocity. Whenever there was an incident like this, there was always an upsurge in violence towards the solders out on the streets in the Nationalist areas who were simply trying their very best to keep the peace.

It certainly wasn't a good time to be a soldier within the Catholic communities of Northern Ireland. The resentment shown towards them was now reaching unprecedented levels, but the Protestant communities still showed their support for the troops. The following poem was sent to 9 Battery HQ from Mount Vernon with a request that it should be published:

---

[*]   Sourced from the author's private collection.

They sit and stare at an empty chair,
And grieve for their daddy who once sat
There.
But grieve on they must for their
Daddy is dead.
From a madman's bullet that shattered
His head.

It's so near Christmas but can it
Be fun,
When your daddy is killed by a terrorist's gun,
Can you laugh like a child and enjoy
Christmas day,
When the daddy you loved has been
Taken away?

They complain of internment, they protest
They object.
Their men are alive, but mine won't
Come back,
If he'd just been interned we'd have
Tried to have fun,
But the 'n' from internment they removed
By a gun.

But we can't go on crying, our eyes
Can't stay wet.
But one thing we can do WE WILL NEVER
FORGET
Nor will we forgive until our dying day,
Those animals who call themselves the IRA.

Belfast (15)

FRIDAY 24th...

In Belfast, the army were warned that two car bombs had been left in the city centre. The first was at Smithfield Square, and the second at Ballygomartin Road. Both vehicles had been booby-trapped in an attempt to kill the bomb disposal teams. Both vehicles were destroyed in a controlled explosion. Back in Andersonstown, a hoax 999 call was made to the RUC Station claiming that a bomb had been planted in O'Kane's Bar at the corner of Finaghy Road North and Ladybrooke Park. A Pig from 9 Battery which was already out on patrol was told to go and investigate. They arrived on the scene, and as soon as the Patrol Commander entered the pub, a burst of machine gun-fire shattered one of the windows. A woman who was in the bar was slightly injured by the bullets and taken to hospital. Shortly after this, the same unit was ambushed again from nearby Trench Street. This time the patrol spotted the gunman and returned fire. They believed they may have hit the sniper.

SATURDAY 25th...

CHRISTMAS 1971

This Christmas, 1971, will be a memorable one for all Loyalists... The terrorists who have tried over the past three years to disrupt our lives and homes have failed in their objectives. The plain truth is that although they have caused much misery and tension in many homes, it has also brought home to the Loyalist what our future prospects would be for Christmas's [sic] to come, if ever we allowed ourselves to become part of a papist Republic.

Christmas is a time of 'Goodwill towards all men', but we Loyalists will not be hypocrites; we have no 'Goodwill' for our 'rebel' enemies, but at the same time we pray to God, that He will forgive them, for what they have done, for we cannot.

To all our Loyalist readers and friends overseas, the staff and the editor of the Loyalist News send to you our warmest 'greetings', wishing you all a very 'Happy Christmas', especially to our many dear and Loyal friends in HM Prison, Crumlin Road, Belfast.

We trust that Christmas 1972 will be celebrated in a different atmosphere.

* Taken from the *Loyalist News*, 25 December 1971.

Christmas Day for the men of 9 Battery in Andersonstown was a day surrounded by a hostile community – and the only outward show of festivity were the few decorations which had been strung up in the accommodation blocks and the cookhouse. An effort had been made with the food to provide a bit of festive fare, but life followed the same routine of patrols and outbreaks of violence. At the top end of the depot was the cookhouse used by 1 and 3 Troop, and just inside the door was a public phone where it was possible to keep in touch with loved ones back home. It was in much use that day, as wives, sons and daughters spoke to their husbands and fathers on this special day. Not all soldiers had to rough it though. For some more fortunate members of the regiment, there was to be a taste of the true meaning of Christmas…

Gnr Pete Hodkinson, HQ Battery

I actually went out for Christmas dinner while I was in Ireland. We went to a guy's house; I think there was four of us and we were at Sunnyside in a Territorial Army Centre. These TA guys that manned the centre had a club room upstairs, and they used to come in with their wives and have a good night. We got very friendly with this couple; they were terrific people. The woman's husband worked there every day, and she was talking to us and invited us over for Christmas dinner. She said her house was only a few minutes away.

Anyway, we sort of poured cold water on it at first – and then we thought: "*OK, well there's no harm in asking*," so we got permission. I think it was someone called Captain D*****, and he agreed and said we could go as long as the people were properly vetted and all the rest of it, so he let us go. It was considered quite a safe area, but we had to take weapons with us. I had a small zip-up case, and we put four SMGs and ammunition in it.

We got picked up by car and went just a few minutes' drive away to this house and went inside. We had a fantastic day. We didn't stay too long, but we had a dinner and we played with the kids and their toys. After about two or three hours they took us back, and it had been brilliant. The sad thing was that once we moved away from Sunnyside, we were told there was to be no further contact for our safety and theirs – and the sad thing was that I never heard from them ever again.

For the Catholic community, Christmas Day was just another day to demonstrate against the soldiers they viewed as a force of occupation in their country. There would be no 'truce', nor any displays of goodwill towards their enemy on this most sacred day in the Catholic calendar. A huge anti-internment rally was due to march towards Long Kesh internment camp, which the Catholics viewed as being a concentration camp. The march-route would take it right past Milltown Cemetery and the bus depot on the Falls Road.

MPS ADDRESS CIVIL RIGHTS ANTI-INTERNMENT RALLY

THE NORTHERN IRELAND Civil Rights Association returned to the streets yesterday, when it held an anti-internment march and rally in Belfast in defiance of a Government ban.

The demonstration, attended by about 5,000, passed off peacefully, but afterwards police said that they had identified a number of people with a view to prosecution.

British troops, who blocked the Falls Road with Saracens near the Whiterock Road junction, allowed the footpaths and later stood by as they entered Falls Park. At one stage, Saracens, forcing their way up through the crowd, were obstructed by teenage boys and girls, who, leaning on the front of the armoured car, allowed them-selves to be pushed forward by it.

As the meeting ended, some 200 youths stoned soldiers positioned in a bus station overlooking the park. A number of rubber bullets were fired to disperse them. There were no counter-demonstrations and none of the marches passed through Protestant areas.

Marchers from five points, the Falls Road baths, Hamill Street, Turf Lodge, Andersonstown and Ballymurphy, converging on Falls Park at 2pm, and were addressed by two SDLP Members of Parliament, Mr Paddy Devlin, Falls, and Mr Austin Currie, East Tyrone, as well as CRA executives. Mr Ivan Cooper, SDLP MP for Mid-Derry, took part in the march, and Miss Bernadette Devlin, MP for Mid-Ulster, attended part of the meeting.

NEW SONG

In the park, banners condemning internment and the Prime Minister, Mr Faulkner, were waved, and a new record, 'Behind the Wire', about Long Kesh, was played and hailed as a new anthem. Halfway through the meeting stewards prevented gangs of youths, who broke away, stoning troops in the bus station.

A huge Christmas card, with anti-internment slogans and 1,000 signatures 'from the people of Ballymun, Dublin' was displayed, and a message of solidarity from the Citizens for Civil Liberties, also in Dublin was read;

'Citizens for Civil Liberties greets the Falls Park rally and pledges full support for the new stage in resistance to internment and detention without trial or charge, North or South of the Border.'

Mr Curry said that the feeling of the meeting was one of victory, despite what Mr Faulkner had said about his side winning. When one listened to people like Mr Paisley and Mr Boal, of the Democratic Unionists, and Mr Dick Ferguson, the former Unionist MP, all of whom mentioned a united Ireland, one knew, he said, that an end to the present regime was near. The SDLP had warned that internment would alienate the entire community, and why should they now talk to Mr Maudling? They would talk, he said, but not until the last man and woman was released from internment.

Mr Devlin said that his party would not let the internees die and he would make no move until they were released. The British Army, he said, had a deliberate policy to terrorise people and provoke the IRA into a battle with them. The army had more firepower, but they were forgetting that they had alienated 40% of the population.

One of the things that appalled him most, Mr Devlin said, was the treatment the army gave to prisoners. They subjected them, he said, *to a kind of torture even the Japanese did not use during the war.**

Mr Rory McShane, of the NCRA Executive, said that their determination did not end with the release of the present internees. They wanted an end to the Special Powers Act and the Stormont Unionist-Orange junta. The whole tradition of Presbyterianism in the 32 Counties, he said, had been Republican and anti-establishment. He believed, he said, that Mr Paisley and Mr Boal would be better off leading the people of the Shankill to join those of the Falls, and thus wiping out Faulkner. Mr Paisley could go down in history, Mr McShane said, as the man who led the Protestant people away from bigotry and into a Republic where everyone would live decently.

Mr Kevin McCorry and Mr Joe Deighan of NICRA also spoke.†

---

*   Author's italics.
†   Sourced from Brian Corser's private collection of newspaper cuttings.

Mr Devlin's comments on the army having a deliberate policy to provoke the IRA into a fight with them seemed a rather sick joke. He conveniently forgot that it was the Catholic community which had asked for the army to go out there and protect them from the Protestants. It was the Provisional IRA who started the killing of the troops when they seized the opportunity to advance their political cause for a united Ireland – and as for implying that the army used torture methods worse than those used by the Japanese in the Second World War, it simply defied belief. The fine words of the NCRA executive, Mr McShane, were just that – and nothing else. There was bigotry from both Protestants and Catholics. The slaughter of people simply because they wanted to remain part of Britain, or because they were Protestant or Catholic, was difficult for many from the mainland to understand – but for the soldier on the ground, they were more concerned with the more pressing problem of trying to keep the peace on the streets of Northern Ireland.

The protesters made their way out of the park and back onto Falls Road. Many youths had gathered at the rear of the bus depot by the high-wire fencing that ran across the back. There was a grassy mound that ran the length of the fencing, and now part of the crowd started to make their way over – and seemed well prepared for what they were about to do. They began to subject the soldiers from 1 and 3 Troop to a steady barrage of bricks, bottles and any other missiles they could lay their hands on. Back at the front of the depot, elements of 2 and 3 Troop were out on the Falls Road being shadowed by film crews from around the world as they monitored the marchers led by Bernadette Devlin making their way up the Falls Road and on to Long Kesh. A barbed wire barricade had been set up across the road to channel the marchers onto the footpaths past the cemetery. A detachment of soldiers manned the barrier as the protesters filed past. Elsewhere, a patrol from 9 Battery spotted a gunman in Finaghy Road North. They opened fire, but he managed to get away.

Gnr Pete Roberts, 2 Troop

I was manning the sangar on top of the building at the front of the bus depot. I saw that fucking cow Devlin leading the procession and I thought how easy it would be for me to shoot the bitch from where I was. Major Harding was stood at the barricade with Sgt Thompson. It was funny really, because Major Harding had this loud-hailer and was asking everyone to disperse; then he wished them all a Merry Christmas! When Devlin appeared in court after her arrest for ignoring the ban on marching, I had to go and give evidence to what I had seen.

Soldiers from 1 and 3 Troop lined the route along the Falls Road as the crowds spilled out of the park – the film crews recording their every move. There was no

The protest rally. Sgt Thompson is third from the left and Major Harding is far right.
(Courtesy of Brian Corser)

trouble here though, probably due in part to all the filming of the proceedings. It would have looked bad for a Christmas Day 'peace march' to break into violence on this most holy of days in the Catholic calendar.

Gnr Steve Corbett, 3 Troop

Our section were over by the wall of the cemetery being filmed by a film crew; I think they were from Sweden. We tried to play it up for the cameras a bit and tried to look as tough as we could. We crouched down with our rifles pointing in the air and sort of scowled at everyone as they went past.

The crowds went on their way and for the time being, everything seemed to be passing without too much trouble – and the troops were able to relax a little – but later that evening it was a different story. The news teams from around the world had long gone as the marchers made their way back down the Falls Road and past the RUC Station. It was now dark, and there was no-one to record the violence which was about to erupt.

Gnr Steve Corbett, 3 Troop

We all stood there and waited for the approaching protesters. I could hear them chanting and singing in the distance as they made their way down the Falls Road. Finally they came into view as they got closer to the front of the bus depot. Someone had just been around delivering the mail to us as we stood there and waited. I remember standing just inside the entrance of the bus depot and reading my letter as the bricks and bottles started to rain down on us as the protesters made their way past.

The crowd finally passed by as everyone made their way home. The new song of 'Behind the Wire' was being sung and grew fainter as the crowds again disappeared into the distance. The men of 9 Battery were at last able to stand down and enjoy what was left of Christmas Day. At around this time, another poem arrived at the Battery HQ – yet another display of appreciation of the risks undertaken by the British soldier to protect the citizens of Northern Ireland…

'SERVICE IN ULSTER'
Out in the cold, the wind and the rain,
Taunted and ridiculed time and again,
Vainly endeavouring peace to maintain –
Who are you? – A British soldier.

What are your thoughts as you stand erect?
Buildings and citizens try to protect.
Every newcomer you must suspect!
Courageous and valiant soldier.

Your chosen career took you over the sea,
Far from you friends and country free;
Way out of sight of your family,
Gallant and brave young soldier.

Hundreds of people you've helped to save,
Thanks to your speedy actions brave.
Alas! Those of your comrades their lives they gave –
We thank you – oh British soldier!

Yours is a debt we can never repay.
Nobody knows how long you must stay.
From morning till evening, from day to day –
God bless you! Oh, British soldier.*

---

*   Sheila Jameson, Edenbrooke Primary School, Belfast – Christmas 1971.

SUNDAY 26th...

The events on Christmas Day had proven to be a very trying time for everyone involved in policing the demonstrations and the resulting riots at the back of the bus depot, but now they had a chance to relax. Patrols were kept to a minimum in an attempt to defuse the growing tension which had been building up over the past few days. The units which did go out reported back that the streets were clear and that they had encountered little trouble.

Gnr Steve Corbett, 3 Troop

I dropped lucky. Sunday was my first rest day, and it just happened to fall on Boxing Day. I remember how knackered everyone was after all the recent incidents and so on. You never got much free time when you were in Northern Ireland. Even on your day off you could be called out if something big was kicking off. You sort of half-expected to get called out at any moment – especially if someone came rushing into the rest room.

MONDAY 27th...

Christmas was now over, and it was back to business as usual. Search teams were again back out on the estates, and in Tullymore Gardens the battery had a rather good find...

ARMY FINDS BOMB KIT

Bomb-making accessories have been found in a house in Tullymore Gardens, Andersonstown. The find, which included fuse wire and timing equipment, was made by soldiers from the 12th Light Air Defence Regiment, Royal Artillery, who were carrying out a routine search in the area. The other 'accessories' included three pounds of gelignite, a half a pound of which was detonated on the spot; three clockwork mechanisms; four batteries; one nail bomb; a home-made fuse, and one stick grenade.[*]

[*] Source taken from *The Troubles* Magazine (Glenravel Publications).

There was the usual gathering of youths as the search teams moved in, but once the soldiers realised the state of the explosives, they quickly cleared the area while bomb disposal dealt with the gelignite on the spot. Such was the state that it was in; there was the very real danger that even attempting to move it could have been enough to trigger an explosion.

TUESDAY 28th…

Up near the Busy Bee, a barricade had been erected across Slievegallion Drive about 50 yards back from the junction with Andersonstown Road. Crowds gathered on the corner by the shops as the soldiers arrived to deal with the situation. The Pigs drew up and blocked the entrance of the junction while the men dismounted and took cover behind the vehicles. Further up the road at the scene of the barricade, a fire had been started and then a few gunmen started to take shots at the patrol. As the soldiers returned fire, they came under attack from the crowds at the side of the shops – and some of the men had to resort to using the riot guns to clear this latest threat. Eventually, the shooting from the barricade died out as the gunmen disappeared and the patrol were able to charge through with their Pigs and remove the obstruction. This was just another routine patrol for the men of 9 Battery.

WEDNESDAY 29th…

It was around this time that 9 Battery was stood down for a few hours to enable the men to have a Christmas meal. Like any soldier they enjoyed their drink, but with being on active service in Northern Ireland, it wasn't often they got the opportunity to relax and indulge in the odd pint of beer. The only time the men got to really wind down was at the occasional discos laid on for the soldiers, but on one night shortly after Christmas, the men of 9 Battery were treated to a Christmas party which was held at RHQ in Lisburn. As was the custom, the men were waited on by all the officers of the battery and the BSM, Don Potter.

Once the food had been served, the BC found a couple of dustbin lids and he and the BSM livened up the proceedings by re-entering the room beating the lids in traditional Rossnareen fashion. Spurred on by this show of 'defiant hostility', the men subjected both of them to a friendly fusillade of bread rolls. Once the BC and BSM realised the hopelessness of their situation, they wisely made a tactical withdrawal in good military order and left the men to enjoy the rest of their party. Some hours later, a rather indignant Chief Clerk complained to the BC that beer was dripping through the ceiling and onto the RHQ clerks who were working below. That night the battery were back out on the streets of Andersonstown and ready for anything. This was the way that 9 Battery did things; nothing would stop them in their determination to wipe out the IRA in their area.

Gnr Phil Gallagher, 3 Troop

I remember the Christmas do I went to at Lisburn with Clancy Campbell. We ended up getting pissed and both of us climbed on stage and sang 'Durham Town' to entertain the troops. Clancy took this girl outside to the allotments to try and get off with her, but she was having none of it and sent him packing. It seems all he got was a: *"Not tonight, Josephine."*

I also remember one time when Ken Turner and Terry M****** did a session of telling jokes. They came on one at a time, and in the end they had to go on with riot shields because everyone was throwing things at them – cans, food, anything they could get their hands on. Their jokes were absolute shite! I can't remember if this happened at the end of our training or at one of the discos though.

Anyway, we all came back half-pissed in the back of a Bedford 3-tonner. It didn't have the canvas on – just the bare metal structure – and we were all hanging over the bars trying to stop ourselves falling over due to our intoxicated state. Any gunman that night would have had a right killing spree if he had seen us.

In Derry, another soldier lost his life trying to keep the peace on the streets of Ulster. Gunner Richard Ham was on a routine patrol crossing some waste ground in the Brandywell district of Londonderry when a gunman fired two shots. He was hit in the head and chest and was pronounced dead on arrival at the hospital.

VICTIMS OF THE TROUBLES WHO DIED THIS DAY

Gnr Richard Ham (20) – The Royal Artillery. Shot dead by the Official IRA while on foot patrol, Foyle Road, Derry.[*]

* List compiled from *The Troubles* Magazine (Glenravel Publications).

THURSDAY 30th…

Jack McCabe – one of the Provos' top men – accidentally blew himself up in an explosion in a garage on the outskirts of Dublin. It is likely that he was assembling bombs at the time and his loss was greatly appreciated by all those who had to witness the devastating effects of these devices. The garage was being used to build and supply bombs to the Provos in the North, and McCabe was one of the top men on the GHQ staff of the PIRA. To hear of an 'own goal' committed by the IRA was always gratifying news to the serving soldiers in Northern Ireland. On the same day that another terrorist died, the men of 9 Battery also had their own success in the fight against the IRA when they uncovered a haul of weapons and ammunition.

ARMS SEARCH IN BELFAST

The RUC and army have come under fire as they carried out a search in the Andersonstown area of Belfast. They found two rifles, a number of holsters and more than 2,000 rounds of assorted ammunition in Slievegallion Drive. When the Security Forces arrived, a number of single shots and automatic bursts were fired at them. Shots were also fired at Navan Green in Andersonstown, and at Albert Street-Durham Street. No injuries have been reported.˙

* Source taken from *The Troubles* Magazine (Glenravel Publications).

The whole battery were out on another search up in the Rossnareen area. The BC was determined to keep the pressure on the Provos and turn the screw even tighter as the year drew to a close. The units moved into their respective positions, and as the search started on Slievegallion Drive, there were bursts of automatic fire and a few single shots directed at them as the Provos tried to gain a little time to remove the weapons from the house where they were hidden. A little while later, the search team uncovered several thousands of rounds of ammunition and two rifles. A unit from C13 arrested several Provo suspects from another location a short time later.

It was around this time that Bdr 'Horace' was conducting one of his 'sneaky-beaky' patrols with Clancy Campbell. They went out with one of the mobile patrols and got dropped off close to one of the estates.

Gnr Clancy Campbell, 2 Troop

I remember the night that me and 'Horace' caught Micky Agnew and Seamus C***, two well-known Provos from the area. I was working with 2 Troop that night. I used to swap and change and just go where I was needed. It was just a couple of weeks before 'Horace' had his big gelly find. We bailed out of the back of the Pig near Koran Ring roundabout and someone opened up on us with a Thompson sub-machine gun. We made a run for it and took cover in this garden, and then these two men came in there and started rooting about. We thought they might be hiding guns or something in the garden or the outhouse, so we stepped out and arrested them. I was pointing my rifle at Seamus C*** to keep him covered, but he started getting a bit cocky and he said to me: "*You wouldn't dare pull that trigger; it would make too much noise and the boys would hear you.*" So I pulls out my SLR bayonet I kept for forcing locks and the like when we did searches, and I held it up to him and said: "*This fucker makes no noise at all.*" His eyes nearly popped out of his head when he saw the bayonet.

We got them both in the back of the Pig and drove off, and we came under fire again from this Thompson machine gun. I don't know how many they fired, but it was a lot – and I was hanging onto Seamus C*** to stop him falling out of the back of the Pig. Anyway, we took them both back to the RUC Station because we thought they were both up to something and we left them for intelligence to sort out.

The ammunition which was found with the weapons. (Courtesy of Brian Corser)

Once inside they were taken up and questioned about their activities. They hotly denied they were up to anything and both claimed to be having a gay relationship with each other and had only met up to spend some time together. Due to the lack of evidence they had to be released, but it wouldn't be long before Micky Agnew was arrested again – and on that occasion he wasn't able talk his way out of it. While Clancy and 'Horace' had been dealing with the two suspects in the garden, there was another foot patrol in the area making their way through a patch of waste ground at the back of a row of houses not far from the Koran Ring roundabout. As the patrol made their way past the backs of the houses, a dog suddenly started barking.

Bdr 'Davey' S*******, 'T' Battery (Shah Sujah's Troop)
There were about eight of us on that patrol. I was still in 'T' Battery at the time and we were doing a foot patrol in 9 Battery's area, but I can't remember why. There was me and the Section Commander, but I can't remember the names of the lads who were with us. Anyway, we were making our way up this patch of land at the back of some houses. It was a bit like a park, and there were all these trees

and patches of long grass. I suppose you would say it was 'dead ground' because it didn't look as though anyone looked after it. We started making our way past the row of houses and then this dog must have heard us – and it started barking – and then this bedroom light came on in one of the houses. The next thing is this guy comes to the window and looks out and he saw us, so we went to ground along some hedges and took cover.

We stayed there for about 20 minutes, and then all of a sudden someone opened up on us. It wasn't high-velocity; it seemed like a Thompson machine gun or something like that, and they had opened up on us from the other side of this park. They took the top of the hedge away with their bullets just above where we lay; then this light came on, or maybe it was car headlights... I can't really remember, but then I saw them – the gunmen – and I can't remember who it was, but he saw them as well. The light had illuminated them, and that's why we saw them. This other guy had the night sight on his rifle, but when we came under fire he dived down and the muzzle of his rifle stuck in the ground and got all bunged up with soil, so he couldn't fire... and so I fired. This other guy watched through his night sight and he said he saw the guy stumble when I fired; well... he went down anyway.

'Horace' and Clancy Campbell were out on patrol on another road around the corner that night, and when the dog started barking and the shooting started, they thought they had been sussed out, but it wasn't them; it was our patrol that got shot at.

There was a lot of shooting in the area that night, and nearly all the patrols which were out on the estates came under fire at some point. It was likely that these two patrols came under fire from separate IRA units who were out in force that evening. It wasn't uncommon for patrols from other units within the regiment to enter the 9 Battery area when called on to do so by the BC if he had something particular planned. The three areas covered by 12th Regiment were different in nature, and all were policed by their respective Battery Commanders in their own way. At times there might have been joint operations between the three batteries mounted in a single area if large searches or other operations had been planned.

VICTIMS OF THE TROUBLES WHO DIED THIS DAY...

Jack McCabe (55) – Provisional IRA. Killed when a bomb he was assembling in a garage in Swords Road, Dublin went off prematurely.*

* List compiled from *The Troubles* Magazine (Glenravel Publications).

FRIDAY 31st...

There were only minutes to go before 1971 drew to a close, and the Provos were determined they would signal the end of the Old Year and the start of the New Year with a bang. At approximately 11:45 p.m. the first explosion occurred when Springfield Road RUC Station was attacked with a nail bomb. This was closely followed by an explosion at a supermarket on the Antrim Road. The final explosion of the Old Year happened just moments before midnight at the Post Office Training School at Fortwilliam Park.

5

JANUARY
An escalation in the attacks

SATURDAY 1st...

Just a few minutes after midnight, two bombs exploded at a printing firm at Whitehouse just outside Belfast. A 20lb bomb was planted in a tobacconists on the Ormeau Road, and a petrol station received extensive damage when two pumps and a kiosk were destroyed in another explosion. The bombings were the Provos' New Year greeting message to everyone. There were no bombs in Andersonstown, but in the city centre the explosions caused widespread destruction to business premises. Fortunately, there were no casualties. The message was clear: the terror campaign was to continue.

The Civil Rights Movement had planned another anti-internment rally for Sunday 2 January in absolute defiance of the government ban on any such parades taking place. The plan was for six separate parades to set off from various parts of Belfast and meet up at Falls Park next to Milltown Cemetery. The West Belfast Protestant Action Association had vowed to stop any Republican parades from crossing the junction of North Queen Street and Peters Hill as they made their way down from the Unity Flats – and the East Belfast branch of the Ulster Loyalist Association demanded that the government took a tougher stance on those people determined to break the ban. Ian Paisley, the leader of the Democratic Unionist Party, again warned of the possible Loyalist reaction to any leniency shown towards the illegal gatherings. Back in Andersonstown at the RUC Station, the worry was that there could be an outbreak of violence far worse than they encountered on Christmas Day.

SUNDAY 2nd...

The protesters set off from their various start points, and all of them had one main rallying point: the park at the back of the bus depot opposite Milltown Cemetery. To the men of 9 Battery, this march appeared to be much larger than the one held on Christmas Day, but the official estimates were only put at around 5,000 people. It started off relatively peacefully; then a group of about 100 youths broke away and moved through the park to the back of the bus depot. Once again the bricks and bottles came sailing over the fence in the direction of the troops defending the depot, but the chain-link fencing surrounding the back of the compound stopped them from entering and the soldiers were able to hold them back. The world's press – on this occasion – were more noticeable by their absence.

MONDAY 3rd...

In Belfast city centre, the Provisional IRA drove a stolen brewery wagon packed with explosives into Callender Street. No warning was given and the bomb exploded with devastating effect in the crowded city centre streets. Forty-two people were injured. At around 11:00 p.m. reports came in of barricades set up on the Glen Road close to the Ulster Brewery and another on the Andersonstown Road next to the Busy Bee. The armoured Pigs of C13 (3 Troop) were following close behind C12 when a gelignite bomb was thrown at their lead vehicle. There was a huge flash and explosion, but fortunately for the occupants there were no injuries. The Pigs carried on their way to the barricades.

Gnr Steve Corbett, 3 Troop

As soon as we got close up to the barricade, there was a volley of shots fired in our direction. We all got out of the vehicles and rushed forward. I was bent down, trying to keep my head low, as I ran towards the barricade with the rest of the lads. You could rarely tell where the shots were coming from, and all you wanted to do was reach the barricade and take some cover. I was too busy dodging all the missiles being thrown in my direction to look where the gunmen were anyway. I reached the barricade and started climbing over it with the others as we tried to get to the rioters. You sort of got swept along by it all; the thrill of the chase and all that. They nearly always did a runner when you got over the barricade, and then they would regroup a short distance off and start pelting you again with rocks, bottles, and darts – anything they could lay their hands on. The gunmen hardly ever stayed around for long; a few shots and they were gone. Some of the rioters were caught as they tried to hide from us in the surrounding gardens. We rounded them up and frog-marched them back to the Pigs and took them back to the RUC Station to be charged.

Back at the scene of the other barricade at the Busy Bee, one of the Pigs from C11 (1 Troop) drove straight at the obstruction and forced their way through. They too had a gelignite bomb thrown at them, and they too were fired at when someone opened up with a pistol as they barged their way through. As the vehicle from 1 Troop drove at the barricade, one of the vehicles from C12 came around the back of the same obstruction and caught the rioters off-guard – and three men were arrested by Sgt Sammy Hulme, the Vehicle Commander. They were put in the back of Sammy's Pig and taken back to the RUC Station for questioning.

Bdr Renzo Peterson Agnello, 2 Troop

On returning to base, a handgun was found in the back of our vehicle, which of course no-one admitted to owning. We had three suspects in the back of the Pig, and one was a good bit older than the other pair – and also our prime suspect. 'Tired Hands' [the late Sgt Hulme] held the pistol to the older suspect's head and threatened to pull the trigger. I was horrified when I saw him do that; it's not the kind of thing you expect to see happen, but it did the trick – and the guy said it was loaded and it was his pistol.

Dermot C**** later admitted that it was his pistol. He also claimed that he was a member of 'B' Company, 1st Battalion PIRA. He said that his orders for that night were to go and watch for army patrols at the Busy Bee. He was told to fire one shot for each Pig that he saw, and was to report back later to the Provo Commanding Officer (Jim), who was in an old white Austin A40 car at the Koran Ring. He added that he had received instructions earlier in the evening when he met a man about the pistol, outside the community centre in South Link.

The Beretta pistol found hidden in the back of the Pig. (Courtesy of Brian Corser)

TUESDAY 4th...

Loyalist discontent concerning the recent parades held by the Republicans continued, and the Black Institution (a Protestant fraternal society) and the Orange Order issued a joint statement to the Stormont Government calling on them to lift the ban on processions. Mr James Molyneaux MP and the Rev Martyn Smyth said:

> Recent events have confirmed suspicion that the ban on processions was directed against the Loyalist organisations and the failure to deal properly with illegal Republican demonstrations forms a strange contrast with the treatment accorded to Loyalists in the past.
>
> We therefore demand that the now discredited ban is lifted forthwith, and we give warning that in future such blatant discrimination in the guise of blanket banning will not be tolerated.[*]

WEDNESDAY 5th...

VICTIMS OF THE TROUBLES WHO DIED THIS DAY...

Pte Keith Bryan (18) – The Gloucestershire Regiment. Shot dead by an IRA sniper while on foot patrol, Ardmoulin Street, Belfast.[*]

[*] List compiled from *The Troubles* Magazine (Glenravel Publications).

THURSDAY 6th...

Mobile and foot patrols operating in the Rossnareen area had spent the past few days keeping a bungalow in Slievegallion Drive under observation, where it was believed that the Provisional IRA were holding regular meetings and training sessions in bomb-making. On the night of Thursday 6 January, several men were observed entering the premises at irregular intervals over a period of about an hour. Back at Battery HQ, the intelligence team were alerted to this latest development and the decision was taken to raid the premises. Several units were immediately dispatched from the base and moved into the area around the bungalows. The back-up team took up their positions a short distance away from their target, and watched as the snatch squads sprang into action.

[*]   Source taken from *The Troubles* Magazine (Glenravel Publications).

FLEEING MEN SEIZED IN SWOOP ON HOUSE

Detectives were today were still questioning seven men held after troops surrounded and searched a house in Andersonstown. It is believed detention orders under the Special Powers Act will be served on the men, who were attending a meeting in the house when the army burst in.

A spokesman for 12th Light Air Defence Regiment (Royal Artillery) which carried out the operation said the house had been under observation for 'some time'.

None of the men taken away lived at the address at Slievegallion Drive, off the main Andersonstown Road, but they all came from the Andersonstown area.

The army said to-day that a marksman shot and wounded a sniper who opened up with a machine gun during the swoop. He staggered away.

The seven men arrested bring the total in the Province in the 24 hours up to eight o'clock this morning to 15. About 15 soldiers took part in the operation last night. Five approached the house while 10 others threw a cordon round it.

Suddenly windows in the house burst open and four of the men tried to make a run for it, but one of the first things they ran into was 18-year-old Gunner John Morrison from Birmingham and the other men making up the cordon. After a brief struggle the fleeing men were held.

Meanwhile inside the house soldiers began to search. In a cupboard they found two men and when they opened a wardrobe door they discovered another. A man passing outside the house was stopped and questioned, but after a short time he was allowed to go.

"He had just walked away from our men when a machine-gunner opened fire on him" the spokesman for the regiment said. "He must have been mistaken for a soldier, but in any case when the fire started he hit the ground and wasn't injured."

An army marksman spotted the gunman and fired. The man was seen to "move awkwardly," the spokesman added. "The soldier believes he may have hit the gunman, but there was no sign of him when we eventually reached his firing position.""

* Source taken from *The Belfast Telegraph*, 7 January 1972.

As the snatch squad moved in on the building, a Provo volunteer spotted them and opened fire on the soldiers with a Thompson sub-machine gun. There was a brief exchange of fire, then the shooting stopped and the Provo was seen to stagger away. As soon as the shooting broke out, the windows of the bungalow flew open and four men tried to make a run for it, but they didn't get far before they were caught by the back-up team. The building was then given a thorough search and two more men were found hiding in a cupboard while another was discovered hiding inside a wardrobe. One man did manage to escape, and that was Patrick L********** – also known as 'The Lecturer'.

Gnr Steve Corbett, 3 Troop

I wasn't on the actual operation, as I had been put on guard at the RUC Station. I was in the top observation post in the roof, which was directly over the interview room. I saw the Pigs return and all these men were taken out of the back and brought into the station. There was a lot of shouting and it sounded like there was a bit of a scuffle as they were taken upstairs and into the interview room just below me. I could hear them being questioned and I remember feeling sorry for the poor bastards at first – and then I thought of the bombing at McGurk's Bar and the furniture shop. These men were being taught how to make the bombs which were being used to slaughter inno-cent people, so I thought: *"Why should I be bothered about what happens to them?"*

The previous day, some more suspects had been lifted in the Riverdale Estate too. The Provos tried to talk down these latest successes against the local IRA units and issued a statement which was published in their mouthpiece, *The Volunteer*:

LIES

The claim by the 'army' that last week's wholesale arrests in the Andersonstown Estate included 'Important IRA officers, blah, blah, blah' would be hysterically funny if it were not for the suffering of the innocent men and boys who were kidnapped. Among the people who were lifted were pensioners, chronically ill men, a few local drunks and a huge amount of young boys with no political affili-ations whatsoever. In their attempts to make 'numbers', it would surprise no-one if the Message Boys started arresting cats and dogs.*

* Source taken from *The Volunteer*.

There was no doubt that the in-house intelligence network set up by the BC was paying dividends – and maybe one of the 'chronically ill men' the Provisionals referred to in their statement published in *The Volunteer* might well have been the man which Renzo Agnello arrested during a search at the house of a suspected Provisional IRA member.

Bdr Renzo Peterson Agnello, 2 Troop

My day started at 3:00 a.m. when some SIB guys turned up. They said that we were going to arrest a leader from the local Provo Brigade, and proceeded to brief us on our target. We had a photo and a description, and I took it that he suffered from chronic asthma. Once briefed, we moved out into the estate and pulled up outside this house. I had been told to go inside the property with others while a cordon was put around the outside of the house. I went upstairs with an RUC man and started to search the bedrooms, and all the time the lady of the house was screaming obscenities at us. "*She protests too much,*" I thought. "*There is definitely someone or something here.*"

We went into a bedroom, and sitting up in bed was this lad with a beard who did not look anything like the photo we had. Also sitting up was a female naked to the waist – and quite a looker. The name we had was Sean, but they all insisted his name was Thomas and that he had nothing to do with any of the Troubles. They all sounded very convincing, but unfortunately for him his inhaler was at his bedside. We took him away; there was no troublesome mob or shooters, which truly surprised me – especially since he was supposed to be quite high in the Provos' chain of command.

Nobody move, an no one will get hurt.

An alternative view on house searching.
(Courtesy of Brian Corser)

FRIDAY 7th...

VICTIMS OF THE TROUBLES WHO DIED THIS DAY...

Daniel O'Neill (20) – Provisional IRA. Died two days after being shot by an army patrol following a gun battle in Oranmore Street, Belfast.*

* List compiled from *The Troubles* Magazine (Glenravel Publications).

SATURDAY 8th...

After the success of the operation on 6 January in which the seven men had been arrested, news came through that one of the men had already escaped custody: Brendan 'Stumpy' Dunlop was on the run...

The incredible facts about how a 20-year-old man escaped from the heavily guarded Holywood Detention Centre has been revealed. It has now been established that the man, named as Brendan Dunlop from Andersonstown, did not casually stroll past army guards at the camp, but in fact used a radio aerial to scale the perimeter fence. He had only just been seized with six other men when the army swooped on a house in Andersonstown. After being taken to the RUC Screening and Interrogation Centre at Holywood Barracks they were questioned about the circumstances of their arrest.

During the interrogation Dunlop asked if he could go to the toilet. He was accompanied from the inter-rogation block 20 yards to a caravan, which is used as a toilet. Dunlop went into the caravan while his escort waited at the door, but he did not emerge again – and when the guard made a search of the caravan he found it empty. The alarm was raised and an imme-diate search was mounted in the camp. Men who made a search of the perimeter believe that he climbed up a radio aerial and dropped over the fence to safety. Road blocks have been set up in an attempt to catch the escaper.*

* Source taken from *The Troubles* Magazine (Glenravel Publications).

The fact that he was able to escape so easily led some to think that he may have had inside help. Within days of the escape, he was in Dublin. Back at the RUC Station in Andersonstown, 'Davey' S******* and his men were in the rest room watching a football match on the TV while they were on standby duty. It wasn't often that time could be found for such relaxation, and so the men were making the most of the moment, but it wasn't long before a call came through after a suspect package had been found at a disused factory on the Falls Road just up from the RUC Station. Rather reluctantly, the men had to abandon watching the game and attend to the latest incident.

Bdr 'Davey' S*******, 'T' Battery (Shah Sujah's Troop)

We were in Andersonstown RUC Station and we were watching the football on the telly. I can't remember his name now... the bloke I was with, but we were on standby and we got called out to a suspect suitcase in the doorway of this disused factory on Falls Road. We went up the road to have a look and we sussed it all out and everything, and they [HQ] told us it would be 30 minutes or so before bomb disposal could get to it, so I climbed up onto the roof and dropped a rock onto the suitcase and nothing happened; it was just a suitcase with a bit of wire sticking out. We didn't want to be waiting around for bomb disposal to come; we just wanted to get back and watch the football – and that's why I did it. It's just as well it wasn't a bomb though when I think about it now. If it had been a bomb I don't think I would be talking about it now.

VICTIMS OF THE TROUBLES WHO DIED THIS DAY...

Peter Woods (29) – Shot dead at home by a Protestant terrorist group, Lowwood Park, Belfast.[*]

[*] List compiled from *The Troubles* Magazine (Glenravel Publications).

MONDAY 10th...

On the Lenadoon and Rossnareen Estates, 58 (Eyre's) Battery and 9 (Plassey) Battery – both from 12th Regiment – conducted large-scale searches as the hunt for weapons and explosives continued. In a garage in Lenadoon Avenue they had a substantial find of bombs and bomb-making equipment. The haul included 5lbs of gelignite, 32 detonators, primers, igniters, incendiary devices, 19 improvised hand grenades and three walkie-talkie radios.

The garage in Lenadoon and the explosives and equipment found on the back seat of the car. (Courtesy of Brian Corser)

TUESDAY 11th...

Most of the battery were on high alert for the funeral of Provisional IRA volunteer Daniel O'Neill, who had died on 7 January – two days after being injured in a gun battle with troops. It was expected that the IRA would try and turn the event into a showcase IRA funeral – and extra patrols were out in case of trouble.

TROOPS SEARCH MOURNERS AFTER FUNERAL

There have been minor scuffles at the gates of Milltown Cemetery as troops using metal detectors searched mourners leaving an IRA funeral at which nine shots were fired. At least four men were detained by troops as they left the cemetery and were taken to Andersonstown RUC Barracks. As one elderly man was taken away, women wielding umbrellas struck at the troops who were escorting them. A few minutes earlier, three men wearing balaclava helmets each fired a burst of three shots at the funeral of 20-year-old Daniel O'Neill who died from gunshot wounds.

As the funeral left the dead man's home in Clonard Street, women wielding raised umbrellas moved in to shield mourners from cameras and photographers. Black flags with white crosses hung from many houses in the street as the tricolor-draped coffin, flanked by eight girls wearing black berets, moved off.*

* Source taken from *The Troubles* Magazine (Glenravel Publications).

One of the patrols took up position in a ditch that ran just outside the cemetery and close to the IRA burial plot. Their intention was to try and identify any Provisionals who were attending the funeral. They had a radio with them so that they could report through to the snatch squad which was waiting at the main gate to move in and arrest any gunmen who fired shots over the coffin. The mourners approached the main gates and made their way to the IRA burial plot. The coffin was placed on the ground while a priest conducted the service and prayed for the soul of the would-be killer. Three men stepped forward, their identity hidden by balaclava helmets, and they each fired a volley of three shots over the coffin. As the soldiers in the ditch watched on, the weapons were quickly passed to accomplices. The gunmen mingled with the crowd, removed their balaclavas and made their escape. As the mourners were leaving, a scuffle broke out as the soldiers closed in and arrested five men and took them across the road to the RUC Station for questioning.

VICTIMS OF THE TROUBLES WHO DIED THIS DAY...

Michael Sloan (15) – A member of the youth wing of the Provisional IRA. Shot dead in an IRA training exercise, New Barnsley, Belfast.*

* List compiled from *The Troubles* Magazine (Glenravel Publications).

WEDNESDAY 12th...

A major disturbance broke out in Tullagh Park on the Rossnareen Estate when a patrol from 1 Troop came under attack from a gang of youths throwing bricks and bottles at the Pigs. The men retaliated with a few salvos of baton rounds, but then they were attacked with several petrol bombs as they tried to pull away. One youth ran up and threw a nail bomb at the rear Pig, but it failed to cause any damage. In other parts of the estate, several terrorist suspects were 'lifted' for questioning.

Back in Lenadoon Avenue in the 58 Battery area, a gunman was seen climbing over a fence into a back garden. The patrol immediately surrounded the house and arrested the two men inside. Up on Norglen Parade, two men claiming to be members of the Official IRA called on a man and took him away to a flat in Ardmonagh Gardens. After a heated discussion he was held down and 'knee-capped' in his left leg. This was a vicious form of punishment where the victim was held down and a pistol held to the rear of the person's knee. A shot would be put through the kneecap – usually resulting in permanent disablement.

VICTIMS OF THE TROUBLES WHO DIED THIS DAY...

Raymond Denham (42) – The Royal Ulster Constabulary. Shot dead by the Provisional IRA at his workplace, Waterford Street, Belfast.*

* List compiled from *The Troubles* Magazine (Glenravel Publications).

THURSDAY 13th...

Sometimes when out on patrol, you would see things that just appeared to be a little out of the ordinary. The average person on the street probably wouldn't even pick up on such innocuous-looking incidents, but the ability to spot things which didn't look quite right often ended up in saving someone's life. A patrol from 1 Troop was out in the area of Falls Road and Kennedy Way when they noticed a car a short distance ahead and decided to investigate. The Vehicle Commander had observed that although the car wasn't marked as a taxi, there were *two* men sat in the back behind the driver. At first glance this may not seem anything out of the ordinary, but normally you would expect two people to get in the front of the car and one in the back. The curiosity of the patrol was sufficiently aroused to pull the vehicle over to check it out.

No sooner had they stopped the car, one of the occupants sat in the back suddenly burst into tears. He started thanking the soldiers profusely for saving his life. He told them that the other two men were Provo gunmen and they were taking him away to execute him. All three were taken out and put in the back of the Pig for further questioning back at base. When they arrived at the station, they were taken inside. Gnr Pete Calder, a member of the patrol, was rooting about in the back of the empty Pig and found a Luger pistol stuffed down the back of one of the bench seats. At first he didn't really think anything of it – after all, it was just a pistol – but then it dawned on him that it wasn't an army-issue weapon and it could only have belonged to one of the men who had just been arrested. He suddenly realised the significance of the find: one of the three men must have hidden it there – and on closer inspection it was found to be loaded with just one round of ammunition. They had indeed saved the life of 'the third man'.

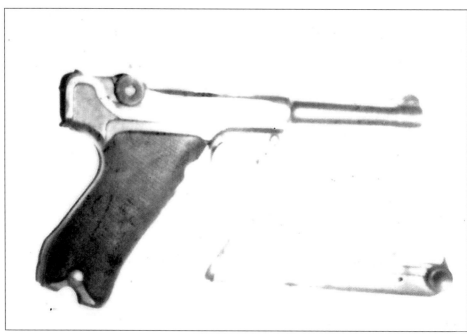

The Luger found by Gnr Pete Calder. (Courtesy of Brian Corser)

VICTIMS OF THE TROUBLES WHO DIED THIS DAY...

Sgt Maynard Crawford (38) – 9th Battalion, The Ulster Defence Regiment. Shot dead by the Provisional IRA while driving along Kings Road, Newtownabbey.[*]

[*] List compiled from *The Troubles* Magazine (Glenravel Publications).

FRIDAY 14th...

Elsewhere in Andersonstown, a foot patrol from 2 Troop had a find of explosives at Glenhill Park during the early hours of Friday morning. It turned out to be by far the largest the regiment had ever uncovered since their arrival in the Province.

LARGE GELLY SNATCH BY TROOPS

A large quantity of explosives and other bomb-making equipment was seized last night by soldiers in the Andersonstown district of Belfast, and in other parts of the city two blasts caused only minor damage.

Almost 60lbs of gelignite was removed from a house and car at Glenhill Park in the Andersonstown district by men of the 12th Light Air Defence Regiment.

The haul also included four walkie-talkie radios, eight detonators, two feet of fuse wire and seven fuses.

While the soldiers were carrying out their search, seven shots were fired at them. They returned one round, but reported no hits. A spokesman for the regiment said today it was unusual to get so much gelignite in one swoop.

And a short distance away, at Creeve Walk, soldiers from the same unit discovered six detonators, wiring and three weapons-training manuals.[*]

[*] Source taken from *The Belfast Telegraph*, 14 January 1972.

Late on Thursday night, one of the special 'sneaky-beaky' patrols led by the Section Commander – 'Horace' – was dropped off by two Pigs. These patrols were used to infiltrate on foot into specific areas, hide up and keep watch on particular houses with known IRA sympathisers – and it carried considerably high risks to the men involved. Once the patrol was dropped off, they were literally on their own and in a very hostile environment. There would be no back-up in the area, and if they were discovered there was never any guarantee of being rescued in time. The patrol had been out for some time, and then in the early hours of Friday morning, a car was observed driving towards them...

Bdr 'Horace', 2 Troop

I had taken the patrol out onto a piece of waste ground at the back of Glenhill Park in Andersonstown. Because of the nature of these patrols, we didn't use the A42 man-pack radios for our communications. They were considered too bulky to use on these 'sneaky' patrols, so we were issued with the Pye two-way pocket radios. The only problem was though that the batteries didn't last very long. I had taken several spare ones with me, but I had used them up – and eventually, I completely lost communications with the base, so I took the decision to do a foot patrol back to the bus depot.

We moved off the patch of waste ground where we had been hiding up and went through the back garden of a house on Glenhill Park. I led my lads along the foot path towards the front gate and then I spotted a car approaching. It pulled up directly opposite from where we were, so we all ducked down and watched to see if we could recognise any of the occupants.

The passenger of the car got out and walked around to the boot, opened it, reached in and lifted out what looked like long thin plastic bags. I quietly opened the gate and walked up behind him and tapped him on the shoulder. I said to him something like... *"What have you got there, mate?"* He quickly turned around and looked at me with an expression of total shock on his face. He muttered to me: *"gelly"* and then promptly dropped the lot on the floor at my feet. I must have presented a right sight to him, because I was all blacked-up with camo paint and armed with a .303 sniping rifle. I suppose the last thing he expected to see was a big hairy squaddie stood behind him!

Gnr Mike Fall, 3 Troop

All I wanted to do was get back to the depot, and then we spotted this car as we started to cross the road. I got my head down and I thought: *"Oh for Christ's sake, come on... hurry up."* I just wanted to get back because I was cold and hungry and that sort of thing, and

The explosives found in the car boot. (Courtesy of Brian Corser)

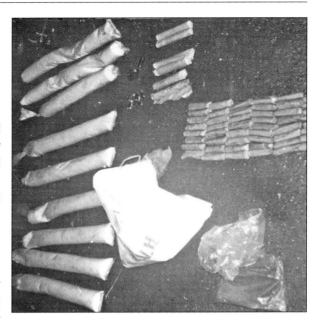

then 'Horace' walked over when this guy got out of the car and opened the boot... and that's when it all kicked off.

Bdr 'Horace', 2 Troop

Some of the other lads dashed over and dragged the other occupant out of the car and down by the side of the house. I was itching for a fight and I told the guy that I had hold of that if he tried to run, I would just shoot him – and that seemed to be enough to make him stay put. I asked him where his guns were, and he said he didn't have any. I asked him where his back-up boys were, and he said there weren't any back-up boys. He had only just finished the words and the bullets started to come over and were hitting the roof of the house directly opposite from where we were. He obviously did have a back-up and we were under fire.

I dragged him down an incline and into a garden, and there I instructed one of my team members to try and pinpoint where the shooting was coming from. He did see some flashes and fired back at them – and then the shooting promptly stopped. I then instructed someone to kick in the door of the house where they were taking the explosives, as we couldn't find a key on the two men. It later turned out that the house was owned by a completely innocent couple who were on holiday in America at the time. The Provos saw it as a good safe house to use for storage while they were away. After we gained entry I told one of the team to phone the RUC Station and ask for transport and back-up.

About 20 minutes later, Tom McShane turned up with two Pigs. We loaded the two men in the back and headed for the RUC Station. One of the lads from the patrol drove the car, still full with explosives, back to the base. It turned out that there were 52lbs of gelignite in plastic bags, four walkie-talkie radios, two feet of fuse wire, seven fuses and a load of made-up blast bombs ready for use – probably about 30 in total.

Gnr Mike Fall, 3 Troop

Tom McShane and S/Sgt Armstrong turned up in a Pig to get these two guys out of the way. We were worried about the car going up because I'm sure the gunmen were firing at the car, and if that had gone up it would have taken half the street with it; I'm sure it would.

When we got to the police station we had quite a welcome party, because there were people from the press, and it was quite a crowd. They took these two guys into the yard at the back to question them before words got out that they had been lifted.

Even the Provisional IRA saw the funny side of how the two men were captured – and they later published a cartoon depicting the incident in one of their papers. It showed the two men being apprehended by the soldiers, and Micky Agnew is saying to Joe Rice: 'All the same Joe, I wish you would get some glasses'. The two men appeared in court on terrorist-related charges a few weeks later.

The cartoon depicting Joe Rice being caught with the explosives. (Taken from *The Volunteer*)

AGAIN REMANDED ON GELLY AND BLAST CHARGES

Two men accused of possessing a quantity of gelignite and two blast bombs were again remanded in custody for a week at Belfast Magistrates Court yesterday.

They are Joseph Brendan Rice (23) bricklayer, Bilston Road, and Michael Agnew (20) painter, Creeve Walk, Andersonstown, and they are charged with possessing 56lbs of gelignite, two 2oz blast bombs (fitted with fuses and detonators), 2 feet of safety fuse and seven General Post Office fuses, at Belfast on January 13th.

At the same court, William McAreavey, Norglen Crescent, was also further remanded in custody for a week, accused of blowing up the home of the parents of a police officer at Stockmans Crescent on October 27 last.*

* Sourced from Brian Corser's private collection of newspaper cuttings.

Directly after the discovery of the explosives – and the return to the RUC Station with two Provos – the Battery Commander, on advice from intelligence, decided to raid the house in nearby Creeve Walk which 'Horace's' patrol had originally been watching. There was obviously something going on there, and the BC ordered another patrol to go out straight away. L/Bdr Danny Coulton, then working for intelligence, was part of the team that went in and searched the place. As they went in, a group of men were making their escape through the back window, but a member of the patrol managed to grab one of them before he managed to get away. After a search of the building they found a couple of weapons, bomb-making equipment and manuals.

There was another find of explosives for 12th Regiment when they found 20lbs of explosives on a patch of waste ground. It was in such a poor condition that it had to be blown up on the spot. This wasn't the first time that explosives had been found in such poor condition. It showed the complete disregard the Provos had for innocent civilians going about their everyday business. The slightest impact could be enough to detonate explosives when they were in such a poor state. The problems which 'Horace' encountered with the Pye radios on that particular patrol were nothing compared to another patrol he once did…

Bdr 'Horace', 2 Troop

I was once out on patrol up on the Riverdale Estate and I was again using the Pye radio. I had it on the 'whisper' setting and had just sent a message through to the RUC Station when I heard this big booming radio transmission coming from inside a house we were passing. It was fairly late on and very dark, and I found this a bit unsettling at first, so I got back on the radio and sent a report – and while I was talking, I heard this booming radio transmission from inside the house again – and then I realised what had happened… my transmissions were being picked up by the television set in the house.

Only hours after the success with the explosives find came yet another discovery of a small cache of weapons:

The army has reported two small arms finds in the Andersonstown and North Queen Street areas of Belfast. In the first search, two revolvers and six rounds of ammunition were found in Orchardville Avenue, Andersonstown. The second find, a .22 rifle, was found in a building at Upper Meadow Street-Spamount Street. The army claim that on both occasions they were acting on information received.

* Source taken from *The Troubles* Magazine (Glenravel Publications).

SUNDAY 16th…

VICTIMS OF THE TROUBLES WHO DIED THIS DAY…

Eamon McCormick (17) – IRA Youth Section (IRAF). Died of injuries two months after being shot by the army during a gun battle near St Peter's School, Ballymurphy, Belfast.

* List compiled from *The Troubles* Magazine (Glenravel Publications).

MONDAY 17th…

This was a relatively quiet day for much of the battery. Patrols were out doing the usual tours around the estates, but everything appeared to be peaceful. Closer to home though, and working off information received from intelligence, a search of a garage in Glen Parade was carried out. The garage being searched was just yards away from the RUC Station. Inside the building the search team found a .22 Remington sports rifle fitted with silencer and also 15 rounds of ammunition. The owner of the garage, who lived in Lake Glen, held a firearms certificate for the weapon, but it was where the weapon was found which caused such concern… The rifle was hidden in the rafters of the unlocked garage – stuffed between a few old mattresses and loaded with one round in the breech. It was the opinion of the intelligence section that the weapon had been deliberately left there for someone else to use. The garage was only 50 yards away from the Falls Road sangar at the RUC Station and it was believed that the weapon was going to be used in an attack on the sangar. The owner of the weapon was immediately arrested and taken to Palace Barracks at Holywood to be questioned.

TUESDAY 18th…

A rather unusual incident occurred in the Bogside area of Londonderry when the Official IRA captured a 21-year-old British soldier from the Scots Guards. He was on leave from his unit in England and had rather foolishly decided to travel to Northern Ireland to visit his fiancée, who lived in the Bogside. Under inter-rogation, the soldier had told his captives that his intentions were to buy himself out of the army and settle down with his fiancée in Ireland. The Officials checked with the girl and even phoned the soldier's parents in an attempt to verify the story.

The Official IRA later released a statement after setting the soldier free: 'We do not believe that the killing of this soldier would have helped the people of this area or the people of Ireland in their struggle'.[*] The Provisional IRA were furious when they found out about the capture and release of the soldier and issued their own statement: 'Words could not describe how we feel about this diabolical action. We are sure the people of Derry and all Republicans are abhorred by this action'.[†] The soldier was indeed a very fortunate man. As a rule, there was only one fate that awaited captured British soldiers. The Provisional IRA didn't take prisoners; they just butchered everyone who was unfortunate enough to be caught by them – and it didn't really matter who they were. Serviceman and civilian alike, a person's religion was enough to seal their fate.

Back in Andersonstown at around midnight, a report came through of a bomb lying in the middle of the road at Culmore Gardens. Patrols from 3 Troop and 2 Troop were sent to investigate. While 3 Troop concentrated on searching along the road and under the hedges, 2 Troop had started searching the nearby maison-ettes for anyone who may have been waiting to detonate the bomb.

---

*   Source taken from *The Troubles* Magazine (Glenravel Publications).

†   Source taken from *The Troubles* Magazine (Glenravel Publications).

TROOPS UNDER FIRE DURING ARMS FIND IN COAL SHED

Overnight searches by troops in the Andersonstown and Falls area of Belfast uncovered arms, ammunition and explosives. Early today, in a vacant house in Norglen Parade, members of the 12th Light Air Defence Regiment found 30lbs of gelignite in a weeping condition, 18 detonators, 10 yards of detonator fuse and a pair of rubber gloves. Three youths were detained, two of whom are helping police with enquiries.

In a coal shed at the rear of Culmore Gardens, Andersonstown, troops found a rifle with a magazine and telescopic sights, a sawn-off shotgun, a Thompson machine gun magazine, 23 rounds of .45 ammunition, 31 rounds of .556 ammunition and an empty ammunition box. Three shots were fired at troops during the search but no injuries were received and the fire was not returned. A .22 rifle and 15 rounds of high-velocity ammunition were found in a garage in Glen Parade. One person is helping police with enquiries.*

* Source taken from The Belfast Telegraph.

As men from the patrol moved along the landing of the block, they spotted a youth coming out – and when he saw the soldiers, he made a run for it. The section immediately rushed to the house and forced their way inside. They were sure they were onto something by the way the youth had taken off the way he did, and so they gave the building a thorough search, but nothing was found.

They trudged back outside and suddenly, Pete Roberts spotted the base of a cartridge case sticking out of the coal bunker on the landing directly opposite the front door. They forced entry and inside, wrapped in newspapers, were a Japanese-made Armalite rifle with telescopic sight and a sawn-off shotgun. There was also a quantity of ammunition and Thompson magazines.

Gnr Pete Roberts, 2 Troop

We were moving away from the house after the search and I just happened to spot a cartridge stuck in an air hole in the door of the coal bunker. I told Sammy Hulme that I thought it might be a marker for a sniper to show him where a gun had been stashed. We forced the door and I went inside and saw something stood in the corner wrapped in old newspapers. There were some bags as well. I went

The weapons
as found in
the bunker.
(Courtesy of
Brian Corser)

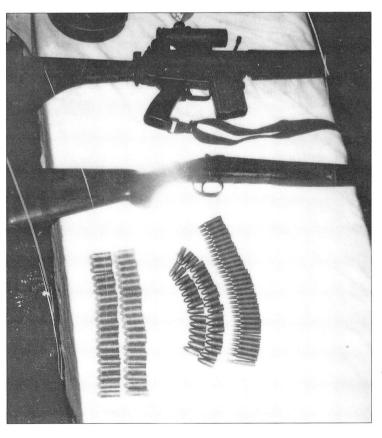

The two guns
on display at the
RUC Station.
(Courtesy of
Brian Corser)

over and started unwrapping them and found an Armalite rifle with a telescopic sight and a shotgun.

Sammy was looking over my shoulder to see what I had found, and as soon as he saw the guns he told me to get out. I was stood there while he went through the bags and uncovered some ammunition and magazines. The fat bastard later claimed all the credit for my find as well. I was bloody furious with him, but there wasn't much I could do about it. After that I never bothered trying to claim recognition for anything again. There just didn't seem any point.

The young lad spotted running away must have been on his way to alert the gunman who had stashed the weapons, because a few minutes after the cache was found, both sections came under fire. Sammy Hulme's men withdrew with the weapons and left 3 Troop to deal with the gunman.

Gnr Steve Corbett, 3 Troop

We never did find the bomb which was supposed to be there – and it's highly likely that the initial report to get us out there was just a ruse to lead us into a trap. Maybe whoever made the call didn't know about the guns hidden in the coal bunker, but thanks to the call, they were discovered by 2 Troop. As Sammy's men pulled away there was a bit of shooting when a lone gunman opened up on us as we prepared to leave. We had a quick search around the area, but couldn't find any trace of the gunman, so we just mounted up and left.

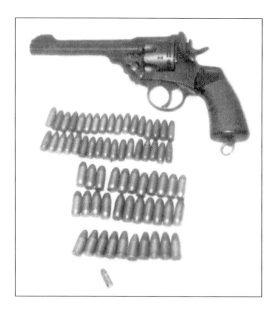

Another arms find: a Webley pistol and ammunition. (Courtesy of Brian Corser)

Later in the day, there was an incident outside the Busy Bee shops when an 83-year-old man came out of Riverdale Park Estate and crossed the Andersonstown Road heading towards the shops. He was struck by a vehicle and killed. The RUC went to the scene of the accident with an escort from 9 Battery to protect them while they investigated the incident, but by the time they had arrived, a sizable crowd had gathered and both troops and police were subjected to a vicious barrage of bricks and bottles. The patrol set up a cordon whilst the RUC tried to get on with their investigation, but it proved impossible and they had to withdraw.

VICTIMS OF THE TROUBLES WHO DIED THIS DAY...

Sydney Agnew (40) – Shot dead at his home at The Mount, Belfast.
   It was believed to be the work of the Provisional IRA to stop him from testifying in court against the terrorists who hijacked the bus he was driving.[*]

[*] List compiled from *The Troubles* Magazine (Glenravel Publications).

THURSDAY 20th...

The regiment had more success when a cache of weapons and explosives were found at Englishtown on the outskirts of Belfast. The haul included a 7.62mm pistol and magazine, three magazines, flares, fuse wire, 99 rounds of ammunition, gun-stripping tools, four nail bombs and four blast bombs. The bombs were blown up on the spot due to the state of the explosives. Around the estates in Andersonstown, the patrols continued – and up on Rossnareen, a patrol from 3 Troop again found itself caught up in rioting as the youths took to the streets. As they returned fire with the riot guns, a lone sniper opened up and fired several shots at the Pigs, but fortunately there were no casualties.

FRIDAY 21st...

At 2:00 a.m. sections from each troop moved out and up to Rossnareen to conduct an arms search. A section from 3 Troop, led by S/Sgt Frank Armstrong, were instructed to concentrate on Ramoan Gardens.

ANOTHER ARMS FIND

AN ARMS cache was found by troops in an early morning search of the Andersonstown area this morning.

In an outhouse they uncovered five revolvers and 260 rounds of assorted ammunition.

During the three-hour operation by men from 12 Regiment, Royal Artillery, three arrests were made.[*]

[*] Sourced from Brian Corser's private collection of newspaper cuttings.

The team made their way down – searching the garages, outhouses and coal bunkers in their allocated area. It looked at first as though it would turn out like so many previous searches.

Gnr Steve Corbett, 3 Troop

I went into a shed that was built on the side of a house and it was packed out with model tanks and aircraft. The owner had made a diorama of a battle scene, and it was absolutely superb. I used to be a model-maker myself, so I knew craftsmanship when I saw it. I forgot for a moment what I was really there for, and then I spotted a ceremonial sword hanging above the models. It was an Orange Lodge sword, and I wondered how the current owner had come by it. I carried on rooting around – hoping that I would find some guns, but there was nothing.

The search continued and still nothing of any significance had turned up. The men moved on to the final few houses – and in the last outhouse to be searched, hidden behind an old washing machine was a small arsenal of weapons and assorted ammunition.

Gnr Steve Corbett, 3 Troop

I got to the last house I was due to check out – number 43 Ramoan Gardens. I climbed over the fencing from the other garden and made my way over to a small brick building which was stood a few yards away from the house. I forced the door with my bayonet and shone my torch inside. There was an old washing machine by the wall at the back, and I seem to remember a chest of drawers by the side of it. I went over and pulled out the washing machine a bit and had a look behind.

Straight away I spotted two Colt .45 automatic pistols and a Webley .455 revolver – as well as a box which was full of .303 armour-piercing ammunition and machine gun magazines. I was just reaching down to grab one of the pistols... this idea entered my head that it would make a good souvenir to keep... and just at that moment, Frank Armstrong walked in behind me and said: *"Right Corbett, I'll take over now."* I thought to myself... *"You bastard."*

I knew straight away what his game was: he wanted the recognition of the find for himself. It was practically the same as had happened to Pete Roberts with Sammy Hulme on the last arms find. All I managed to keep hold of was a few rounds of the .303 AP, but when I think about it now, maybe Frank guessed what I was going to do.

The outhouse where the guns were discovered was now given a thorough search. In the official report covering the find were listed the following items:

At 21 0200 an operation was mounted to search all the outbuildings in the Rossnareen area. In the outhouse / coal shed at 43 Ramoan Gardens, the following were found:

1 × .45 Webley revolver (loaded)
1 × .38 Spanish revolver (loaded)
1 × 9mm Star automatic pistol
2 × .45 Colt automatic pistols
2 × Armalite magazines (one loaded)
1 × Thompson magazine (loaded)
110 × .303 rounds
72 × 5.56 Armalite rounds
63 × .45 rounds (pistol and revolver)
4 × .45 dum-dum rounds
13 × .38 rounds

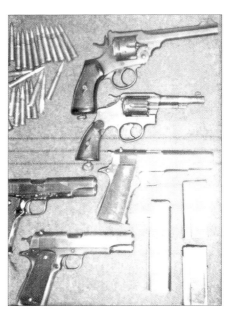

The pistols and ammunition discovered in the outhouse by the author.
(Courtesy of Brian Corser)

It was quite an impressive haul. In another part of the building, a two-way radio and a Morse radio set were found. There was an ice-cream van at the side of the property which was also searched. The team then turned their attention to the house and arrested three men who were in possession of several thousands of pounds, which they claimed was money made from selling the ice-cream! The search drew to a close and the teams returned to base at 7:30 a.m. On return to base, S/Sgt Frank Armstrong was congratulated for '*his*' find. Some weeks later, the following article appeared a Belfast-based newspaper:

---

3 IN FAMILY REMANDED

A man and his two sons accused of possessing arms and ammunition were further remanded on continuing bail until March 8 at Belfast Magistrates Court yesterday.

They are Robert Knocker (45), plasterer, Robert Mark (20) and John (17), all of Ramoan Gardens, Andersonstown.

They are charged with possessing a Spanish revolver, a Webley revolver, an automatic pistol, two US Army Colts and 300 rounds of ammunition at their home. The three were granted bail in the High Court earlier this month.*

* Sourced from Brian Corser's private collection of newspaper cuttings.

On the border, the Provisional IRA exploded three mines near Derrynose as a mobile patrol from the Devon and Dorset Regiment approached. The unit had been providing cover for a group of army sappers. Pte Stentiford was killed instantly in the triple blast. He was the second soldier to be killed since the beginning of the year.

On the mainland – in London – a parcel bomb was delivered to the Westminster office of Labour MP Mrs Judith Hart. In Belfast, the IRA bombed a city office and then a factory. Army bomb disposal experts were called to a third device containing 25lbs of explosives, and this was safely defused. The bombing campaign was a constant source of worry to those who worked in the city. Every kind of establishment within Belfast was considered to be a legitimate target by the IRA. People were living on their nerves – wondering if they would be caught up in the next explosion. For one family, it always seemed to them that every time their mother left the house, something was sure to happen.

'Moira' – Belfast resident

My mother was a jinx. Every time she went to town a bomb went off, or there was trouble or something – and it got to the stage where we would say: "*Mother, tell us when you're going out, because we're not going to town if you're going to town.*" Now a couple of times she was sat in a restaurant near St Anne's Cathedral, and... a hearse was outside… and luckily they'd sat at the back of the restaurant, and… the hearse was full of explosives and went off – and all the glass came in and the people sitting at the table got covered; and they were sat at the back, so you can imagine the state she was in when she came home.

Another occasion she was going for the bus at Shaftesbury Square, and… somebody put a bomb in a shop or a bank … I don't know. She was going across the zebra crossing and it went off, and she was blown across the crossing. Her glasses went that way and her teeth went that way. She was on her hands and knees and all these people rushed to help her… and she was on her hands and knees and they said: "*Can we help?*" and she said: "*Just find my teeth, my glasses*" – and she was so embarrassed, because her teeth… the force of it… her teeth flew out. So they managed to get her teeth and her glasses and… they wanted to take her to hospital, but she wouldn't go. She said: "*Just take me to the bus stop,*" so they took her to the bus stop – and I came home and saw she was in a state… because she was covered in debris, and she had come home on the bus looking like that.

Once she got home, then it hit her. Luckily she wasn't injured, but I think her hearing was affected after that, because of the noise… the blast of the bomb… so that's a couple of incidents that we used to say: "*Mother, you're a jinx… Do NOT go into town,*" but… you can't stop living; you have to keep going – but not long after that, we moved; we moved to County Antrim – and that was a lot better, because we were out of the city.

VICTIMS OF THE TROUBLES WHO DIED THIS DAY…

Pte Charles Stentiford (18) – The Devon and Dorset Regiment. Killed by the Provisional IRA in a landmine attack while on army foot patrol; Keady, County Armagh.[*]

[*] List compiled from *The Troubles* Magazine (Glenravel Publications).

SATURDAY 22nd…

The Provisionals in Andersonstown were stung into action by the previous day's success by 3 Troop and the haul of weapons they found in the outhouse. Whenever there was a significant find of weapons, the Provos would retaliate in some way to try and counter the publicity generated by the latest find. Reports came filtering back to BHQ from the various mobile patrols that went out in the afternoon that much of Rossnareen and the surrounding estates were sealed off by barricades. It could well have been that other arms caches were being moved around in an attempt to stop them being discovered by the search parties. The battery had been having quite a bit of success just recently, and it must have been hurting the Provos to lose so many weapons.

Gnr Steve Corbett, 3 Troop

Our Pigs were sent up towards the Busy Bee after reports of large crowds gathering outside the shops. As we got closer, the Pigs came under attack from both sides of the road. They were throwing all kinds of stuff at us. The vehicles were taking an absolute pasting from paint bombs and rocks. They used to aim for the windscreen with the paint bombs to try and obscure the driver's vision.

There was a barricade on one of the roads and we had to smash our way through it. I fired a few shots with the riot gun at some youths who got too close to the back of our Pig and was well pleased when I saw one of them drop to the ground. I was quite worn out by the time we got back to base and was looking forward to a rest, but it didn't happen. While I had been out on patrol, there had been a bit of a riot in front of the bus depot and our troop was sent out on a cleaning-up detail to shift all the rubble.

Down at the bottom end of Andersonstown Road, there was a huge battle between rioters and troops as a search team entered the Whitefort Inn. The covering party ended up firing around 25 rounds of rubber bullets to try and disperse the crowds as the search continued inside. They eventually arrested several people and took them back to the RUC Station for questioning.

SUNDAY 23rd…

Just after lunch, reports came through of yet another large gathering outside the Busy Bee – and again 3 Troop were sent to investigate.

Gnr Steve Corbett, 3 Troop

We were just leaving Rossnareen Avenue when we got diverted to the Busy Bee after reports of large-scale rioting. It was like a rerun of the previous day. The Pigs took another pasting from the paint bombs as we got near the shops, and again we replied with our rubber bullets.

That evening, I went out with about seven other lads in the back of two Pigs and we got dropped off in Rossnareen to do a foot patrol. We were out there for over two bloody hours trying to dodge groups of youths who were stoning us. I was lumbered with the A42 radio on my back and Frank Armstrong had us cutting through gardens and climbing over fences. It was murder trying to keep up with the lads. The aerial kept getting stuck in the branches of trees.

I hadn't been back at the depot that long before I was dragged out again on another incident: we were sent up to Lenadoon Avenue to help out 58 Battery. They were caught up in a major disturbance, and there were that many rioters they were finding it hard to cope. We all jumped out of the Pigs and got stuck in. I had the riot gun and was blasting away for all I was worth. Some of my shots went wild and smashed a fair few windows in the houses. The locals thought that we deliberately targeted property on the estates, but these riot guns were notoriously inaccurate and it was anybody's guess where your shot might end up. You just fired at the target in front of you, and the last thing on your mind was the possibility of damaging someone's house. You were more interested in looking after yourself and your mates than worrying about smashing some bloody windows.

As always, the constant worry in these situations was the hidden gunman. A choice had to be made whether to go in with riot shields and batons and confront the rioters, or to go in with the rifle and use the butt if anyone had a go at you. It was brutal and bloody. The rioters would try and separate soldiers from their comrades and try to seize their weapons to turn against them.

TUESDAY 25th…

Evening entertainment for the off-duty British soldier based in a Catholic area was totally out of the question. To leave the safety of the base would be akin to signing your own death warrant, but in the Protestant area of Carrickfergus were a group of women who were dedicated to supplying some home comforts to the troops. This magnificent group of women were known to all as the 'Cake Ladies'. They laid on discos for the troops, organised the pop bands to entertain them, and even encouraged their own daughters to go so that the off-duty soldiers would have someone to dance with.

Gnr Steve Corbett, 3 Troop

I remember going to one of those discos. Obviously we had to take it in turns to attend these things, and my day for going was the 25th of January. Some of the lads who had been to the previous ones had

'Bill and Ben –
The IRA Men'.
(Taken from
The Loyalist News)

Republican humour.
(Taken from *The Volunteer*)

told me how good they were, and I was really looking forward to it. A group of us arrived at this hall and we were taken inside. There was a stage at one end with a record player on a table, and at the other end there was beer on sale.

We waited for 'the talent' to turn up, but all we got was some WRACS and a few from the WRAF. I'm not saying they were rough, but you wouldn't have liked to meet up with some of them on a dark night! They spent all their time dancing with each other as well; they just didn't seem to want to be bothered with us, so we all concentrated on the beer instead. It was nice to be able to wind down and relax without having to watch your back.

At one of these discos, a certain NCO got fed up of waiting for the army transport which was laid on to take the men back to their bases. He took it upon himself to use the public transport and returned back to Andersonstown on the next available bus. This rather irresponsible action cost him his stripes and he was reduced to the ranks.

Just occasionally there might be the odd show of support towards the men of 9 Battery from the Catholic community in Andersonstown, but such displays of tacit sympathy were quite rare. Tony 'Sammy' Symonds recalls one woman he occasionally met when out on foot patrol…

Gnr Tony 'Sammy' Symonds, 2 Troop
On occasion a lady would pass. No speech would pass our lips; no look at each other, but she would push a couple of sweets into my hand. Not all wanted trouble.

It was around this time that the battery was visited on two separate occasions by television film crews doing documentaries for their respective TV channels. The first crew were from ITV's *Look North* and they spent a few days filming and following 2 Troop as they went about their duties. The documentary covered the discos laid on for the troops and the 'Cake Ladies' who organised them. Special patrols were laid on so that the cameramen could capture images of the men out on foot patrol and mobile, but in truth the vehicles and the men never ventured far away from the RUC Station. There was too much risk involved venturing further out, and nobody wanted to see any of the TV crew getting injured. The sole purpose of this exercise was to let the people of the North-West of England see what 12th Regiment were actually doing in Northern Ireland. Their recruiting ground was throughout the Granada TV region, and they were well known as the 'Lancashire and Cumbrian Gunners'.

Back in Lancashire and the surrounding districts, the exploits of the men of 12 Regiment and their successes against the Provos were reported in several of the local papers, and the BBC decided that they too would like to do a documentary about the men of 9 Battery. Eventually, a film crew from the *'Panorama'* programme turned up and spent a few days filming 1 and 3 Troop. Mick McHale was assigned to the task of driving the cameramen around the area.

Gnr Mick McHale, 3 Troop

We had been told that the BBC's *'Panorama'* team were coming over to do a documentary about the battery. They duly arrived and we were called in to our sleeping accommodation at the bus depot to meet them. I was told I would be driving the lead Pig when we took them around, and so we went outside with the camera crew to sort out where they would be in the vehicle. It was a bit of a tight squeeze really, because the cameraman was sat in the middle right next to me, and then the guy with the microphone sat in the Vehicle Commander's seat while the sound engineer sat cross-legged with his box of tricks in the footwell in front of him.

We were briefed by the BC where we were allowed to take them. The names escape me now, but it was the cushiest and safest areas where we used to patrol. After driving around for perhaps 30 minutes or so – and getting pissed off by the lack of action and offers of cups of tea and biscuits from the locals – the film crew asked the Vehicle Commander who was sat in the back of the Pig if we could go somewhere a bit more lively. The Commander got on the radio to the RUC Station and asked for permission to do the 'hard' tour. The BC got back to him and gave the OK providing we didn't let the cameraman shove himself through the vehicle cupola, and we were told we had to keep battened up.

Anyway, I drove up to Rossnareen Estate to give them a taste of what we

Tony 'Sammy' Symonds being filmed by one of the Granada camera crew. (Courtesy of Tony 'Sammy' Symonds)

really put up with every day. On arrival we got the usual treatment. First it was the verbal abuse, and then the stones and bottles; then the paint bombs and acid bombs started coming over; and then the women put on a show – rattling their dustbin lids and blowing their whistles. Sadly for the film crew there was no gunfire, but it did get their adrenaline flowing! Watching it all on TV the following night was a bonus. The cameraman had filmed me in profile, and then panned down to my hands on the steering wheel. Don Potter [the BSM] was watching the film and spotted that I was wearing officers-style leather gloves – and that wouldn't do at all! He gave me a right old bollocking for that.

WEDNESDAY 26th…

Activity in the area had been picking up over the past few days, and the patrols were increased to keep a check on what was going on. There were the occasional gatherings on street corners, but nothing of any great significance seemed to be happening – and then later that evening, a report came in that a barricade had been set up at the junction of Glen Road and Ramoan Gardens.

In Belfast, a Claymore-type mine exploded near a car which had been used as a barricade at Glen Road and Ramoan Gardens.[*]

* Source taken from *The Troubles* Magazine (Glenravel Publications).

Two Pigs were sent to the scene. They moved into Coolnasilla Park and pulled up while a patrol from 3 Troop dismounted and moved in on foot. The ground sloped upwards towards Glen Road at that point, and between the Pigs and the road was a small wooded area. The patrol was instructed to move forward through the woods and clear it of any gunmen who may have been hiding near the barricade. The fear was that if a mobile approached from the roadway, they could be driving into yet another IRA ambush. Also in the area was a patrol from 2 Troop. They too had heard the report about the barricade and went up to have a look. They moved into the grounds of the Ulster Brewery, gained entry to the office building and went out on the roof to keep an eye on the barricade.

Gnr Pete Roberts, 2 Troop
We got inside the building and went up on the roof and lay there watching the barricade. It was just to the right of us across the road at the junction of Ramoan Gardens. I seem to remember it was a van or lorry blocking the road, but there was a small fire next to it.

The foot patrol from 3 Troop slowly made its way through the woods from the opposite direction. Just ahead was the road, and clearly visible was the barricade. Both patrols were completely unaware of the presence of each other.

Gnr Steve Corbett, 3 Troop

We entered the woods and started moving forward towards Glen Road. It was pitch-black in there and you could hardly see anything. As we got closer, I could see the road looming above us. A couple of street lights were still working and the glow from them was illuminating the barricade up near the junction. There was a red van there, which I think was a Post Office van, and there appeared to be a fire underneath it. It was really eerie in that wood. There wasn't a sound to be heard, apart from us making our way through, and a crackling coming from the barricade.

  We got closer and then all of a sudden there was a rush of hot air and a blinding flash, followed by a bang like a clap of thunder as a bomb went off. A few seconds later I could hear all the debris falling through the trees around us. The branches were snapping as bits of the barricade came crashing down. We all stopped and crouched down low in an attempt to avoid all this stuff that was falling around us. When everything had settled down, the van and the barricade had gone. All that was left was an engine block in the road. It wasn't really worth checking out after that, as the bomb had cleared the barricade for us, but we moved forward and had a look just in case any civilians had been caught up in the blast.

Gnr Pete Roberts, 2 Troop

We lay there watching, and then there was a fucking big blinding flash and an almighty bang and the van disintegrated. Nobody knew we were up on that roof; we weren't even supposed to be there, so we didn't stand up or anything like that because no-one would have known who we were and we might have ended up getting shot.

Back at the barricade, the patrol surveyed the damage; their work was done. The bomb had effectively removed the road block for them. They went back to their Pigs and returned to base. This was yet another near-miss for the patrol. The probability was that the barricade was a trap for any mobile approaching it on the Glen Road. Somewhere there would have been someone waiting to detonate the bomb if any vehicles had approached it. Had one of the vehicles been next to that when it exploded, it would have obliterated it. The bomber must have spotted the foot patrol approaching through the woods, lost his nerve and detonated the device just a bit too soon.

The buildings from where Pete Roberts kept watch on the barricade.
(Courtesy of Brian Corser)

Although the exact date isn't recorded, there was a similar incident as this a few days earlier when a mobile patrol was making its way up Shaw's Road. Earlier in the day there had been a phone call made to the RUC Station claiming that weapons were hidden in a flat at 40 Greenan. As the patrol entered Shaw's Road from the Stewartstown Road, they had only gone a few yards when there was a huge explosion by the side of the road. Both vehicles escaped the force of the blast and remained undamaged, but the crews were badly shaken by the incident, which left a hole by the side of the road almost four feet across and two feet deep.

After the explosion, the vehicles drove to the flat and the men smashed their way into the building as they searched for the device used to detonate the bomb. The owner claimed he saw a youth running into Tullymore Gardens just after the bomb went off.

VICTIMS OF THE TROUBLES WHO DIED THIS DAY...

Peter McNulty (47) – Provisional IRA. Killed by a premature bomb explosion while taking part in an attack on Castlewellan RUC Base, County Down.[*]

* List compiled from *The Troubles* Magazine (Glenravel Publications).

PEOPLE RESENT IRA BOMBS – ARMY

There is growing resentment among people living in the Andersonstown area against what is described as 'The IRA's bungling methods'.

According to the army, two IRA explosions in the Glen Road area shortly after midnight last night provided great resentment.

The two charges, each between two and five lbs, exploded in the area of a burning car which had been set up as an obstruction in the road. Although there were no casualties, there was considerable damage to windows and doors in nearby houses.

An officer on the scene reported: "People came onto the street angrily protesting about the IRA's bungling methods. They left us in no doubt as to how they felt about men who place explosives where they endanger lives and wreck homes. Their language was out of this world."

The army say this is the second incident of this nature in this area of the city in the past few days.[*]

[*] Sourced from Brian Corser's private collection of newspaper cuttings.

THURSDAY 27th…

In Londonderry, the Democratic Unionist Association (DUA) advised the RUC that they intended to hold a religious rally at Guildhall Square on the afternoon of Sunday 30 January. The Civil Rights Association also planned to hold a huge anti-internment rally on the same day, and it was also due to end in Guildhall Square. The government ban on such parades was still in force and the DUA had made it quite clear that they fully expected the authorities to stop the illegal march planned for the same day by the Civil Rights Association…

The Rev James K. McClelland, Minister of Londonderry Free Presbyterian Church and Vice President of the Londonderry and Foyle Democratic Unionist Association, said: "The civil rights march is not legal and it is our intention to have a properly organised legal meeting in Guildhall Square. The authorities will have to keep their word and stop the civil rights march and give us protection." He said they expected about 1,000 to attend their meeting, which he would address along with the Rev William McCrea, Minister of Magherafelt Free Presbyterian Church.[*]

[*] Source taken from *The Troubles* Magazine (Glenravel Publications).

The potential for trouble was obvious should these two rallies be allowed to meet up. In Belfast, all troops were put on high alert after reports came through that a soldier had been kidnapped by the IRA in the Short Strand area. The army eventually admitted that one of their soldiers was 'absent without leave'. The Provisional IRA continued with their attacks, and at Forkhill, probably the longest gun battle ever recorded took place between members of the Scots Dragoon Guards and the IRA. Over a three-hour period, the Dragoon Guards fired over 4,000 rounds of ammunition at gunmen who were holed up in a house just over the border. Throughout the Province the bombing campaign went on, and in a 30-hour period there were at least 26 explosions recorded.

VICTIMS OF THE TROUBLES WHO DIED THIS DAY...

Peter Gilgunn (26) – The Royal Ulster Constabulary. Shot dead in a Provisional IRA gun attack on his patrol car in Creggan Road, Londonderry.

David Montgomery (20) – The Royal Ulster Constabulary. Shot dead in the same incident.

The men died when their patrol car was climbing up Creggan Road to Rosemount RUC Station. Three gunmen were lying in wait, and as the car slowed down to negotiate the steep road, one of the gunmen stepped forward and opened fire at point-blank range with a Thompson machine gun on the five occupants. The two men were killed instantly, and a third was injured.[*]

[*] List compiled from *The Troubles* Magazine (Glenravel Publications).

FRIDAY 28th...

VICTIMS OF THE TROUBLES WHO DIED THIS DAY...

Raymond Carroll (22) – The Royal Ulster Constabulary. Shot dead by the Provisional IRA while at a garage, Oldpark Road, Belfast.[*]

[*] List compiled from *The Troubles* Magazine (Glenravel Publications).

SATURDAY 29th...

Mobile patrols were sent out to the Rossnareen area after reports were received of a large gathering of people. Upon their arrival they were met by a hostile crowd of around 30 youths. The two Pigs drew to a halt and a small section of the crowd broke away and moved to the rear of the vehicles Some of the rioters managed to get close enough to the back vehicle to pelt the occupants with rocks through the open doors, and two of the crew were injured, but not seriously. A little further up the road, the vehicles pulled into the side of the road while the men dismounted and took cover behind the open rear doors as the stoning continued.

ARMY BREAK UP MOB

Troops used rubber bullets to break up a mob of about 30 youths throwing bottles and stones at soldiers in Rossnareen Avenue, Andersonstown today. An army spokesman said: "The mob was dispersed."[*]

[*] Source taken from *The Belfast Telegraph*, 29 January 1972.

According to the press release, the soldiers dispersed the mob, but this was far from the truth. Only two rubber bullets were fired by the patrol and they threw back a few paint bombs which had failed to smash. The rear vehicle fared even worse – and in this encounter the youths actually got the better of the patrol, and it was decided that the best thing to do was just to withdraw from the estate before things got too far out of hand.

In Londonderry, preparations for the huge anti-internment rally to be held by the Republican movement on Sunday 30 January were complete – despite the government ban on such gatherings taking place. The organisers of the rally were left in no doubt whom would be held responsible if violence broke out, when the army and RUC issued a joint statement making their position quite clear on the matter:

Experience has already shown that the attempted marches often end in violence and must have been foreseen by the organisers. Clearly the responsibility for this violence and the consequence of it must rest fairly and squarely on the shoulders of those who encourage people to break the law.[*]

[*] Source taken from *The Troubles* Magazine (Glenravel Publications).

The Protestant Democratic Unionist Association in Londonderry had also planned to hold an open-air religious rally in Guildhall Square, but after receiving assurances from the authorities that the planned civil rights march by the Republicans would be halted by force if necessary, they decided to call off the service. They appealed to all Loyalists to stay out of the city on Sunday, but they also issued a warning to the Government:

> We are prepared to give the government a final opportunity to demonstrate their integrity and honour their promise, but warn that if they fail in this undertaking they need never again ask Loyalist people to forfeit their basic right of peaceful and legal assembly.[*]

The army and RUC again warned the organisers of the Republican protest march that the authorities had a duty to act against those deliberately breaking the law:

> In carrying out their duty, the Security Forces are concerned to avoid or reduce to an absolute minimum the consequences of any violence that may erupt from the confrontation between sections of the community or between the Security Forces and those taking part in an illegal march.
>
> The Security Forces choose the time and the place at which to intervene and its policy, which is clearly in the public interest, allows the possibility that marches may, in some cases, proceed for some distance before being stopped. This does not, however, mean that participants will be allowed to break the law with impunity.[†]

The organisers were now under no illusions about the possible consequences of going ahead with the protest. Back in Andersonstown, the men of 9 Battery were not unduly concerned by the events which were rapidly drawing to a head in Londonderry. They had already dealt with two illegal gatherings – and despite some small-scale rioting on both occasions, there had been no serious incidents.

SUNDAY 30th... 'BLOODY SUNDAY'

The terrible events of 'Bloody Sunday' are probably remembered more than any other incident which happened during the whole of the Troubles in Northern Ireland. On that day 30 people were shot while they were attending a civil rights demonstration which had attracted an estimated crowd of around 15,000 people. Of those shot, 13 of them subsequently died. Another person who was wounded

---

[*]   Source taken from *The Troubles* Magazine (Glenravel Publications).
[†]   Source taken from *The Troubles* Magazine (Glenravel Publications).

during the demonstration was to die more than four months later. The Paratroop Regiment, who were policing the march, claimed that they had been subjected to attacks from IRA gunmen and had only responded to defend themselves from those attacks. They also claimed that at least 200 rounds of ammunition had been fired at them, and they had only fired back at identified targets.

The civilians, for their part, produced scores of witnesses who claimed that the Paratroopers had opened fire first. It is doubtful if the truth of what really happened on that day will ever come out. Any Official or Provisional IRA volunteers who were out on the streets during the protest rally – and who may have been involved in any of the shooting that day – are hardly likely to own up to the part they played in the massacre of so many civilians.

Had the organisers of the rally took heed of the warnings that were issued before the march was held, all the loss of life could have been avoided, but they chose to carry on in direct defiance of the ban. The fact that such clear warnings were issued by the military and the RUC is often conveniently overlooked by those who hold the Paratroopers solely to blame for the tragedy which happened that day in Londonderry. When word started to spread of the gunning down of the protesters in Londonderry, there was an outbreak of violence on the streets of Andersonstown of such a magnitude that it came perilously close to overwhelming the soldiers of 9 Battery – and it continued for several days afterwards. Back at the bus depot, those who were not out on patrol were sat watching the TV coverage of the civil rights march in Londonderry.

Gnr Steve Corbett, 3 Troop

I thought it was great when I heard about all the killing in Derry. I wasn't alone in my thinking either. I thought back to Christmas Day when we had our so-called 'peace rally' led by that gobshite Bernadette Devlin. That ended in violence at the back of the depot, although there was no shooting or anything like that. As far as I recall, we all just assumed it was Provo gunmen who had been shot dead by the Paras in Londonderry – and we thought it was no more than the bastards deserved. Better them than us was my opinion at the time.

Bdr 'Horace' – a Section Commander of 2 Troop based at the front of the bus depot – recalls how his men reacted to the news of the shootings.

Bdr 'Horace', 2 Troop

I was sitting in the house at the bus depot watching the TV with the rest of the lads. They were all cheering as the Paras went in, and they were saying things like: *"Go for it, the Paras – get stuck in."*

They were taking great delight at watching them blasting away at the IRA in Londonderry. This is how we saw it at the time, but even then I knew there would be repercussions for all of us when news reached through to the IRA units in our area – and I remember saying to them quite clearly: "*I wouldn't cheer too loud lads, because we're all going to get it in the necks before tomorrow*" – and I couldn't have been more right.

The expected trouble actually came sooner than 'Horace' thought. At around 10:30 p.m. a mobile patrol near the Busy Bee shopping precinct on Andersonstown Road reported on their radio the presence of a large crowd of about 200-strong. Most of the shops had been torched and buses and cars had been hijacked and used as barricades across the roads.

Gnr Steve Corbett, 3 Troop
S/Sgt Burton took our section out and up Andersonstown Road to see what was going on – and as we drew closer to the Busy Bee shops, I could see a glow in the sky from all the fires. There were the skeletal remains of buses and cars which had been torched – littering the road – and there were large crowds milling about on the streets. The sound of gunfire filled the air as we drove through. I'd never seen anything like it in my life; it was truly a very frightening sight to see.

The Pigs slowed down to a crawl, and as we passed the shops, the bricks and bottles began to shower the vehicles from both sides of the road. I remember looking out of the back of the Pig as a crowd of rioters started to charge up towards us and pelt us with all kinds of stuff. The whole area was illuminated by the flames from all the buildings which had been set ablaze. We pressed on further up the road and turned into Finaghy Road North and drove down a short distance, and then we turned around and parked up at St Joseph's Training College. Some of the section started to take pot-shots to extinguish the street lights so that the darkness would give us some cover from the rioting mobs.

The patrol was split into two sections: one section was detailed to guard the Pigs while S/Sgt Burton took three men up onto the hill in front of the Training College. To the left of their position was the fork in the road where Shaw's Road ran parallel with Tullymore Gardens. Directly in front of the hill and on the other side of Andersonstown Road ran an open stretch of grassed land which was about 450 yards long. To the left were a group of houses situated on Tullymore Gardens and Glassmullin Gardens, and to the right of this strip of land were a line of bungalows along Glenshane Gardens. At the top of this road was Slievegallion

Drive, which passed in front of a row of shops fronted by a low brick wall. Looking directly to the right, it was possible to see down a fair length of Andersonstown Road towards the Busy Bee shops. The whole sky beyond the shops and the back of Slievegallion Drive appeared to be glowing from the numerous fires around the estates; the sound of gunfire and explosions filled the air.

Gnr Steve Corbett, 3 Troop

We made our way on foot up the drive of St Joseph's Training College and on to the top of the hill which overlooked the junction of Andersonstown Road and Shaw's Road. There was a wide grass verge on the other side – and just beyond that was a group of houses with a low brick wall in front of them which were maybe about 150 yards away from our position – and we settled down to watch. I remember this street light just a few yards in front of me, and it was illuminating the top of the hill. I was getting a bit worried about being spotted because of the glow from it, and so I decided to take a shot at it and put it out. I lined up my rifle and squeezed the trigger – and missed! Mick Burton turned towards me and gave me the look of death. I felt a right idiot for missing, but I really felt exposed by its light and I just wanted to put it out.

Mick Burton's men were eventually spotted. The Provo volunteers started to move in and took up firing positions – and then the shooting started. Some of the gunmen had moved up behind the wall in front of the shops on Slievegallion Drive, and others were positioned around the low garden walls around Tullymore and Glassmullin Gardens.

Gnr Mick McHale, 3 Troop

I remember lying there and listening to the bullets as they went just over the top of us. Bits of twigs were falling on our heads as they cut through the trees.

Gnr Steve Corbett, 3 Troop

I was looking over towards the houses at the bottom end of Tullymore Gardens as the shooting started. It seemed to be coming from all over the place. All you could hear was 'crack-crack-crack' as the bullets passed over our heads, and now and again you would hear a rifle being fired. It all pointed to the gunmen being very close to where we were hiding up. I always remember being told by a training instructor that if you heard a crack and then the bang of a gun being fired, it was time to get your bloody head down and take cover. In front of me I could see someone moving about between two of the houses just across the way, and every so often there would be gunfire coming from that area, but I couldn't be sure if the man I saw was a gunman – and so I didn't open fire. I was mindful of our Rules of Engagement – as we all were – and I didn't want to be finding myself on a charge of murder. In fact, none of us returned fire, so I assumed I wasn't the only one who was unsure about the activity between the houses.

It was a dreadful sight to see. All of the Busy Bee looked as though it was on fire. Crowds of people were roaming around and smashing things up and the sky seemed to be glowing red.

S/Sgt Burton decided to pull us back from the hill. By that time we had been up there for over an hour – and all the time we were there, we were being shot at. It seemed obvious to me the Provos knew we were up there because of all the gunfire that was aimed at us, but I don't think they knew there were only four of us. If they had known, well… it doesn't bear thinking about.

The patrol fell back towards the safety of the Pigs; they moved out and entered into the estate near Rossnareen Avenue. Mick Burton decided to go along the road and lift the drain covers to see if there were any weapons hidden down there. The men dismounted and started making their way along and Mick Krasnowski got to one particularly stubborn cover and used his rifle barrel as a lever to free

it. Some weeks later, when on the rifle ranges, he was to discover the folly of his actions. When checking the zero on his rifle, he couldn't even hit the target at 50 yards. On examination of the barrel of his rifle, it was found to be bent.

At the time, it was still assumed by everyone in the battery that those killed in Londonderry were Provo volunteers shot dead in gun battles with the troops. By the end of January, the men of 9 Battery were two months into their tour and all of them had become accustomed to the violence on the streets of Andersonstown, but they had never experienced it on this scale before; the sheer ferocity and volume of it all had come perilously close to overwhelming all the patrols out on the streets.

The author.
(Courtesy of Steve Corbett)

Gnr Steve Corbett, 3 Troop

Sunday night was an absolute nightmare. I have never experienced anything like it in my life. Even after all these years, I find it hard to believe that the army would just open up on innocent protesters on that march in Londonderry. Something must have happened to make the soldiers believe that they had come under attack. I can only speak from my own experiences when I came under fire from IRA gunmen. Many times there would be civilians in close proximity to us when the shooting started. Most of us were only in our late teens or very early 20s, and we had never experienced combat before. It is very unnerving to come under fire from hidden gunmen. You start looking around; trying to work out where the shots are coming from – and all the time there are entirely innocent people dashing about amidst the gunfire trying to get out of harm's way.

There are those who hold the theory that the IRA were happy with the outcome of the protest rally in Londonderry. The shooting of so many civilian protesters caused such outrage amongst the Catholic community that many rallied to the IRA cause. This gave the Provos a huge boost to their recruiting figures and a further increase in financial backing and weapons supplies from the Irish-Americans who viewed the terrorist attacks as some kind of patriotic war against the British aggressors. All it did for the men of 9 Battery was to turn the following days into an absolute nightmare of never-ending attacks from the Provisional IRA.

THOSE THAT DIED AS A RESULT OF THE DISTURBANCES WERE...

John Duddy (17)
Kevin McElhinney (17)
Patrick Doherty (31)
Bernard McGuigan (41)
Hugh Gilmour (17)
William Nash (19)
Michael McDaid (20)
John Young (17)
Michael Kelly (17)
James Wray (22)
Gerry Donaghy (17)
Gerald McKinney (35)
William McKinney (26)

All had been shot dead in the vicinity of Rossville Street, Bogside, Londonderry.

There was another death on this day…

Major Robin Alers-Hankey (35) – The Royal Green Jackets. He died four months after being shot by a Provisional IRA sniper in Abbey Street, Bogside, Londonderry.*

* List compiled from *The Troubles* Magazine (Glenravel Publications).

MONDAY 31st...

The rioting had continued throughout the night, and by now there were trucks being hijacked at the rate of around one every 15 minutes by the Provo volunteers and the residents of Andersonstown. All the entrance roads to the estates were being blocked off by huge barricades. A large arsenal of weapons was also smuggled into the area to arm the volunteers who were waiting to launch their attacks against the soldiers. Every street that the patrols entered seemed to be blocked off by hijacked trucks. Every time they approached them, they came under withering fire from the Provos standing their ground – fiercely determined to stop the patrols entering the estates. As they approached, the armoured Pigs were hit by fire from the volunteers armed with machine guns and high-velocity rifles. The telltale sound of the .45 Thompson machine guns hammered out as the bullets raked the armour plate with a 'clang-clang-clang' – the air pierced with the 'crack' of high-velocity rounds fired from rifles.

S/Sgt Burton's patrol finally pulled out shortly after 2:00 a.m. and returned to base. They drove up Shaw's Road and on to the Glen Road to avoid the rioters who were still on the rampage around the area of the Busy Bee. By now it was snowing very hard and it just added to the soldier's misery as they tried to deal with the rioting and clear the barricades from the streets. The shooting and bombing continued as the troops tried to restore order.

FLAMES LIGHT UP BELFAST'S NIGHT SKY

Flames lit up the night sky over Belfast last night with a big down-town office ablaze, a bank at Andersonstown burning following an explosion, and hijacked lorries on fire in several districts including the Upper and Lower Falls and the Markets area.

Between 6pm and midnight, Belfast Fire Brigade turned out in response to 18 calls. Earlier in the evening a brewery was badly damaged and 30 vehicles were hijacked and burned along the length of the Falls Road.

Barricades were thrown up at Andersonstown and in the Lower Falls area and bursts of gunfire were directed from Albert Street at the British Army post at Northumberland Street without causing any casualties.

At least 10 people were hurt in one of two bomb blasts in Belfast city centre yesterday. The injury blast was at British Home Stores in Castle Place.

Two victims were RUC men. One who lost a leg was described in hospital as 'serious'. Two of the eight civilians were also 'seriously' hurt.

It was thought that the bombers hijacked a van belonging to British Home Stores, placed a bomb in the back and then drove it to the rear of the store, where it was abandoned.

A police spokesman said that the two RUC men went back into the shopping complex after hearing that some people might still be left in the premises near the British Home Stores. As they went in to warn of the danger, the bomb went off. The people inside were not injured.

An army expert estimated that the bomb contained about 100lbs of explosives.

Early this morning 13 Saracen armoured personnel carriers, several Whippet cars and an army barricade breaker were reported to have moved into the Andersonstown / Glen Road area where streets were still blocked by barricades thrown up yesterday.

The second blast was at a milk bar in Great Victoria Street. A bomb weighing about 20lbs was left outside in a suitcase. Damage to the building was described as only 'superficial'. There were no casualties.

BLACK SMOKE

Huge clouds of black smoke hung over the city as the Ulster Brewery building on the Glen Road burned.

Six masked men held up the staff and after sprinkling the office block with petrol set it alight. Extensive damaged was caused, but the production end was unaffected. No-one was hurt.

Firemen were hampered in reaching the outbreak by barricades erected in the neighbourhood. A public house in Albert Street was also set alight and barricades of hijacked cars blazed throughout the city. In the afternoon a Falls Road cinema was extensively damaged by fire.

The Union Street office block only yards from the city centre and previously damaged by an explosion was completely gutted by an inferno that sent flames roaring from the four-storey building. Firemen were able to confine the outbreak but were unable to save the building. The fire burned until early this morning.

The Ulster Bank at Andersonstown, scene of

several fires the previous night, was wrecked by an explosion and the building was gutted by the blaze that followed.

Two soldiers were shot in Belfast yesterday but their injuries were said to be 'not serious'.

The first, from the 12th Light Air Defence Regiment, was helping remove a barricade in Glen Road when he was hit. The same was said of a soldier hit in the Flax Street Mill observation post.

In Grosvenor Road men from the 1st Battalion Gloucestershire Regiment claimed to have shot an armed man trying to steal a van. "He was dragged away before they could reach him," an army spokesman said.

A patrol in Springfield Road came under machine gun fire, but no-one was hurt.

Troops claimed another possible hit when they returned fire in Rossnareen Avenue, Andersonstown.

Shots were fired at an army patrol in the Crumlin Road and on the edge of Ardoyne a patrol came under machine gun fire. There were no casualties.

As trouble flared throughout the city as part of the backlash to the previous day's Derry killings, many city services were stopped and police advised motorists to avoid West Belfast.

Children who found 46 rounds of .303 ammunition and three rounds of 9mm ammunition handed it to a military patrol (Gloucester's) an army spokesman said last night.*

* Sourced from Brian Corser's private collection of newspaper cuttings.

The newspaper reports made grim reading. The backlash from the shootings in Londonderry had spread far and wide. Much of Belfast was under siege from the Provisionals as they sought revenge for the 13 protesters shot dead the previous day. At first light, two Pigs from 2 Troop left the safety of the bus depot and ventured out towards the estates to check for barricades. Sergeant Sammy Hulme was leading the patrol, with Dave Bamford as his driver. In the back were Bdr Renzo Agnello, Steve Gerald, Pete Roberts and Bdr 'Horace'. Lieutenant Dick Burland was in command of the rear Pig, with Paddy Keane at the wheel. They made their way up Andersonstown Road and turned into Slievegallion Drive just by the Busy Bee. Directly ahead, the road was completely blocked by several large vehicles.

Bdr Renzo Peterson Agnello, 2 Troop

We arrived in the Pigs, debussed and were on foot at the end of the road that had the barricade; then we came under very heavy fire and I took cover behind a lamppost. You could hear the 'pst-pst-pst' as the rounds flew around you. Other troops were already on the ground and returning fire when we arrived. I remember it was snowing quite heavy, which may have spoilt the accuracy of the shooters and saved us from casualties. We then got back into the Pig to attempt the removal of the barricade, which was the main reason we were there, and then we broke through.

The two Pigs forced their way through and travelled a short distance up Slievegallion Drive before turning around and coming back out onto Andersonstown Road. They then turned right and headed towards Shaw's Road to check for anymore barricades – and as they passed Tullymore Walk they came under fire, but Sammy Hulme ordered the Pigs to carry on. The patrol reached the top, turned right into Glen Road and then started to make their way back down towards the bus depot.

As the lead vehicle approached the junction with Ramoan Gardens, Sammy Hulme spotted a barricade at the bottom end of the road and ordered Dave to turn in and drive down while they checked it out. They had just reached the lower end near the barricade when a gunman suddenly jumped up from behind it and fired off a few shots with a pistol at the windscreen of the Pig. One bullet pierced the armoured glass with a tremendous crack and caused absolute chaos within the confines of the vehicle as it ricocheted off the armour plate. As it entered the vehicle, it took the button off the cuff of Dave's jacket before grazing the cheek of Sammy Hulme – and then Renzo was hit; the bullet cutting a deep furrow across his shoulders. Next in line was Steve Gerald, with the bullet travelling the length of the Pig, just missing his skull and passing through his beret – making holes in the back and front. Much to the amusement of one of the crew, he could see Steve's hair sticking out of both holes. The bullet then struck the back of the Pig, flattened to the size of a 50 pence piece, travelled back towards the front of the vehicle and hit Renzo again – this time in the back of the head – and knocked him off his seat.

Gnr Pete Roberts, 2 Troop

I looked at Steve Gerald and saw his hair sticking out through the holes in his beret, and I started laughing; then I looked around at Renzo. He was slumped forward… not moving, with all this blood coming out of the back of his head – and I remember thinking: "*Fucking hell – he's dead.*"

Bdr Renzo Peterson Agnello, 2 Troop

The Pigs had come under sustained fire near Tullymore Walk as we travelled up Shaw's Road, but we carried on our way. We then turned onto Glen Road and were just approaching the brewery when Sammy spotted the barricade at the bottom of Ramoan Gardens. I remember the Pigs turning down and approaching the barricade, and everything was strangely quiet. Suddenly I felt as though I had been hit by a sledgehammer. There was no pain as such, but I knew I had been hit. I heard a Welsh voice [Pete Roberts] saying: *"Renzo's dead,"* and I thought: *"No I am not, but I will be if you don't get me to hospital."* I could see all the blood running down both my arms. Thankfully, 'Horace' took command and got the vehicle to Musgrave Park Hospital.

'Horace' looked down at Renzo as he lay there slumped over the bench seat. His combat jacket had a bullet hole in it and blood was pouring down his collar. At first 'Horace' thought that Renzo had been shot right through the body. Sammy was still shaken up by his own close brush with death, and so 'Horace' took command and ordered Dave to turn around and drive to Musgrave Park Hospital. Dave slammed the Pig in reverse, hit the accelerator and roared backwards away from the barricade. There was a sudden crunch and the rear of the vehicle lifted in the air as it hit a concrete post – the rear wheels screaming as they lost their grip on the tarmac. He slammed the gearstick into first, but the vehicle wouldn't budge. The rest of the crew moved right to the back of the vehicle to transfer the weight onto the rear axle and get the wheels back on the road. For a few tense moments the Pig remained there impaled on the concrete post as Dave rocked the vehicle back and to, before finally breaking free. They roared off and made their way to Musgrave Park Hospital with the badly injured Renzo.

When they arrived, one of the crew went in and brought out a Marine Medical Orderly. He didn't seem to fully understand the urgency at first, but when Renzo was lifted out of the back of the vehicle and the Orderly saw all the blood, the colour drained from his face and he immediately realized that Renzo was quite badly hurt.

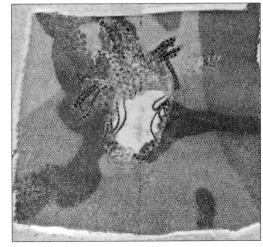

A piece of material removed from Renzo's jacket, which clearly shows the bullet hole. (Courtesy of Brian Corser)

Once inside they took off Renzo's jacket and saw that his jumper and shirt looked as though they had been cut through with a meat cleaver. They gently removed his clothes to expose the injuries to his back. The bullet had entered Renzo's body on the upper right of his torso, and a deep furrow had been cut the full width of his right shoulder blade, exposing the bone. The bullet came out of his flesh and re-entered at his left shoulder blade, and again cut a furrow down to the bone. As the medical orderlies dealt with Renzo, the bullet which had caused so much damage fell out of the collar of his shirt as it was being cut away.

By a strange coincidence, Renzo's brother just happened to be at Musgrave Park Hospital installing a new antenna on the roof of the communications post when Renzo was brought in.

Sgt Paul Agnello, HQ Battery

I was at the command post in the grounds of Musgrave Park Hospital when Renzo got plugged. I was up on the roof installing a telescopic antenna when I heard the 'phut-phut-phut' of low-velocity rounds just over my head. A split-second later I heard the 'rat-a-tat-tat' sound of a Thompson from the direction of the Andersonstown underpass. This was the same day my brother, Renzo, got shot.

Sammy Hulme got his crew back on board the Pig and left Renzo in the safe hands of the medical orderlies, but before they left, 'Horace' swapped his rifle magazine for that of Renzo's. They were good friends and 'Horace' was determined that at the next opportunity, he would get a gunman with one of Renzo's bullets. Lt Burland decided to return to the depot so that a full account of the incident could be given to the BC. A short time later the men were out on patrol again, and this time 'Horace' was travelling with Lt Burland. The two vehicles travelled up Glen Road, turned down Shaw's Road, and again they came under fire from Tullymore Gardens. The Provo volunteers had chosen their spot well. They had taken up position in front of a row of three houses next to a shop. From their firing position they could see straight down Tullymore Walk and onto Shaw's Road, which was about 150 yards away. Any military vehicles travelling along that road were within easy range of the Provo gunmen. 'Horace' recalls what happened next…

Bdr 'Horace', 2 Troop

When we left the depot I looked at Lt Burland and pleaded with him to stop the Pig the next time we came under fire. I was beginning to get a bit claustrophobic, and I told Lt Burland that I would sooner face the bastards in the open rather than be confined to the insides of the Pig. We drove along Shaw's Road and passed the entrance to Tullymore Walk again and the gunmen were still there at the top

– just waiting to direct their fire at us. Dave slammed on the brakes while Dick Burland jumped out of the cab and came racing around to the back of the Pig just as I was about to get out. The Provos immediately opened fire with what sounded like a Thompson and a high-velocity rifle, and the bullets were raking across the side of the vehicle. Dick Burland had to take shelter behind the open door to save himself and he kept jumping up and down to try and avoid the bullets that were going under the door.

Sammy Hulme pulled up behind us and the rest of the lads dismounted and took cover behind the bonnet at the side of the Pig. They were leaning over and engaging a target they had spotted at Tullymore Gardens about 150 yards away. I asked them where the target was and they pointed to a low brick wall in front of some houses situated just to the left of a shop. I spotted two gunmen, and one of them was wearing a light coloured duffle coat. I got hold of Lt Burland and urged him to come forward with me. We ran across the grass verge and took cover by the corner of some houses in Tullymore Walk – and as we ran across, the gunmen carried on firing at us, but by now we had closed the gap down to around 100 yards.

I looked around the side of the houses and saw one gunman break cover and start to run. I took aim and shot at him, and I saw a puff of brick dust as my bullet hit the wall just behind his head, so I swung my rifle over a bit further to the right in the direction he was running and took aim again. I fired off four quick shots, and the gunman seemed to be launched through the air. I don't know whether it was through my bullets hitting him, or whether he just dived for cover. We then made our way through about six gardens and worked our way around to the shop at Tullymore Gardens where the gunman appeared to be heading. We eventually linked up with members from 58 Battery, who were there with a Ferret armoured vehicle from the Blues and Royals. The shop was all boarded up, and no-one would answer our hammering on the shutters.

A few minutes later, a Sergeant from 58 Battery ordered the Commander of the Ferret to drive through the front doors – and as I looked inside, I saw a group of women sat about on the floor. As soon as they saw us, they all started screaming and getting hysterical – no doubt they had been fed on stories of our supposed brutality and feared the worst – but amongst the women sat a man, and he was sweating profusely as though he had been running. There was no doubt in my mind that he was one of the gunmen, but I had no way of proving it. We searched the premises but found no weapons and no bodies, so to this day I don't know if I hit the gunman I saw flying through the air after I fired my shots. I remember Lt Burland talking to me some time later about the shooting, and he told me that as we both ran forward, he was more worried about being accidentally shot in the back by our own men who were returning fire than he was about the gunmen who were shooting at us.

At around noon a patrol from 3 Troop ventured back out onto the streets to assess the situation. This was the first time they had seen the trail of destruction in daylight, and it was a scene of utter devastation. The two Pigs made their way up Andersonstown Road and picked their way through the twisted remains of burnt-out buses and cars. The snow continued to fall as they made their way towards the shopping precinct. The blackened charred ruins of buildings and gutted vehicles stood out even more against the white carpet which now covered the ground.

Gnr Steve Corbett, 3 Troop

It was a terrible sight to see. There were plumes of thick black smoke everywhere; the roofs of some of the buildings had completely gone. All that was left of the double-decker buses was the metal framework and they just reminded me of huge cages. The tyres on the vehicles were still burning and the air stank of charred rubber. When we returned to base, someone told me about Renzo getting shot. That was the fourth one from the battery since we had arrived at the end of November.

The other gunman is thought to have been hit near Rossnareen Avenue when troops came under heavy automatic fire, possibly from a Thompson sub-machine gun and a Bren gun. An army marksman fired one round and, according to a spokesman, he believes that one of the IRA men may have been hit. About 40 rounds were fired at soldiers near a barricade at the spot, but there were no military casualties.

Sentries at the Glen Road bus terminus also came under fire, but neither of the two shots struck a target.[*]

[*] Source taken from *The Troubles* Magazine (Glenravel Publications).

By now much of Andersonstown was sealed off. There were barricades across most of the main routes into the estates, and the Provos were determined to keep the troops out. There were still large groups hanging around on street corners – waiting to take on any soldiers who came near. Shouts of: "Murdering British bastards" filled the air as they drove past.

Soldiers again came under fire at Shaw's Road and at Rossnareen Avenue. On one occasion, troops fired nine rounds at a sniper, but he was not hit. More shots were fired at the army post at Flax Street and at troops who moved in to recover four of the six lorries taken from the Ulster Brewery at Glen Road. The soldiers fired 23 rounds to put out the street lights after the gunmen opened up.[*]

[*] Source taken from *The Troubles* Magazine (Glenravel Publications).

The patrol continued on its way – surveying all the damage done over the past 24 hours. It had been an absolute nightmare and there appeared to be no end in sight. The section that 'Horace' had been with at the time had come under fire on no less than nine separate occasions in that 24-hour period – and two of those attacks were launched with a Bren gun. It was later estimated that there had been a total of 27 separate shooting incidents on the battery as a whole. Another patrol from 3 Troop was turning into a cul-de-sac somewhere near Rossnareen Avenue after they had spotted several cars on fire. As soon as they tried to enter, they immediately came under attack from a large crowd of rioters.

Gnr Gordon 'Addi' Adamson, 3 Troop

I went out to a riot up near Rossnareen Avenue and I was driving the lead Pig with BSM Don Potter in charge. He was a cracking bloke, and in my opinion one of the best men in the whole of the battery. We got up there and we were turning into this cul-de-sac when Don Potter spotted these three cars burning away in a barricade, and he told me to ram them and shift them off the road. I had three attempts, but I couldn't budge them. In the end he told me to leave them and back out, but I was having none of that. I thought to myself: *"I'll just have one more try,"* so I backed up maybe 20 yards or so and then put my foot down. The BSM looked at me as though I had gone mad, and then we shot forward and hit the cars at speed. I hit them so hard that I went straight through the barricade and pushed one of the cars through a brick wall and into someone's front garden. Don Potter sat there looking totally stunned, and after a moment or two he turned to me and said: *"OK Adamson, well done."*

The estates in Andersonstown had become one huge battleground. Everywhere the men of 9 Battery went there was confrontation on a scale they just hadn't seen before. Every patrol that went out met up with rioters or gunmen roaming the streets. All the men were absolutely shattered through rushing from one incident to the next. As the final hours of January drew to a close, the patrols were able to pull back to the safety of the bus depot and get some well-earned rest. They had been on the go since Sunday night and had hardly had a break – such was the scale of the violence. Things had been bad, but over the next few days they were destined to get even worse…

Back at the headquarters of 39 Brigade, the situation in Andersonstown was viewed so seriously that two infantry battalions of extra troops had been earmarked to go in and clear the barricades, but the BC did not think much of this idea. He thought it was better by far to act overnight. He knew 9 Battery were becoming very tired, but he also knew that they would always do what was asked of them – and they did. By dawn, despite some stiff opposition – and with the help of two troops of the Blues and Royals and some Royal Engineers, with their Scooby Doos* – all of the barricades had been cleared.

---

* 'Scooby Doo' was the nickname given to a large armoured tractor used by the Royal Engineers for the removal of barricades and burnt-out vehicles.

6

FEBRUARY
All-out war

TUESDAY 1st...

At around 2:00 a.m. the Pigs of 3 Troop again ventured out into the estates to try and remove the barriers and burnt-out wagons. The temperatures had plummeted, and it was absolutely freezing. The two vehicles pulled up while the men dismounted and went in on foot to do a recce of the area. The Royal Engineers' driver and Scooby Doo was called in to remove the remains of the buses, while the Pigs rammed through the smaller barricades and pushed the wrecked cars to the side of the road. By 6:30 a.m. they were done and returned to base.

The prime focus of the trouble in terms of shootings had seemed to be centred on the Rossnareen Estate and the area of Tullymore Gardens – and it was the roads leading to this part of the estate which had the highest concentration of barricades. The main entry point off the Glen Road was Ramoan Gardens. The next entry point was on Shaw's Road at Green Avenue, which then changed to Edenmore Drive and then Slievegallion Drive. The road curved in a large loop which linked up at the bottom with Andersonstown Road, and at this junction was the Busy Bee shops. Over the next few days, these roads were to be the scene of heavy fighting between 9 Battery and 1st Battalion, PIRA.

The entry point to the Riverdale Estate was on the Andersonstown Road almost opposite the Busy Bee. This particular stretch of Andersonstown Road bore the brunt of much of the rioting and looting around the shops. On Finaghy Road North were three more entrances onto the Riverdale Estate.

It was, by now, approaching 9:00 a.m. and back at the bus depot the Protestants who worked in the engineering workshop were starting to turn up for work. Dick Rothwell was on guard at the main entrance, waiting to check the vehicles as they approached the gateway. Further up Glen Road, a Provo gunman lay in wait...

Gnr Dick Rothwell, 2 Troop

It was around 9:00 a.m. and I had just stopped a car at the main gate to the compound at the bus depot. I checked the driver's security pass and we walked around to the rear of his car while he opened his boot for me to look inside. Other workers were passing through the gate on foot, and all of a sudden I heard a 'crack-crack' as two

The entrance to the depot where the shooting took place.
(Courtesy of Richard Rothwell)

high-velocity bullets whistled through the air close to where I stood. I took cover as best as I could and adopted the prone position – lying flat on my stomach behind the curb stones at the entrance to the bus depot – and when I got back up I saw that the driver had jumped in his car and drove off to get out of the line of fire. The other workers had scattered as well – and I can't say I blamed them either.

Rothwell had a lucky escape. The attacks continued all over Belfast as the Provos and the residents of the Nationalist estates sought revenge for the killings in Londonderry. At around 5:30 p.m. a patrol from 3 Troop was out yet again after being called to the scene of the latest barricades to be thrown up by the rioters. The sheer size of some of the obstructions defied belief.

Gnr Steve Corbett, 3 Troop

We got called out again, and I couldn't believe it. We were back at the same spot where we had been earlier and the barricades were back up. I was beginning to think that it was a complete waste of time removing them. When you had spent all that time shifting them, you did get a bit frustrated when you saw them back up again. We got to one barricade, and it was absolutely enormous. There were two articulated lorries, a milk float and four cars – and the whole lot was blazing like mad. The cars had been put on the back of the lorries and they had been driven across the road and completely sealed off the entrance to the estate. As we approached it, we came under fire from a couple of gunmen and I took cover behind one of the Pigs. We eventually got the barricade shifted with the aid of Scooby Doo and moved onto the next one. Every time we approached them, I used to get a knot in my stomach. You just sort of knew that you were going to get shot at – and I began to think that maybe this time I might get hit.

The assistance given to the men of 3 Troop by the Royal Engineers' driver and his 'Scooby Doo' tractor – while under constant fire from the Provo gunmen – led to him receiving a well-earned Military Medal for his actions during this period.

It was 10:00 p.m. by the time the men of 3 Troop had broken through and approached the final obstruction. As the patrol moved in and started to dismantle the barricade, they were once more subjected to harassing fire from the gunmen who had taken up positions in the houses overlooking the street. The flames from the burning vehicles illuminated the men as they set about their work. Gradually the shooting died down and the mobs had started to congregate on the other side of the barricade – just waiting for the chance to have a go at the soldiers with their stocks of rocks and bottles.

Gnr Steve Corbett, 3 Troop

The next barricade was only a small affair and we soon had it shifted, but by then there was a sizable crowd gathered and they started attacking us with anything they could lay their hands on once we had broken through. We all took cover behind the Pigs and I brought out my riot gun and started firing back at them. Just ahead of us there was a bit of a dip in the road. We were one side of it and they were lined up on the other. I could see them running from behind the houses and fetching crates of milk bottles to use against us. When the rioters threw the bottles, they made a kind of fluttering sound as they toppled through the air – and just occasionally I caught sight of them as they passed through the glow cast by a single street light which was still working, and then the next thing all this glass would be flying about all over the place.

I remember watching as I saw someone lighting something in the porch of a house – and to my horror I could see that it was a young boy, and his mother was stood behind him encouraging him. I remember the papers reporting the next day that it was a nail bomb that had been thrown, but I seem to remember it being a petrol bomb. Even so, if anyone had shot the young boy they would have been screaming: "*Murderers*" at us again. I found it quite disgusting the way some parents of very young children encouraged them to take part in the rioting. When they ended up getting seriously injured, they always blamed us for it and claimed we deliberately targeted them.

VICTIMS OF THE TROUBLES WHO DIED THIS DAY...

Cpl Ian Bramley (25) – The Gloucestershire Regiment. Shot dead by an IRA sniper while opening a barrier at Hastings Street RUC/Army base in the Lower Falls, Belfast.*

* List compiled from *The Troubles* Magazine (Glenravel Publications).

WEDNESDAY 2nd...

ARMED YOUTHS HIJACK VEHICLES

Several armed hijackings have taken place in Belfast, including a bus and an oil-tanker. Three buses have been hijacked; one is reported to have been set on fire by a group of children outside the Glen Road terminus, and two others are blocking the road. On the Andersonstown Road, a 5,200 gallon oil-tanker was hijacked and at Fruithill Park, a bread van was taken. Elsewhere, lorries were hijacked at Finaghy Road North, Monagh and Glen Roads as well as Divis Flats.*

* Source taken from *The Troubles* Magazine (Glenravel Publications).

On Tuesday 1 February the Northern Irish Prime Minister, Mr Brian Faulkner, appeared on the BBC Northern Ireland television programme 'Scene Around Six'. A sombre-looking Mr Faulkner issued a statement to the people of Northern Ireland:

This is a very grave moment indeed in the history of Northern Ireland. Mounting hysteria and unreason surround us on every side. Impossible and outrageous demands are being made. In this situation I believe that, we as a government, have two responsibilities. Amidst the emotionalism and hysteria, we must continue to speak with the voice of reason. We must continue our readiness to sit down at any time with any of our fellow citizens, who wish to discuss the situation with us, in a realistic and reasonable spirit – but we have another responsibility too – and that is to speak for that body of Ulster people; the vast majority who have borne months and years of disorder with incredible fortitude; and whose very restraint could too easily be mistaken for disinterest.

Today, when it is clear that a campaign to achieve a United Ireland without our consent is being mounted both by parties in Northern Ireland and by the government of Mr Lynch, it is right that I should sound a most solemn note of warning. The Unionist community in Northern Ireland will not tolerate such a proposition. We are more than ready to discuss how the institutions of Northern Ireland may be framed on a renewed basis of general consent and to develop the most friendly and co-operative relationship with our neighbours in the South, but there it ends – and because there are difference of opinion on many matters amongst those who support the union with Great Britain, let us not be supposed that they are incapable of united action in the face of a threat to their freedom and to their democratic rights. It will continue to be our aim at all times to seek a peaceful way out of the present situation, but if overtures are rejected and we are faced with a continuing defiance of lawful authority and an attempt to overthrow the State, then this government – and this parliament – will demand to be heard over any camera in the streets to assert that those we represent also have their basic rights and we'll defend them.

The signs for peace in the Province didn't look promising; neither side was prepared to compromise. The poor squaddie on the ground had little interest in the politics of Northern Ireland. All they knew was that suddenly they were caught up in the middle of what appeared to be all-out war on the streets of Andersonstown.

Up on Finaghy Road North, a patrol from 1 Troop came under fire as they negotiated the turn towards Shaw's Road. No-one was injured and they didn't return fire. Another patrol which had dismounted from their vehicles and moved in on foot towards a barricade also came under fire and the men scattered and took cover. This prompted the Patrol Commander, 'Budge' B*****, to scream out: "The next man that moves will be put on a charge!" Needless to say, no-one in the patrol was going to stand around and get shot at – and they continued to take cover where they could find it.

At around 3:15 p.m. other patrols were out in force conducting Operation *Yobbo*. The BC used to have pet-names for some of the patrols, and 'Operation *Yobbo*' was one of them. The Pigs would cruise around the estates waiting for trouble to break out and then move in, but it would appear that on this occasion there were no disturbances. There were a few groups congregating on the street corners, but nothing like there had been over the past few days. Even the rioters were beginning to grow tired; they had been building and manning the barricades since the previous Sunday, and they too were in need of a rest.

Up near the Busy Bee shops, a Ferret scout car (U31) approached a barricade strung across the Andersonstown Road. It consisted of a burnt-out car, old railings and large chunks of rubble from some of the wrecked buildings. As the Ferret scout car tried to negotiate its way around the obstruction, it knocked down a young girl who was stood close by. An ambulance was sent for, but due to all the obstructions in the road it had great difficulty in getting through to her. She was yet another tragic consequence of the rioting, and again the soldiers were blamed for her injuries. The shootings continued as more patrols from 9 Battery came under attack…

The other two soldiers were wounded in the Andersonstown area of the city.

One was hit in the hand when a gunman fired eight shots at a patrol of the 12th Light Air Defence Regiment, but his injuries are not serious.

The incident happened at Tullymore Gardens and a short time later another soldier received a leg wound when a gunman opened fire on troops from the same unit at Rossnareen Avenue. Later, when soldiers searched an abandoned car in the area, they discovered a rifle and Sten gun with a silencer.

* Source taken from *The Troubles* Magazine (Glenravel Publications).

Phil Gallagher on guard duty. (Courtesy of Richard Rothwell)

The soldier wounded in the leg wasn't even aware of his injuries until the patrol got back to base. He looked down and spotted the red stain on his combat trousers. Elsewhere, a section of men from 3 Troop made their way into the estates on foot after dismounting from their Pigs…

Gnr Phil Gallagher, 3 Troop
Our section moved in on foot after being dropped off by the Pigs, and there was a lad from REME with us called 'Tiny'. He was a big lad and when he had an SLR in his hand it looked like a kid's toy. Well, we came under fire from some gunmen and we all took cover, and Tiny rushes over to this little brick wall and crouches down to protect himself from the gunfire, but he was that tall and wide it was like an elephant trying to hide behind a small bush. I remember thinking at the time that he was an ideal candidate for a sniper's bullet, because the wall he was behind gave no cover for a man of his size!

At the top end of Andersonstown, a patrol from 2 Troop was on its way to investigate reports of barricades near the brewery. They turned off Shaw's Road and edged up Glen Road to the scene of the latest incident. The two Pigs arrived at the scene and were confronted by a large wagon which had been parked across the width of the road. Just before it – and to the right – was the turning for Ramoan Gardens, which sloped downwards towards the junction of Edenmore and Slievegallion Drive. It was the same spot where Renzo Agnello had been shot just a few days earlier. The patrol pulled up just short of the turning and 'Horace' and a few other men dismounted to investigate.

'Horace' and Pete Roberts. (Courtesy of Steve Corbett)

Bdr 'Horace', 2 Troop

I was in the front Pig with Lt Burland and Sgt Hulme was in charge of the rear Pig. We pulled up a few yards from the barricade and I got out to go and have a look at the wagon. I can't remember what was going through my mind at the time – it's so many years ago now – but I seem to remember having this crazy idea that I might be able to drive the truck out of the way. I started walking towards the truck, and all of a sudden there was a burst of gunfire to my right. The bullets went just over the top of my head.

Gnr Pete Roberts, 2 Troop

We got near the barricade and some of us got out of the back of the Pig as 'Horace' went over to the wagon. I remember hearing a crack and a bang, and then all this snow came falling down as the bullet passed through the branches of the tree just above our heads.

By now the rest of the patrol were already out of the vehicles – and one of them, a REME technician who had gone along with them for the ride, spotted the gunman towards the bottom end of Ramoan Gardens. He took aim and returned fire – and immediately the gunman stopped shooting. Two men were then spotted jumping into a red Morris Marina saloon and driving off rather erratically. Lt Burland ordered his men to mount up and they gave chase.

Bdr 'Horace', 2 Troop

I jumped into the back of one of the Pigs and we shot off down Ramoan Gardens. Dick Burland saw the car turn right into Kenard, but by the time we got there we had lost sight of it. We thought the bastards had got away from us for a minute, but when we turned into Tullymore Gardens, there it was – abandoned in the middle of the road. Dick Burland and Sammy Hulme rushed over; it was just stood there with both its doors wide open and the engine ticking over. There was no sign of the gunmen, but when the car was searched, Dick found a rifle and a Sten sub-machine gun fitted with a silencer in the boot. There was a horrible stench of marzipan as well, so it looked as though the car had also been used to transport ANFO * bombs.

At around 7:14 p.m. there was a huge explosion just outside the battery area. The situation was really coming to a head now, and it was nothing short of all-out war. At 9:30 p.m. 3 Troop were called out to assist C12 while they carried out a search, but due to difficulty finding their way around the barricades, by the

---

*   Ammonium-nitrate / Fuel-oil.

The rifle and Sten gun found in the boot of the Morris Marina car.
(Courtesy of Brian Corser)

time they got up there the search had already been completed. Elsewhere on the estate, Andersonstown Road was shut off close to the Busy Bee and some of the roads leading to Rossnareen Avenue had barricades strung across them again. The patrol tried to return by using Glen Road, but that was also barricaded. It wasn't that long since it had been cleared after the shooting incident involving 'Horace' and 2 Troop.

Gnr Steve Corbett, 3 Troop

We turned up Glen Road to head back to the depot and came across another barricade blocking the road, but as I recall, we just rammed it and carried on our way. We hadn't been back at base that long before we were sent out again to Rossnareen Estate to do another search. We were going along the footpaths – checking under the hedges for anything stashed away. All the time we were doing the search, gangs of youths were following us and pelting us with bricks and bottles – and then we moved onto the maisonettes to check out the coal bunkers while 1 Troop concentrated on the garages.

The whole battery had entered back into the estate to conduct a large-scale search of the maisonettes, garages and coal bunkers. The men of 2 Troop patrolled the Andersonstown Road by the Busy Bee and along Shaw's Road, while 3 Troop put a cordon on Slievegallion Drive as the search teams of 1 Troop moved in.

Gnr Steve Corbett, 3 Troop

We finished our search and then formed the cordon for 1 Troop while they searched the garages. I was stood by the shops on Slievegallion Drive looking towards where the flats were. The road curved to the left just there as it changed to Edenmore Drive. I was watching the houses and noticed that some of the bedroom windows were open on several of the properties, and every so often something would be poked out. In the failing light it looked just like someone pointing a rifle at me. I kept watching and expected to hear gunfire at any moment, but I was ready for it though, and I put a bullet up the spout of my rifle just in case I had to return fire. I thought about it afterwards and came to the conclusion that perhaps someone was deliberately trying to provoke us into opening fire. We had already been accused of firing our weapons in a reckless manner once before.

INDISCRIMINATE SHOOTING, SAY RESIDENTS

Three young children narrowly escaped death in Andersonstown on Saturday, in what is claimed to have been one of the worst acts of indiscriminate shooting by British soldiers in the district since the Troubles began.

At about 4.30pm, soldiers were shot at in Knockdhu Park. An army Saracen then drove down into Edenmore Drive and pulled up outside two houses. They began firing into the house from a distance of a couple of feet. One of the bullets narrowly missed the window of one of the houses where the children were standing inside.

The Saracen then drove down to the bottom of Edenmore Drive and in the meantime a crowd of people had gathered outside the two houses which had been fired on. The Saracen drove up again at about 50 miles an hour and the people had to dash for safety.

Following a complaint by a resident, an army officer said that they had fired the shots because they thought they saw a sniper in a garden.

But from the position in which the Saracen was in, it would be impossible to either see a sniper or to fire into the gardens, said the resident. The resident said that he could produce witnesses to prove that the army had shot at the house deliberately and were not aware of any sniper in the gardens behind.[*]

* Sourced from Brian Corser's private collection of newspaper cuttings.

This particular undated newspaper report could have been referring to an incident which took place on Saturday 2 January when a patrol from 1 Troop came under fire from a hidden gunman. The newspapers often referred to the Humber Pigs as being 'Saracens', but occasionally there would be mobile patrols of Paratroopers entering into the battery area, and many of the men in 9 Battery thought they appeared to be a law unto themselves at times. Back at Slievegallion Drive, the search continued as the men of 9 Battery searched for weapons and explosives.

Gnr Steve Corbett, 3 Troop

I was moved further down the road as the search progressed and I ended up stood close to the BC. I just happened to be looking down towards Andersonstown Road when there was a long burst of machine gun fire from that direction. The idiot who opened fire gave his position away though, because the stupid arsehole had used tracer ammunition. The BC turned around and looked at me, started muttering to himself and shook his head in disbelief; then he started strutting up and down with his thumbs tucked into the armpits of his flak jacket. I watched as the bullets appeared to slowly rise through the sky before speeding up and going over the rooftops of the bungalows just across from Slievegallion Drive. I always found the actions of the BC to be so reassuring. When I saw him strutting about like that, I just knew we were in safe hands and that I would come to no harm.

Down on Andersonstown Road, 'Horace' was conducting his own search at the back of a pub with a few of his men who were manning the cordon.

Bdr 'Horace', 2 Troop

I took a few of my men around the back of a pub more or less opposite the Busy Bee. There had already been some shooting and I was just making sure the area was clear. There was a wall around eight feet high with a dustbin next to it, and I told one of the 'Thomas twins' to climb up and have a look into the back. He had just got up, looked over the top and a long burst of tracer went over the top of his head. I said to him something like: "*Did you see that?*" He jumped down and said to me: "*See it? It nearly took my bleeding head off!*" When we got back to base later, I was talking to Dai M*****. He had seen the tracer as well and he told me he had returned fire exactly where it had come from. He told me he saw the windows rattle as he fired back and then the shooting stopped.

The search teams were called in and the units set off for base. As they pulled clear, they met up with a hostile crowd of youths who subjected the Pigs to a ferocious barrage of paint bombs and milk bottles. Back on Shaw's Road, the cordon had also been told to mount up and return to base, but one man remained at his post. He had been told to stay where he was and that the Pig would return for him once the search was over – but it didn't.

Gnr Dick Rothwell, 2 Troop

We headed up Andersonstown Road in the Pigs to do a search and lift operation and just after the junction with Finaghy Road North, our Pig pulled up. The Bombardier in charge said that I and another bloke would be acting as sentries. I was to get out and take cover in a ditch. I think it was near the junction with Shaw's Road and Andersonstown Road. The other sentry was taken further up the road out of my sight and I couldn't be sure exactly where he was. I was told not to worry when I saw the Pig moving away from me, as it would return to pick me up when the search ended.

The search had dragged on for several hours as the teams worked their way through the garages and outbuildings, but Rothwell stuck to the task he had been given. Even when he saw the other men mount up further up the road, he wasn't unduly concerned. After all, he had been told that his vehicle would return and pick him up. The Pigs returned to base and the men dismounted and unloaded their weapons. Suddenly a cry went out: "Where the fuck's Rothwell?" A quick headcount took place and it suddenly dawned on them that he'd been left behind! A Pig was quickly dispatched to search for him. While all this was going on, Dick was still lying there in the ditch.

Gnr Dick Rothwell, 2 Troop

I heard the call to mount up and I remember hearing the doors of the Pigs slamming shut in the distance; the engines started up and they drove away. At first I wasn't too concerned, as I had been told someone would definitely come back for me. I just assumed that the search had moved around the corner from me. After maybe about 30 minutes I began to think that maybe something WAS wrong, as everything seemed too quiet, and it was then that I realised they were NOT coming back… they had forgotten about me. I was terrified. There I was, stuck on the edge of the worst estate in Andersonstown, and I had no way of getting back to camp.

I lay there in the ditch for a while wondering what to do. I could hear people talking and walking up and down close to where I lay. I was very concerned that they may discover me because I knew what I could expect if they caught me – and then after what seemed like a lifetime, I could hear the Pigs approaching in the distance. They drew up near where I lay. I heard them dismount and I recognised Sgt Lawson's voice. A few others got out of the back and they appeared to be looking in my direction. I didn't dare just stand up with it being so dark in case someone from the patrol thought I was a gunman and shot me by mistake, so I'm lay there going: *"pssst, pssst!"* trying to attract their attention. At last they turned and looked towards me as I called out to them. I never felt so relieved in all my life as that moment when they spotted me.

When we got back to base, I was taken over to the RUC Station for the CO to interview me. I told him what had happened and how the NCO had told me to stay where I was until the Pig came back for me. The NCO insisted that when he shouted 'mount up' he meant everyone – and he denied ever saying that he told me to stay where I was until the Pig came back for me. It was my word against that of an NCO, and I wasn't believed.

As far as I was concerned, the NCO was the one responsible for the men under his command in that Pig. He should have personally checked we were all back in it before he gave the order to drive off, but he didn't. Every time Dave Lawson saw me that day, he went: *"pssst, pssst"* and started laughing. I couldn't see the funny side of it though – and if the Provos had got their hands on me, I would have been lucky if I had only got a bullet in the back of my head.

The Patrol Commander's responsibility was to check that all his men were back on board the vehicle before driving off. This he clearly failed to do. Gnr Rothwell admitted to hearing the order to mount up, but he chose to stay where he was because that is exactly what he was told to do. As far as the BC was concerned, Gnr Rothwell came out of this incident with considerable credit. He could hardly have been in more danger, but he kept a cool head. In fairness to the Vehicle Commander, he would have expected the crew of his vehicle to notice if anyone was missing and to alert him, but ultimately the responsibility for his men was his alone.

On 4 March 1973 – and in similar circumstances – 19-year-old Warrington soldier Pte Gary Barlow, from The Queen's Lancashire Regiment, was left behind after a search at the Divis Flats in Belfast. After the search teams had finished, they mounted up in their Saracen armoured vehicles and were just about to drive away when a shot was heard. Everyone immediately debussed and took cover as they tried to locate the gunman. A soldier manning an observation post on top of the flats thought he saw where the gunman was hiding and the search teams were ordered to move in. Unable to gain entry to the garage where it was suspected the gunman was, the order was given to ram the garage doors with the Saracen and Pte Barlow and another soldier were sent in to search the building. By this time hostile crowds were starting to gather, and night was starting to set in – and so the officer in charge decided to withdraw his men. The call was given to mount up, and the officer asked the two NCOs to check that all the men were back. Pte Barlow's Vehicle Commander is said to have asked if everyone was back on board, and someone reputedly shouted back: "Yes."

A short while after the vehicles had returned to base, Pte Barlow's comrades realised that he was missing. At around the same time, two young Catholic girls from the Divis Flats had courageously taken the decision to go to the base and report that a soldier had been left behind at the garages. Such a simple act of humanity could well have cost the young girls their lives at the hands of the Provos had they been observed entering the army base. A patrol was quickly sent back to the flats to try and rescue Pte Barlow, but it was already too late. He had been shot through the head at close range and died early the next day. This was the kind of sadistic brutality which was the hallmark of the Provisional IRA. They didn't take prisoners. Dick Rothwell was indeed a lucky man the day he was left behind. If he had been captured, there is no doubt that he would have suffered the same fate.

On another search held by the battery, a rather disturbing incident happened to Gnr 'Snowy' H*** of 2 Troop when he was part of the cordon providing cover for the search team.

Gnr 'Snowy' H***, 2 Troop

I was part of a cordon up in Rossnareen where the battery was carrying out a big search. We were all given our positions on where to go, and I was crouched in this doorway. It was like two doors, and I was next to the left door as you look at it. I had been there about 20 minutes and then all of a sudden the doors flew open and I was dragged inside by these two guys. They grabbed me from behind and got hold of my belt and just dragged me inside. I started screaming out and 'Horace' and another guy came rushing over and pulled me back out. The two men who grabbed me got away though.

'Snowy' H***.
(Courtesy of 'Snowy' H***)

Only for the timely intervention of 'Horace' and the other soldier, it could have been a grisly end for 'Snowy'. It was, by now, 12:15 a.m. and everybody was just glad to get out of the estates in one piece. As the other patrols returned, the talk was just about all the rioting and the shootings taking place all over Andersonstown. Even those not out on patrol in the estates were facing attacks from the snipers as the Provos launched attacks against army posts all over Belfast. There seemed to be an all-out assault on anything wearing khaki.

It had been another terrible day. More wagons from the Ulster Brewery had been taken and used as barricades throughout much of Andersonstown. Parts of the Busy Bee had been torched again. Anti-British demonstrations were being held in the Republic as the backlash over the killings in Londonderry continued. A gelignite bomb was thrown at the British Embassy in Dublin, and the passport offices were almost destroyed by a huge blaze. Some British-owned shops also became targets of the protesters.

More than 30 vehicles, including lorries and vans, were hijacked during the day and last night to form barricades in the Falls and Andersonstown areas.

Vehicles were set on fire and burned as the violence increased and the premises of Caroline Records at Andersonstown were badly damaged by fire.

Two shops on either side were slightly damaged. Two other buildings, as well as the Busy Bee supermarket – only a short distance away – were also damaged by fire.

During a bomb scare at Andersonstown yesterday afternoon, a small boy – the army claimed he was between eight and 10 – threw a nail bomb at troops.

A shot was also fired at the soldiers, but no fire was returned.[*]

* Source taken from *The Belfast Telegraph*, 2 February 1972.

VICTIMS OF THE TROUBLES WHO DIED THIS DAY...

Thomas McElroy (29) – Shot dead in Divismore Park by a British Army sniper in Henry Taggart Army Base.

Louis O'Neill (49) – Killed in a bomb explosion when a Loyalist terror group blew up the Imperial Bar, County Tyrone.[*]

* List compiled from *The Troubles* Magazine (Glenravel Publications).

THURSDAY 3rd...

The battery was now entering its fourth day of rioting. Barricades were still being thrown up at an unprecedented rate. Another barricade consisting of cars and wagons had been put across the Glen Road by the brewery. The entrance to the Riverdale Estate by the Busy Bee was shut off, as well as the other entrance situated on Finaghy Road North. Kennedy Way was also sealed off by a blazing barricade which the Sappers were trying to remove with the aid of their tractor, Scooby Doo. A small bomb was detonated outside Casement Park, but no soldiers were injured.

A number of vehicles were set on fire in the Falls and Andersonstown areas last night.[*]

[*] Source taken from *The Belfast Telegraph*, 3 February 1972.

Everyone was, by now, feeling the pressure of the past few days. The men had been out attending incidents with hardly a break. Shootings were taking place continuously all over the battery area, and one soldier from 3 Troop almost lost his life when he was caught up in a riot at a barricade on the Andersonstown Road.

Gnr Gordon 'Addi' Adamson, 3 Troop

One time we were at a riot and Mick McHale got hit on the head by a brick and was knocked out stone-cold. The poor bastard was lying there sprawled out with these rioters closing in on him. The Patrol Commander spotted what was happening and shouted for someone to grab him back, so Phil Gallagher starts running towards Mick and he shouted across to me to give him a hand. Some of the others from the patrol started wading in with their batons and riot guns to keep the rioters away as me and Phil got hold of Mick and carried him back to the Pigs. I'm sure they would have finished him off if they had got hold of him. They were like a pack of wild animals when they saw him lying there in the road.

In a rather bizarre twist to all the hijackings of the vehicles around Andersonstown, the Provisional IRA issued a statement which was published in one of the evening newspapers:

IRA WARNING TO HIJACKERS

The 2nd Battalion of the Belfast Command of the IRA in Andersonstown issued a warning last night to those responsible for the burning of shops and the hijacking of motor-vehicles in the Andersonstown area that such conduct would not be tolerated in the future.

In a statement the IRA said that they were committed to the defence of the people not only against Crown forces, but against all anti-working class elements.

"We hereby give notice," said the statement, "to all those responsible for the burning of shops and the hijacking of private cars and lorries conveying necessary supplies to the area that a recurrence of these activities will not be tolerated by the Irish Republican Army."

The statement claimed that following the killings in Derry, units of the IRA in Andersonstown had engaged British forces on several occasions in the area wounding five, and according to their latest intelligence reports, one of these has since died.*

* Sourced from Brian Corser's private collection of newspaper cuttings.

The IRA warning was just another stunt in the ongoing propaganda war. After all, it was *their* members who were orchestrating the hijackings, and it was *their* gunmen manning the barricades constructed from the hijacked vehicles. At around 7:30 p.m. Operation *Yobbo* took to the streets on yet another patrol in search of the troublemakers who were roaming the estates – and at approximately 10:15 p.m. a call was received by C13 from C12 who were caught up in a major disturbance in Rossnareen. There were large crowds of rioters who had penned in the Pigs of 2 Troop and they needed assistance. The rioters were throwing everything they could at the stranded vehicles as the men fought back with salvos of rubber bullets to defend themselves. It was truly a frightening situation.

Gnr Gordon 'Addi' Adamson, 3 Troop

I was driving the lead Pig, with Mick Burton in charge. We got up to where the riot was and it sounded as though someone was already firing rubber bullets before they even got out of the Pig. Clancy Campbell, Mick Krasnowski and a few others were in the back waiting to jump out with the riot guns, and I wanted to join them and get stuck in, but Mick Burton wouldn't let me leave the Pig. I had to stay there and guard it.

Gnr Steve Corbett, 3 Troop

I donned my tin hat and grabbed my riot shield and baton as we mounted up. As we approached the estate, I could see the large crowds trying to push forward to the Pigs of C12. Bricks and bottles were raining down all around them as the lads trapped in the open took whatever shelter they could from the missiles. Our Pigs screeched to a halt and we piled out of the back – screaming and shouting as we surged towards the rioters. I lashed out with my baton at those who got in my way – using my shield to protect myself from all the bricks and bottles which were being thrown at us.

Gnr Clancy Campbell, 3 Troop

I jumped out of the back and ran forward with the rest of the troop – blasting away with my riot gun as I went. I didn't bother with a shield, as it would have just got in my way. When we got closer to the crowd, I realised I had run out of ammo; then this bloke came running towards me. I guess he must have spotted me searching my pockets for more rounds. He reached out to grab me, so I swung the riot gun and hit him over the head with it. I don't know what happened to him after that because I just lost sight of him in the crowd.

The rioters began to fall back as the men pressed forward, and finally they reached the stranded Pigs. Apart from a few cuts and bruises, there were no other injuries; they had again got off lightly. The sections mounted up and the Pigs returned to base. It was only 10:45 p.m. when they got back. The whole riot could have only lasted a matter of minutes, but it seemed to drag on forever.

Elsewhere, on another part of the estate, patrols from 1 Troop were also trying to force back rioting mobs. There seemed to be no letup in the violence. Sgt Bob 'Scouse' Thompson was wading in with his men, fighting from the front. He built himself a fearsome reputation in Andersonstown. He never held back – whatever the situation – and it was for his courageous actions in Andersonstown that he was later to be awarded the Military Medal. In a letter sent to him on 30 September 1972 Lieutenant-General Sir Harry Tuzo said:

Dear Sergeant Thompson,
I am writing to congratulate you on your award of the Military Medal for your performance while serving here with your battery from November 1971 until March this year.

I know that you served as a Section Commander in one of the worst areas of Belfast, and throughout your period here your determined and aggressive leadership have been an example to all who served with you. Your success in capturing a number of leading terrorists and your courage when, with complete disregard for your own safety, you saved the life of a civilian are a credit to you and your regiment.

I am delighted that your leadership and courage have been recognised by this well-deserved award.

Yours sincerely,

Harry Tuzo[*]

'Addi' Adamson remembers an incident when he was out on patrol with Lt Dick Burland and Sgt Thompson…

Gnr 'Addi' Adamson, 3 Troop

One day I was out on patrol driving our Troop Commander, Lt Burland. We had been told that an IRA gunman had been seen in some flats just off Shaw's Road and we went up there to have a look around. We pulled up about 100 yards away from the flats and dismounted, and then Sgt Thompson spotted the gunman behind a window and opened fire. Lt Burland said: *"Did you get him Sgt?"* and he replied: *"Yes, I think so, Sir."* I think the hit was later confirmed. Sgt Thompson was a very good Commander and Lt Burland was very young and straight out of Sandhurst College and still learning, but again, he was another good Commander.

An anonymous officer from 9 Battery was later to pen this ode to Sgt Thompson…

An heroic saga of the raw guts and courage of the men of 1st Assault Troop, 9 (Plassey) Bty in general – Sgt THOMPSON in particular:

When the men grow old, and the wind blows cold
On the heads where hair once grew
When their teeth decay and their beards go grey,
Then they'll tell you a tale or two.

They'll tell you a tale of the Belfast trail
With the mud and the blood and the mire,
And they'll tell of the bang from the gun in the hand
Of the kid from the Liverpool Shire.

---

[*]   Reproduced with kind permission from Sgt Bob Thompson MM.

'Twas a blustery day and the skies were grey
As Bob and his crew hit the town,
And the IRA knew that their days were few
As he looked around with a frown.

Bob slapped his thigh and was heard to cry,
"Right Wacks, let's sort 'em out!"
And with a snarl and a sneer, he grabbed the ear
Of the likeliest looking lout.

But the BC yelped like a bitch in whelp
As his ear was near torn from his head,
And as he turned with a growl and a black-browed scowl –
Bob knew his promotion was dead.

With his name in disgrace and scars on his face
From the Major's quite reasonable fury,
Bob climbed on his 'Pig', with his heels gave a dig
And rode off to the Ulster Brewery.

'Twas at the brewery gate that Bob met his fate
In the shape of the Belfast kids,
Where the cool crisp air was rent with despair
And the clang of the dustbin lids.

As the whistles blew and the bottles flew
And the sun was cut out by the stones,
Bob's mighty frame on the riot scene came
And the crowd quaked with terror and groaned.

"Hand me my gun, you stupid bum!"
Bob yelled at the nearest man,
Which hurt the Colonel's pride, but he knew inside
That Bob was an honourable man.

With an ice-cold heart and a reckless laugh
Bob loaded up his riot guns,
And he drew a bead and took no heed
Of the rocks and the shots and the puns.

His shot rang out and hit the snout
Of a yob who at once bit the dust,
And the huge mob ran, whilst a nearby band
Played 'Ernie' in praise of Bob's guts.

So young girls swoon and singers croon
O'er the tale of those heroic shots,
And spend your days in honest praise
Of Bob from the Liverpool Docks.

FRIDAY 4th...

As morning broke the whole of Andersonstown was enveloped in a thick fog, but even that couldn't hide the scars of the previous four days of rioting. Many of the roads were lined with burnt-out wrecks of cars which had been pushed aside by Scooby Doo. The Ulster Bank was a ruin; it had been destroyed in an explosion the previous Monday. Shops had been badly damaged by fire and emptied of their contents as looters went on the rampage. Everywhere was littered with bricks and shards of glass.

At around 8:00 a.m. a mobile from 3 Troop ventured out of the depot and up the Andersonstown Road. The Pigs from 1 and 2 Troop were in Riverdale Gardens and Glen Road checking on the situation there. Everywhere was deathly quiet as the patrols probed the area. Just one fresh barricade confronted the Pigs of 3 Troop and they were able to smash their way through. The rest of the day remained quiet. At around 7:15 p.m. a patrol from 3 Troop ventured into the Rossnareen Estate. Every house appeared to have its porch light on and every household was out there staring in defiance as the Pigs slowly cruised around. It was as though each side had fought themselves to a standstill.

Back at Musgrave Park Hospital, Renzo Agnello – still recovering from his injuries sustained on 31 January – had a visit from the military. He was handed a plastic bag containing the bullet which had hit him and asked to sign for the contents, and then it was taken away from him and sent to the forensics lab for examination. They told Renzo that it would be returned to him after they had finished with it, but he never did get it back; the IRA saw to that: they blew up the forensics lab to destroy all the incriminating evidence from previous attacks they had launched. A short while later, Renzo had another visitor... Bdr 'Horace' was out on patrol near the hospital and decided to pay Renzo a visit to see how he was.

Bdr 'Horace', 2 Troop
I walked into the room and straight away I could see he was on the mend. I asked him how he was and brought him up to date with

what had been going on over the past few days. I could see that he seemed quite pleased to be out of it all and away from the danger; then he made a comment to me: *"The only Fenian* [Catholic] *in the back of the Pig, and the bastards had to hit me."* I could see he hadn't lost his sense of humour, and I asked him if there was anything I could get him. His reply was: *"Yes, a compensation form and a pen."*

SATURDAY 5th...

After the lull in the rioting the previous day, the youths were again out in force and waiting for the patrols to re-enter the estates. That afternoon, a patrol came under heavy attack from groups of youths as they entered the Rossnareen Estate. The men retaliated with a volley of shots from their riot guns and the youths fell back.

BOY INJURED BY RUBBER BULLET IS IN HOSPITAL

A 12-year-old Belfast boy is in the Royal Victoria Hospital suffering from severe eye and other facial injuries as a result of being hit at close range by an army rubber bullet on Saturday afternoon. He is Sean Smith, Kenard Avenue.

His father said yesterday that the white of his eye had to be stitched and that other surgery has to be carried out when swelling subsides.

Mr Smith stated that he reported the incident at Andersonstown Police Station and was told that they had no knowledge of the matter at the time.

He said he had kept the boy in the house as there were a lot of army vehicles in the area. When he thought they were gone he sent his son a message, and it was in the short time he was out he received his injuries.[*]

[*] Sourced from Brian Corser's private collection of newspaper cuttings.

The belief at the time between many soldiers was that these youths seemed to think it was some kind of 'game' when they launched these attacks on the patrols. It is also true to say that some were actively encouraged by their parents to get involved in the stoning. An inevitable consequence of these attacks was that at some stage someone was going to get seriously hurt by these rubber bullets.

'Moira' – Belfast resident

I remember a friend of mine being injured by a rubber bullet. There was some rioting going on in the street where she lived and a young soldier was lying down in her front garden. My friend opened the door to watch what was going on and the young soldier spun around, thinking that the rioters had got behind him. He was absolutely terrified, and in his panic he fired his rubber bullet and hit my friend in the face. She was blinded for life, but she never bore any grudge against that young soldier.

Such were the tragic consequences of the riots at times. At 5:30 p.m. two Pigs moved out on Operation *Basset-Hound*. This was an intelligence-gathering patrol which over the past weeks had brought remarkable success to the battery in terms of weapons finds and Provo members taken off the streets. In the back of the lead Pig was someone working with an intelligence officer from Palace Barracks. The two of them would make notes and point out suspects to the Patrol Commander as the vehicles drove around Andersonstown. When a likely suspect was spotted, a message would be radioed through to the rear Pig which was following some distance behind. A snatch squad would jump out and take the suspect off the streets and he would then be questioned at Palace Barracks. These operations had no connection with the Military Reaction Force (MRF) or any other organisations which were working undercover at that time; they were done purely at regimental or battery level to gather intelligence in the local area – and *Basset-Hound* was nothing more than a name given to these types of patrols mounted by 9 Battery. Sometimes there would be a radio link between the Pigs and a 'Q' car which would also be in the area. The 'Q' cars were unmarked civilian vehicles used by many of the intelligence teams who roamed around much of Belfast. James 'Slim' Murray, who was attached to the Intelligence Section run by 12th Regiment, recalls how the system worked:

Gnr James 'Slim' Murray, RHQ

With being in Headquarters Battery, I spent most of my time with the Intelligence Team based at Lisburn. I occasionally went out in the 'Q' cars which drove ahead of the snatch squads in the Pigs. I always used to feel on edge, as for obvious reasons we had to wear civvy clothing and keep our weapons well out of sight. I don't suppose there would have been much hope for us if we had ever actually been caught out by the locals on the estates. You tried not to think of such things. I remember on one occasion when I filled up the 'Q' car and managed to put the wrong fuel in. We didn't get very far before the car came to a grinding halt – much to the horror of those of us inside it!

Normally we would drive into Andersonstown and look out for any known suspects on the streets. If we saw someone, one of us would get on the radio to the snatch squad who were following at a distance. They would drive up and just take them off the streets and put them in the back of the Pig. After that they would be driven up to an office we had where they could be questioned. We would follow them up in our car and when we got there, we had to dig through our intelligence reports to try and identify them.

Several members of 9 Battery also undertook these more dangerous 'undercover' missions from time to time, as well as their normal operational duties. One such man was L/Bdr Danny Coulton, who would often be seen sporting a beard when in uniform and out on patrol. The next time you saw him might be when he was behind the wheel of a civilian car speeding through a vehicle check point. Phil Gallagher remembers one incident which took place on Andersonstown Road when a few men from 9 Battery were travelling around in an unmarked civilian car...

Gnr Phil Gallagher, 3 Troop

I remember an incident that happened on Andersonstown Road. Danny Coulton and Mick were out in an unmarked 'Q' car cruising down the road past the Busy Bee. They were doing a bit of undercover work for our Intelligence Section. Danny looked in the rear-view mirror and spotted a car following them, so they speeded up a bit. The next moment, this car had dropped a gear and the driver must have floored the accelerator because he was now alongside Danny's car and the passenger leans out and points a Thompson machine gun at them. Danny's driver slammed on and caught the other driver unawares, and when the gunman opened fire his bullets were hitting the road in front of Danny's car. The Provos took off down Andersonstown Road with the 'Q' car chasing them. Danny picks up the Sterling sub-machine gun and leans out of the passenger window to return fire – and the bloody magazine falls off!

On another occasion, a more novel approach was tried out by 'Davey' S******* and Clancy Campbell when they were out on a lift operation. The pair of them were dressed in tracksuits and hiding in the back of a Pig.

Gnr Clancy Campbell, 3 Troop

We went out on Operation *Basset-Hound* once, and me and 'Davey' S****** were in the back of the rear Pig with our tracksuits on. We spent some time driving around Andersonstown looking for anyone we recognised on the 'wanted' list and after a while, I can't remember where it was, but we spotted this group stood on this road and we got a call from the front Pig to go after a certain bloke in the group. The Pig slowed down and we threw open the back doors and jumped out; then we started running towards these people and the daft bastards thought we had escaped from the back of the Pig, and they were waving at us and cheering as we ran towards them. Anyway, we got up to them and grabbed this bloke we were after. You should have seen the look on his face; he didn't have a clue what was happening. We ran back to the Pig with him, carrying him under his armpits, and everyone just stood around watching. They were that surprised by what we had done.

On another occasion I was chasing two blokes down the road when I was wearing my tracksuit. I kept shouting at them to stop, but they wouldn't, so I pulled out this .32 pistol the RUC had given to me for protection and I fired about three shots in the air to try and make them stop. I got a right bollocking off the BC for that.

Gnr Phil Gallagher, 3 Troop

Sometimes me and 'Taffy' M***** would travel up to Palace Barracks to pick up the intelligence men before going out on *Basset-Hound* and we got to know two MRF guys. One was a Welsh lad who we obviously called 'Taffy', but I can't remember the name of the other. We had more to do with 'Taffy' than the other. We used to pick him up off the street, drive around and drop him off at a different location – having gained 'intelligence' information off him.

Anonymous NCO, MRF

It's no secret the British Army in Northern Ireland used undercover troops – be it at regimental or brigade level. Commencing late 1971, I served in an undercover role in and around the Belfast area. Our primary role was intelligence-gathering operations and, indeed most of the time, this would be the remit of any such unit… this and, if required, acting on any suitable intelligence gathered. In the words of Chairman Mao: "*In counter-terrorism, power comes from intelligence; not the barrel of a gun.*"

Undercover work – in some people's eyes – can evoke a glamorous pastime; believe me, it isn't. It can be routine, with long periods of boredom and short periods of adrenaline-rushing highs… Parallels with being on the streets in uniform come to mind. Undercover, you have to undergo a metamorphic transition. Rank, generally, is not an issue and you have more autonomy in the decision-making process.

Strategically, you would have a better understanding of the bigger picture with more parts of the jigsaw. Again, as on the streets in uniform, it's much the same; you are dependent on your mates to watch your back. Friendships forged on the streets in a conflict situation will last a lifetime.

I remember the very first time I walked the streets of Belfast in civvies. I felt extremely vulnerable and felt that everyone was looking at me. Of course, they weren't and I soon learnt how to blend in. It quickly just became second nature; you wore anonymity like a cloak. Situational awareness was your watchword. We would work in three or four-men squads both in mobile and foot surveillance operations. Other tasks could be Close Protection and Close Personal Protection duties. Observation post surveillance operations were also a big part of the job and could be tedious; days spent waiting for the proverbial to hit the fan. Still, it was all part of the role – and when things came together, it could be very satisfying.

You have to remember that in some parts of Belfast and the surrounding areas, law and order was non-existent. In some areas, the law was provided by vigilantes. Kneecapping or tar and feathering were some of the least punishments handed down. The IRA ruled with an iron fist; the Provos were judge and jury. If members of the Security Forces were caught in any of these areas, retiring to collect your pension wasn't an option – big boy games, big boy rules! In certain instances, our operations were compromised. Anyone that underestimated the Provos were very foolish; their intelligence was excellent and a strange vehicle or individual in these areas would be clocked immediately.

We operated in Andersonstown quite often. It was a very staunch Republican area and we used to call in at the bus depot situated at the top of the Falls Road opposite Milltown Cemetery. Members of 12th Light Air Defence Regiment were based there. I think they were split into 1 and 2 Troop or something like that, but they didn't really seem to function in the same way as we infantry guys did. A cup of tea was always on offer – that and a natter about the latest security and intelligence status. Andersonstown, at that time, was a very dangerous place – and the troops situated there did a fantastic job in the very proactive manner that this area was managed. No-Go areas on this patch simply wasn't an option. For us, contacts in this area weren't unknown. However, our own operations could be fraught with difficulty in any area we operated in – and encountering army patrols could be problematic. VCPs could be a nightmare – especially where Rent-a-Mob was in attendance.

On many occasions, our unit was compromised by army VCPs. After all, they didn't know who we were. Our vehicle registrations used to be provided to all units on a weekly basis; however, we used to frequently change these. Many a time we had been asked to step out of the car and frisked, with the rifles behind being cocked with the accompanying cry of: "*They are tooled up*," or "*carrying*." When this happened, we had to be taken out of the area by the troops; they couldn't just let us go.

Another area favoured by the Security Forces in Andersonstown was Milltown Cemetery. This was overlooked by an army sangar on the Falls Road side – ideal to get photos of the mourners that used to attend the Republican funerals there. I remember attending one of these funerals in person, but having to leave rather quickly. Another plus for the Security Forces was the ingress and egress into the Andersonstown area via the peripheral roads, which were excellent. However, this also applied to the IRA and road cordons could be a security issue. Speed was the key. Once into the estates, it became a nightmare. I remember going into one particular estate early Monday morning just after 'Bloody Sunday'; I think it was Rossnareen. Early morning, driving through a burning barricade, when the vehicle steering became unresponsive… The cause? Two punctured tyres. We managed to drive out and, as ever, our always dependable back-up provided us with armed cover and replacement wheels.

Obviously on our travels we encountered persons that did not have our best interests or health at heart, and then we had orders to engage them. We were not a murder squad as some people like to claim, and I have never knowingly shot at an unarmed person. Generally, and when circumstances allowed, we operated within the law – but I would refer you to the framework of the Yellow Card.

In essence, a soldier could only open fire if he thought his target presented an immediate danger to life. This, crucially, never meant that a target had to be armed with a gun or anything at all. A petrol bomber or a man driving a car at a group of soldiers or civilians with the apparent intention of running them over could be met with lethal force. If an unarmed man tried to wrestle your weapon away from you in a riot, he could be shot lawfully if there was no other way of stopping him. Likewise, if an individual soldier or a group became cut off in a riot and feared for their lives, they could – if necessary – shoot unarmed civilians. Even if an unarmed group were beating up a member of the public, he was entitled to fire if it was the only way of saving that person's life. In legal terms, the state of the mind of the soldier was crucial. If he thought, reasonably, that a target posed a threat to anyone's life, then he could pull the trigger.

After all these years my memory has dimmed somewhat, but one image that never leaves me is remembering watching a scene of a shredded human torso – minus head, together with other body parts – being shovelled into a sack and thinking: *"This was once a human being."* This was in Belfast city centre in early 1972 after a bomb was very recently detonated – a somewhat daily occurrence. That incident typified to me man's inhumanity to man. Was it worth it? I would suggest the jury is still out; only history can judge.

As is so often the case in many conflicts, there are claims and counter-claims made by the opposing forces as they try to outdo each other in the propaganda war, but there was one rather bizarre claim made by the Provisionals that 9 Battery had used a helicopter to ferry troops into the Rossnareen Estate. The author has no recollection of any such tactics ever being used, and neither have any former members from 9 Battery, but the following article appeared in a copy of the IRA newspaper *The Volunteer*:

HUNS DROP IN

Raids by the British Army continued throughout the week in the ……… A number of people were lifted for reasons unknown to anyone but those who seem intent on complete oppression of the people.

One of the more novel features of the Friday raids in the Rossnareen area was the use of a helicopter to drop terrorists in Shaw's Road. We would like to let the military authorities know that we are duly impressed and will definitely consider giving up the fight.

PS – Why don't you try using motors like everybody else?*

* Source taken from *The Volunteer*.

The 'helicopter' claim was made shortly after a successful operation planned and mounted by the Battery Commander. For some time, the BC had become concerned that the 'opposition' were monitoring all patrol movements in and out of the bus depot so closely that it was becoming impossible to achieve the element of surprise on certain operations. The BC had planned one certain operation for Rossnareen and rather than take the usual expected routes of Andersonstown Road or Glen Road, he sent the men in the direction of the city centre. The men then did a 'wide loop' to come in to the target area on the blind side. The ruse worked so well that it led to speculation amongst the Provisionals that the only way the soldiers could have got there unnoticed was by helicopter.

VICTIMS OF THE TROUBLES WHO DIED THIS DAY...

Paul McFadden (31) – Died of injuries six days after a bomb inside a van exploded outside Castle Arcade, Belfast. The Provisional IRA failed to give adequate warning of the bomb.

Phelim Grant (32) – Provisional IRA. Died when a bomb being transported on a sand barge blew up.

Charles McCann (28) – Provisional IRA. Killed in the same incident.*

* List compiled from *The Troubles* Magazine (Glenravel Publications).

SUNDAY 6th...

It was now a week since the killings in Londonderry, and still the rioting continued on the streets of Andersonstown. After the statement issued by the Provisional IRA about the hijacking of vehicles and destruction of buildings, it was the turn of the clergy to make a direct appeal to the people...

FALLS PRIESTS CONDEMN DESTRUCTION

Priests in the Falls Road and Andersonstown area of Belfast – in a statement read out at masses on Sunday – said that they were appalled that the dignified mourning in the areas for the events in Derry on Sunday week last were disfigured by wanton destruction and damage.

The statement said that the priests were ashamed that the destruction and suffering had come from within their own areas and they appealed to all to join together to end this destruction.

"The burning and destruction of shops," added the statement, "has virtually deprived the people, especially those without transport, of everyday necessities."

The burning and destruction of business premises has resulted in even fewer jobs in a notorious [sic] jobless area. The burning and hijacking of lorries and vans and buses had resulted in the stoppage of deliveries of essential goods and services.

The priests say that the tragic consequences of the burning and destruction was suffering and misery inflicted on all – and in particular on all those already suffering most in the community.

The priests ask the people responsible for the damage to think particularly of the old-age pensioners and mothers of large families.

* Sourced from Brian Corser's private collection of newspaper cuttings.

The 'dignified mourning' mentioned by the priests seemed a bit of a sick joke to the men of 9 Battery. If there had been any, they certainly hadn't seen any signs of it! The only 'dignified mourning' appeared to be the hanging of black flags from houses and shops. For the past week they had been subjected to a constant stream of attacks from both the Provisionals and the community as a whole. There had also been some evidence to suggest that even the Catholic priests supported the fight against the army.

The men that were not already out on patrol had been placed on immediate standby. A protest rally had been planned for Newry and the fear was that if there was a repetition of the events of 30 January Andersonstown would again erupt in violence. It was only in the past day or so that the situation had calmed down a little, but it wouldn't have taken much for the district to descend into a confrontation almost like a civil war once more. Back at the RUC Station, a large crowd had gathered outside to stage one of their 'dignified' protests.

Gnr Robert Isherwood, T Battery (Shah Sujah's Troop) HQ

I remember the Sunday after 'Bloody Sunday' and going down to Andersonstown Police Station. There were big crowds outside hanging black crosses on the fencing in protest about what had happened in Londonderry the week before. This Sergeant detailed me and 'Jock' ***** to go outside to move them on. The pair of us were only about 5ft 2in tall, and to me it seemed our SLRs were almost as big as us! We got out there and started to try and shift them, and then all of a sudden a gap appeared in the crowd. This usually meant a gunman had put in an appearance, so I grabbed 'Jock' by his flak jacket and dragged him into the sangar. I remember the Sergeant calling us all the names under the sun and trying to get us out to finish the job. Happy days!

Up on the Springfield Road, another unit from 12th Regiment came under attack during the evening. As the patrol made its way along the road, there was a burst of automatic fire which entered the Pig through the open rear doors and went through the front windscreen without hitting any of the occupants. The crew of the Pig returned fire, but were unsure if they had hit any of the gunmen. There had been numerous incidents where gunfire had entered the rear of the Pigs while out on patrol. The doors were almost always kept open while conducting these patrols. It was highly dangerous, but did allow for rapid deployment of the soldiers when the situation arose. There had already been several incidents where the occupants found bullet holes in the radio battery packs after returning from patrol…

Gnr 'Snowy' H***, 2 Troop

Me and Dave L*** were sat in the back of a Pig doing a mobile around the Rossnareen Estate when we came under fire. Somebody said that it was five shots fired at us, but there's a saying that you don't hear the one that hits you – and me and Dave only heard four shots. There was a radio battery in the back that we had been using as a seat a bit earlier and we were both resting our feet on it – and when we got back to base, we found a bullet stuck in it. That must have been the shot we didn't hear.

VICTIMS OF THE TROUBLES WHO DIED THIS DAY…

David Seaman (31) – An Englishman also known as Barry Barber. Found shot dead at Cullaville, near Crossmaglen, County Armagh.

* List compiled from *The Troubles* Magazine (Glenravel Publications).

MONDAY 7th…

The fear of a repetition of the violence seen at other marches prompted the government to take action, and on this day Brian Faulkner introduced his Public Order Act banning marches for the next 12 months. Whether anyone would actually take notice of this edict remained to be seen. Back in Andersonstown, in a rare show of co-operation between the locals and soldiers, a cleaning-up team was formed to sort out the mess caused by all the recent rioting on Andersonstown Road.

The men from 3 Troop worked side by side with the local women to clear away the rubble and remains of barricades. Fortunately for the troop, no-one took advantage of the situation and the cleaning-up carried on without incident, but it would take more than the removal of wrecked cars to remove the scars of the rioting which had been going on for the past few days.

ANDERSONSTOWN VOLUNTARY SERVICE SCHEME

A voluntary service scheme has gone into operation in the Andersonstown area of Belfast, the aim of which is to provide more amenities for the people. Teams will be set up in each street to sponsor all kinds of activities which will include decorating the homes of old people and providing guidance and help for those with personal problems.

At 9am tomorrow, 50 young people will be engaged in cleaning up the area and removing unsightly vehicles. Messrs, Eastwood have given the loan of four lorries to help in the work.

Mr Sean Hicks, the secretary, said last night that in the long term they hoped to send groups of children to the Irish and Scottish Gaeltacht and to set up knitting and handicraft classes.*

* Sourced from Brian Corser's private collection of newspaper cuttings.

TUESDAY 8th...

The attacks on the patrols continued as the Provos tried to claim their first proper 'kill' on the men of 9 Battery. Down near the Kennedy Way roundabout, a foot patrol from 3 Troop were making their way around the area and moved onto a patch of waste ground close to the Lucozade factory. As they crossed the ground, one of the men spotted a small wooden box with a wire leading away from it.

Gnr Phil Gallagher, 3 Troop

We were out on patrol with Bob Wilson, near the Lucozade factory, when he suddenly stopped us. Just in front of him was a small wooden box. I wasn't sure what it was at first, and then I noticed a wire leading away from it towards the bottom of the waste ground. It was then that I realised that I was stood near a bomb of some kind. I nearly shit myself when I thought about what could have happened. We all scattered in case anyone was waiting to set it off, and Bob got on the radio for Felix [bomb disposal] to come and deal with it.

It wasn't long before Felix turned up – and after following the wire back to the detonation point, they moved back to the bomb and dismantled it.

Gnr Phil Gallagher, 3 Troop

After they opened the box up I could see the gelignite inside. The ordnance officer told me it was about 7lbs of explosives. On the other side of the box was a load of nails. There was liquid coming from the explosives and I can remember the smell of marzipan. They took it out of the box and blew it up a few yards away from where we were – and before they left, one of them gave the box to Bob as a souvenir. It ended up on our 'trophy wall' back at base.

These devices were capable of inflicting appalling injuries – and even death. In 1974, Marine Rivenberg was on foot patrol in New Lodge when he stepped on one of these mines which had been hidden on a patch of waste ground. Both his legs were blown off. A short time later, signs were painted on walls in the Lodge… 'HARD LUCK RIVENBERG'. He went on to make a remarkable recovery and, in a show of true determination, he refused to marry his fiancée until he could walk down the aisle unaided, which he eventually did do.

VICTIMS OF THE TROUBLES WHO DIED THIS DAY…

Bernard Rice (49) – Shot dead from a passing car while walking past shops on Crumlin Road, Belfast. Attack carried out by members of the Protestant Red Hand Commando (RHC).*

* List compiled from *The Troubles* Magazine (Glenravel Publications).

WEDNESDAY 9th…

The Civil Rights Movement had designated 9 February as 'D' (for 'Disruption') Day, but it all turned out to be a bit of a flop. A crowd of about 150 gathered outside the Busy Bee to show their support, but the protest went off without incident. The Provos had threatened to inflict 'severe punishment' on anyone who ignored the protest – a sure sign that the locals had no choice but to comply with the wishes of the Republican thugs who claimed to be fighting for the cause of freedom. It was rather ironic that the cause of freedom didn't actually extend to allowing the citizens of Northern Ireland to choose for themselves if they wished to take part in this protest. That so many did choose to ignore the warning in Andersonstown was seen by some to conclude that maybe the Provos were losing some of their authority over the people.

VICTIMS OF THE TROUBLES WHO DIED THIS DAY...

Patrick Casey (26) – Killed by an unknown Republican terrorist organ-isation. He died of injuries sustained three days previously in a bomb explosion at council offices at Keady, County Armagh.*

* List compiled from *The Troubles* Magazine (Glenravel Publications).

THURSDAY 10th...

Two British soldiers went missing from their unit in the north, and all patrols in Andersonstown were asked to watch out for them. There had always been inci-dents of soldiers deserting their units for one reason or another. Some claimed they did not agree with what the troops were doing in Northern Ireland, but anyone deserting ran the very real risk of being executed by the IRA if they were caught. Meanwhile, in Coalisland, two other soldiers were injured – one quite badly – when their armoured vehicle was blown up by a landmine while removing a barrier at Annagher crossroads: a stark contrast of two soldiers carrying out their duty, and another two running to save their skins.

Back in Andersonstown, the patrols were out in force and keeping their eyes open for any sign of the two missing soldiers. A mobile from 3 Troop was cruising around Riverdale Estate when a report came over the radio about a huge fire up near Rossnareen Avenue. Such calls had to be treated with caution, as there was always the danger that it could just be a setup to lure soldiers into an ambush. It was a common tactic used by the Provos, as they knew the soldiers had to go and investigate every such call. The Pigs moved up and started searching the area, but no smoke could be seen. The streets were unusually deserted for that time of day, and it wasn't yet lunchtime. It had all the hallmarks of an ambush, and so the two Pigs withdrew.

As they left the area, they stumbled upon a car being pushed by two youths. When stopped and questioned, they claimed they had found it abandoned and had decided to take it home to see if they could get it going. The car had been fitted with a set of false plates and it was highly likely that it would have been used as a means of transporting a bomb to some target in the city centre.

VICTIMS OF THE TROUBLES WHO DIED THIS DAY...

Joseph Cunningham (26) – Provisional IRA. Shot dead in a gun battle between the IRA and RUC at O'Neill's Road, Newtownabbey, County Antrim.

Sgt Ian Harris (26) – The Devon and Dorset Regiment. Killed by the Provisional IRA in a landmine attack on their mobile patrol, Cullyhanna, County Armagh.

Pte David Champ (23) – The Devon and Dorset Regiment. Killed in the same incident.*

* List compiled from *The Troubles* Magazine (Glenravel Publications).

FRIDAY 11th...

Late in the evening, a patrol was cruising around the Riverdale Estate when the Commander of the lead vehicle suddenly spotted the figure of a man carrying a rifle sprinting across the road. The vehicles had just turned into Riverdale Park North when the figure darted out of the shadows and down the side of a house. The men quickly debussed and rushed over to the houses while the second Pig drove around to see if they could locate the gunman further around the back. The gardens in the immediate vicinity were searched, but no trace could be found of the elusive figure and the men resumed their patrol.

Elsewhere in Belfast, a woman was injured when Provo gunmen opened up on soldiers in Divis Street. In the Ardoyne, a gunman shot up an observation post manned by The Queen's Lancashire Regiment. They returned fire and believe they may have injured the gunman; traces of blood were found at the scene. In Londonderry, troops came under attack from nail bombs and snipers during a riot.

SATURDAY 12th...

The two army deserters who had absconded on 10 February turned up at a press conference given by the IRA. The men were members of The Queen's Lancashire Regiment and they claimed that they had been ordered to shoot on sight three top Provisionals who appeared on the 'wanted' lists if they ever came across them. The army denied such claims and a spokesman said: "That's their opinion."

It is difficult to understand why any soldier would take the risk of deserting while in Northern Ireland – especially when still in uniform – but there was once an incident when a soldier from 9 Battery went missing while on patrol. The soldier, known as 'Kid Curry' to his mates, was out on foot patrol when he apparently 'lost his bottle' and disappeared. The Section Commander got in touch with HQ to report him missing and extra patrols were sent out to look for him. A short time later he turned up at the RUC Station after having travelled back on a double-decker bus – still in possession of his SLR rifle. He was promptly arrested and disarmed. No-one is sure what happened to him, but it was rumoured at the time that he was court-martialed and kicked out of the army.

Up the far end of Andersonstown, two Pigs from 3 Troop were driving down Shaw's Road when the Vehicle Commander looked over to his left and noticed a car parked up in Tullymore Walk. When the driver of the car saw the Pigs, he ducked down – and this raised the suspicion of the patrol. They decided to check him out to see what he was up to.

SOLDIERS BEAT ME – CLAIM

Police are investigating allegations that a man was beaten up after being lifted by the army on Saturday afternoon near his home.

In a complaint to the police and to Army Headquarters, Mr James Nesbitt, of Tullymore Walk, Andersonstown, said that he had just returned from shopping on Saturday afternoon and was sitting in his car when he was pulled out by men of the 12th Light Air Defence Regiment who put him into the back of an armoured personnel carrier.

He alleged that he was kept in the armoured car from 4.10pm until 5.30pm and during this time was beaten by the soldiers.

Later, Mr Nesbitt contacted General Sir John Anderson, the Col Commandant, UDR, and asked who he should complain to about the incident.

Mr Nesbitt said: "The General was an officer in my old regiment. The army have apologised to me but that is not enough. They humiliated me in front of my neighbours."

Police confirmed that Mr Nesbitt made a formal complaint to the Andersonstown Police Station and said that it would be investigated. It is known that Mr Nesbitt also telephoned Army Headquarters.

A spokesman for the 12th Light Air Defence Regiment said: "As far as we are concerned we have not apologised.

"We were in the area looking for a man on the wanted list who had been seen a short while before. A mobile patrol passed the car in which Mr Nesbitt was sitting and he ducked down. The patrol did another tour of the area and the same thing happened. The patrol then took it upon themselves to check him out.

"At the time some 50 youths were stoning and bottling, and so Mr Nesbitt was asked to get into the Pig so that he could be questioned in a quieter area.

"He refused and was lifted out of the car by soldiers who placed one hand under each armpit. He was then taken round the corner and headquarters were contacted to check him out. After he was cleared he was driven back and released as close to his vehicle as was possible. He was only in the carrier for between five and 10 minutes."[*]

* Taken from the author's collection of newspaper cuttings in his Belfast diaries.

Such incidents as this did happen from time to time, but it wasn't often that it was reported in the papers. When the patrol had pulled into the cul-de-sac to investigate, it was only a matter of moments before the youths started to gather. Some of his neighbours came out to see what was happening, and that was when he started to get a bit aggressive. He obviously didn't want to lose face in front of his neighbours. The soldiers were left in an impossible situation when they asked him to get out of the car and he refused. They were left with no alternative but to forcibly eject him.

The door of the vehicle was opened and Nesbitt started lashing out as one of the patrol removed him from the car. They took him to the waiting Pig to question him, and that's when the situation started to escalate. The crowd of onlookers began stoning the patrol and they had to withdraw a short distance while they continued to question Nesbitt. Had he been more co-operative, the whole episode could have been avoided. The soldiers were pushed to their limits at times by the extreme levels of provocation they encountered virtually every single day they went out on patrol. The fact that they never massively overreacted was a testament to their discipline and self-control.

By 12 February the battery had been involved in around 200 shootings and bombings since arriving in Andersonstown on 25 November. At least 40 of these shootings happened in the immediate vicinity of Rossnareen Avenue. In the Falls Road area, a soldier from the Gloucestershire Regiment was shot and injured by a Provo sniper. The Provisionals also blew up the house of a man who ignored the warning not to ignore the planned strikes on 'Disruption Day' on Wednesday 9 February. A group of men turned up at his home at around 11:00 p.m. and ordered him, his family and immediate neighbours to evacuate the houses while they planted a 15lb device in his house. One of the gunmen reportedly told the council road sweeper that his house was being destroyed because: "You swept the streets of Beleek on Wednesday."[*]

Source taken from *The Troubles* Magazine (Glenravel Publications).

SUNDAY 13th…

In the early hours of Sunday morning, a call was made to the RUC Station claiming that a bomb had been left in the depot. All the men not out on duty were immediately hauled out of their beds to conduct a search of the entire complex. As was to be expected, nothing was found, but the response had to be the same to all these calls. The IRA often used to say: "We only need to be lucky once. You need to be lucky every time" – and it was quite a true saying. There was always the chance that the next call could indeed be for a genuine bomb. Gradually the base returned to normal and the soldiers carried on with their patrols. At 4:30 p.m. a section from 3 Troop went out to the Rossnareen Estate to conduct two lift operations. The vehicles reached their first intended target and the men moved in.

Gnr Steve Corbett, 3 Troop

I was detailed to go around the back of the property with three other lads while the search team went in through the front door. We had only been there a minute or so before a large crowd started to gather around the house and they started to put us under a tremendous hail of bricks and bottles. I crouched down and took cover as best as I could, but I was stuck in the open with my back to the building and nowhere to hide from the missiles being thrown.

On the opposite side of the hedges at the bottom of the garden, the rioters were lined up and throwing everything they could lay their hands on at us – and then they started pouring into the gardens on either side of the building. A bottle hit me on the knee and exploded in a shower of flying shards of glass. Many others missed me by mere inches, and the other three lads with me fared no better. I could hear the windows behind me shattering under the impact of the volley of bricks and bottles.

The rioters were screaming at the tops of their voices as they attacked us; then the officer in charge opened the back door from the inside and signalled for us to enter, as it was impossible to get around the side of the building. We fled through the hallway as the barrage of bricks and bottles continued behind us. I made my way to the front door with the three lads and the officer. Someone opened the door and we hesitated for a moment when we saw all the youths gathered there. There was nowhere else to go, and so we made a break for it and dashed out together to try and board the Pigs.

As the five of us came out of the front door, we again ran into a hail of missiles. All you could hear was the sound of breaking glass and screams as the rioters tried to hem us in. The situation was truly terrifying and I feared for my life. We were vastly outnumbered by the crowd, who had us completely surrounded. We charged towards the gate – keeping as close together as possible. Some of the crowd were trying to grab us and drag us into their ranks.

Once outside on the road, I saw a crowd of about 40 youths in front and behind the Pigs. They were throwing everything they could at us, and on entering the Pig I was hit again on the back of the leg. The rest of the lads couldn't get in because of the rioters, so one of the Pigs slammed into reverse and charged at them at speed to make them scatter. They still came at us and we had to fire salvo after salvo of baton rounds to disperse them. We finally managed to get into the back of the Pigs and get away. It had been absolute hell, and we still had another lift to do.

The patrol reached their final objective and managed to complete the lift without any further trouble. When they reached base, it was still only 4:55 p.m. The whole nightmare experience from leaving camp to their return had lasted just 25 minutes. There was nothing more frightening than to be caught out in the open and surrounded by a rampaging mob intent on killing you. The proof that these people would indeed kill you given half the chance was graphically displayed for all the world to see when on 19 March 1988 Corporals Robert Howes and Derek Wood – both dressed in civilian clothes and in an unmarked car – were travelling up Andersonstown Road when they got caught up in an IRA funeral procession which was travelling in the opposite direction towards Milltown Cemetery. The actual reason for them being there is unclear, but their mistake cost them their lives.

The crowd of mourners believed they were under attack from a Protestant paramilitary group and surrounded the vehicle. Despite the fact that at least one of the soldiers was armed, they did not fire their weapon into the crowd to try and save themselves. Corporal Wood opened the window of the car door, partially climbed out and produced his pistol. He fired a shot into the air in an effort to scatter the crowd. They briefly fell back before surging forward again and dragging the two men from their vehicle. Howes and Wood were then bundled into a taxi and driven away. They were then subjected to a savage beating before being executed and dumped naked behind some shops not far from where they had been abducted.

It is difficult to say how other soldiers would have acted in similar circumstances, but there can be no doubt that some would have been prepared to sell their lives dearly – and who could really blame them when they were facing the possibility of being killed? There was once an incident in Andersonstown when a foot patrol from 3 Troop were dropped off near Rossnareen Estate. The Ferret scout cars of the Blues and Royals were supposed to provide the back-up for the four-man team, but because of some mix-up, the scout cars withdrew...

Gnr Clancy Campbell, 1 Troop

I remember one time when we went out on patrol. There was me, Leon K*********, 'Scouse' A**** and A.N. Other. The Blues and Royals did a runner on us and left us four in the middle of a rise. They were supposed to be our back-up and they just left us out there on our own. There were about 100 people there and just four of us. The next thing is we had a big riot on our hands and I really thought we had shit it. We made a break for it and went under this underpass by a block of flats, so I cocked my rifle and shoved a round up the spout and I told the others that if there was anyone on the other side – and if they got in my way – I was going to start shooting. I said: *"I don't care; they're not going to get me."* I remember Leon saying to me: *"You can't do that!"* and I said: *"Who fucking can't? I'm not going to end up dead for anyone."*

Anyway we ran to the road, I can't remember the name of it, but we ran out and I stood in the middle of the road and pointed my rifle at a car that was coming up. It stopped and I was just about to get the driver out and this Pig comes tearing around the corner. It stops, and out steps Tom McShane with a big grin on his face, but I would have just shot my way out of it if that Pig hadn't turned up when it did because the Blues and Royals did a runner and just left us in the lurch.

Clancy Campbell would have been perfectly within his rights to open fire if he thought his life was in danger from the hostile crowd. The Yellow Card, which was issued to all soldiers, clearly states: 'You may fire after due warning if there is no other way to protect yourself or those whom it is your duty to protect from the danger of being killed or seriously injured'.

VICTIMS OF THE TROUBLES WHO DIED ON THIS DAY...

Pte Thomas McCann (19) – The Royal Army Ordnance Corps. Shot dead by Republican terrorists near Newtownbutler, County Fermanagh, while off duty.*

* List compiled from *The Troubles* Magazine (Glenravel Publications).

MONDAY 14th...

The lift operations around Andersonstown continued as the pressure was kept on the Provos. The occasional sniping at patrols still occurred, but the large-scale

'Frenchy' C***** points to the bullet hole in the Land Rover.
(Courtesy of Brian Corser)

attacks seemed to have died down. One incident which took place happened when a soldier from the battery was being transported to Aldergrove Airport to start his R&R leave. As the Land Rover approached the Kennedy Way roundabout, a single shot was fired. The bullet hit the top portion of the metal frame surrounding the windscreen and went out through the canvas side-screen. It had missed the driver's head by just a few inches.

TUESDAY 15th...

In Belfast, the IRA bombing campaign continued and devices were planted in two business premises. In the first incident, a gunman walked into Sawyer's food store and handed the startled shop assistant a duffle bag, telling her: "It's a bomb, and you have 10 minutes to get out." Before leaving, he ordered her to place it behind the counter. The resulting explosion destroyed several parts of the food hall and blew out windows in adjoining properties. The callous indifference of the Provisional IRA bombers to the safety of the general public when planting these devices was once again laid bare for all to see.

In the second incident, the bombers were believed to have sprinkled petrol around the premises of the Kennedy & Morrison Ltd. engineering store in Union Street before planting the bomb. The explosion ignited the petrol and the resulting fire destroyed the building. Meanwhile, on the Fermanagh border, troops attended an incident at the Aghalane customs post after reports of an explosion. As the soldiers arrived, they came under heavy fire from gunmen operating from across the border.*

WEDNESDAY 16th…

At 7:30 p.m. a patrol commanded by an officer known to all as 'Sydney Slug' moved out into the Rossnareen Estate and was immediately ambushed by a large mob who had been lying in wait. 'Sydney Slug' ordered the vehicles to pull to one side while they took on the rioters.

Gnr 'C', 3 Troop
We pulled to one side and started blasting away with the Fed riot guns. We wanted to get out and have a go at them, but 'Slug' wouldn't let us; then we moved on to the Riverdale Park Estate and we got stoned again. Albert Manners let off this cracking shot and brought down this woman, but if the stupid cow hadn't been there rioting, she wouldn't have got hurt would she?

By this stage of the tour, none of the men really cared whether they caused serious injury with the riot guns. Their reasoning was quite simple: If the thugs didn't come out on the streets and take on the soldiers, they wouldn't end up getting hit by rubber bullets and hurt.

'DEAR SNIPER'

HOW DO YOU FEEL DEAR SNIPER,
WHEN SNIPING JOBS ARE DONE:
DO YOU REALLY FEEL A HERO,
WITHOUT YOUR SNIPER'S GUN?

YOU POSE THROUGHOUT THE LIGHT OF DAY,
AN UPRIGHT REPROBATE,
COLLECT YOUR DOLE-ASSISTANCE PAY,
FROM SOMEONE THAT YOU HATE.

YOU MUST FEEL BIG TO HEAR THE NEWS,
THE BOY YOU SHOT IS DEAD:
YOUR ROTTEN SOUL MUST COUNT YOUR DOLE
AS THIRTY BITS OF LEAD.

---

*   Source taken from *The Troubles* Magazine (Glenravel Publications).

THE BOY YOU KILLED LEFT LOTS OF GRIEF,
BUT THEN – YOU'RE NOT TO BLAME:
YOU STOLE HIS LIFE, THE FINAL THIEF,
AND ONE WHO KNOWS NO SHAME.

AT LEAST THE BOY CAME OUT TO FIGHT,
BUT CRAVEN CUR AND BASE:
YOU'D NOT THE GUTS TO COME OUTRIGHT,
AND FIGHT HIM FACE TO FACE.

AN UPRIGHT LAYABOUT AND TRUE,
YOU HIDE BEHIND THE KIDS,
WHO SET THE AMBUSH UP FOR YOU,
WHILE MOTHERS RATTLE LIDS.

YOU SKULK IN DARKNESS AT THE REAR,
A YELLOW SWEATING SKUNK:
TAKE ONE QUICK SHOT THEN DISAPPEAR,
A HERO FULL OF FUNK.

YOU MUST FEEL GOOD – NOW DON'T YOU
A VIRILE RAT AND STRONG:
LIKE OTHERS OF YOUR WITCHES BREW,
WHO USE THE GUN AND BOMB.

BUT HERE'S A LITTLE FOOD FOR THOUGHT,
THAT YOU MIGHT CONTEMPLATE:
SOME VERMIN RUN BEFORE THEY'RE CAUGHT,
BUT GUNNER TIGERS FEAR FOR NOUGHT,
AND RATS EXTERMINATE.*

This poem was also distributed throughout Andersonstown to the homes of known members of the Provisional IRA.

---

* This poem originally appeared in *The Belfast Telegraph* and was reprinted for all members of 9 (Plassey) Battery; our mascot was the Bengal Tiger.

VICTIMS OF THE TROUBLES WHO DIED THIS DAY...

Pte Thomas Callaghan (45) – The Ulster Defence Regiment. Abducted by the Provisional IRA while driving a bus and later found shot dead at Foyle Road, Derry.

Pte Michael Prime (18) – The Royal Army Pay Corps.

Shot dead by a Provisional IRA sniper while on mobile patrol near the Moira roundabout, M1 motorway, County Down.*

* List compiled from *The Troubles* Magazine (Glenravel Puublications).

THURSDAY 17th...

After the recent lull in the fighting, the rioters were back out on the streets again in force and virtually every patrol that entered the estates was met by hostile mobs waiting for a chance to attack the vehicles. They knew that the battery was close to the end of its tour, and they were determined to cause as much trouble for them as possible. At 1:00 p.m. a patrol from 3 Troop met heavy resistance when they entered the area of Tullymore Gardens. As the Pigs negotiated the turn at the bottom of Edenmore Drive, the youths sprang out and launched a volley of paint bombs and other missiles. The men in the lead vehicle dismounted and started to lay down salvos of rubber bullets as a snatch squad from the rear Pig rushed forward. They managed to capture one of the youths and he was taken back to the RUC Station to be charged.

In an attempt to crack down on the sudden upsurge in the disturbances, the BC devised a plan to teach the youths a lesson. At 8:00 p.m. Operation *Yobbo* swung into action as men from all three troops moved into the estates to confront the rioters. A patrol from 3 Troop, under the command of 'Sydney Slug', was sent out to drive around the area and maintain radio contact with the other units. The patrol was instructed not to get involved in any clashes with the mobs, but to keep a respectable distance and to leave the other patrols to deal with the rioters. Once other units had made contact with the mobs, they were to dismount and confront them and hold station while Sydney Slug's patrol drove into the area and then moved in on foot. The idea was that they would close in on the mobs from behind and attack as the other units started to move forward and drive the rioters back. The units moved in to the estates and it wasn't long before 2 Troop made contact with a large crowd of youths. A radio message was sent to Sydney Slug's patrol to move in and hold station in the next street while 2 Troop drove the rioters back towards them.

Gnr Steve Corbett, 3 Troop

We dismounted and went in on foot. I could hear all the racket in the next street and then gradually the rioters started falling back to where we were waiting for them. 'Sydney Slug' kept coming over to me and grabbing the microphone while he asked for radio checks. You could see by his actions that he was all flustered and unsure what to do. We should have moved in as soon as we saw the rioters falling back, but 'Slug' kept hanging on; then we got spotted and they started to scatter in all directions. We had to get stuck in then and we charged forward. I grabbed hold of a young lad; he could only have been about 12 years old or so. Someone else knocked him to the ground and then he was dragged off towards the Pig by two others. When the other troop saw what was happening, some of them came over and started battering him. There was no need for it. The lad had been captured and was offering no resistance. He was so terrified that he wet himself. It was an awful thing to see, but there wasn't much that I could do to stop it.

That was the only time I ever saw something like this happen. I heard of other things which were supposed to have taken place, but you never knew if it was true. At times we faced extreme provocation, and not everyone can hold back their anger when the chance to retaliate presents itself, but even so, there was no excuse for such behaviour. What I saw that day made me feel ashamed of the actions of some of my comrades.

VICTIMS OF THE TROUBLES WHO DIED THIS DAY...

Elizabeth English (65) – Shot dead by the Provisional IRA. She died seven days after being shot when the IRA attempted to ambush an army foot patrol in Barrack Street, Lower Falls, Belfast.[*]

* List compiled from *The Troubles* Magazine (Glenravel Publications).

FRIDAY 18th...

At approximately 7:30 p.m. a patrol from 3 Troop went out on Operation *Yobbo*. The front Pig was commanded by 'Sydney Slug', with Les as the driver. The rear Pig was being driven by Mick McHale, with Tom McShane acting as Vehicle Commander. The two vehicles spent some time cruising around the estates and then received a call that a man had been shot through both kneecaps; had been tarred and feathered; and dumped in the road opposite the Ulster Brewery. The patrol was immediately dispatched to investigate. There had already been one incident that night when a man had been covered in blue paint and shot through the kneecaps by an IRA punishment squad. The patrol which attended that incident found him lying in the road. Because of the previous shooting, it was expected that this latest incident would be yet another victim of the punishment squads who were out that evening.

In Belfast, terrorists used a dummy filled with explosive in an attempt to injure troops.

A patrol went to Glen Road after reports of a 'body' lying in the road. This turned out to be a dummy and it exploded when the soldiers arrived. Some shots were also fired at the troops. One civilian was injured in the blast.*

* Taken from the author's collection of newspaper cuttings in his Belfast diaries.

The two Pigs arrived at the scene and Sydney Slug's vehicle parked directly opposite – and just 10 feet away from the 'body', which was tied to some railings bordering a school playing field. Tom McShane halted his vehicle some distance short of the 'body' and kept watch. 'Slug' sat there for several minutes wondering what he should do, but it soon became apparent from his actions that he couldn't decide how to deal with the situation. In the end he told one of his men to get out and have a look at the civilian to see if he was still alive.

Gnr Steve Corbett, 3 Troop
I was sat on the left side of the Pig at the front and immediately behind 'Slug'. I was looking over my shoulder at the 'body' tied to the railings and I could see that it was dressed in some kind of military clothing. It was only about the width of the pavement away from our Pig – maybe 10 feet or so – and I think we all knew straight away that it was a bomb. Even though it was quite dark, we could clearly see it was a tailor's dummy dressed up and covered in paint and feathers, but 'Slug' wanted someone to go out and check it anyway. None of us were that keen to get out and take the risk, and me and Albert Manners were arguing about it and trying to tell 'Slug' it was just a dummy and that it was a setup, but he wouldn't listen to us.

In the rear vehicle, the crew watched and wondered what the delay was in checking out the 'body' – and then they heard raised voices as the men in the front vehicle tried to warn 'Slug' that it was a setup. They listened to the heated argument with some amusement, still unaware that the 'body' was, in actual fact, a tailor's dummy.

Gnr Mike Fall, 3 Troop

When we reached the location, the vehicles stopped and Mick McHale turned off the engine. We could hear the other guys in the Pig in front of us arguing about who was going to get out and check this guy tied to the railings. It was really funny at the time, because what we could hear was the guys saying to 'Sydney Slug': *"Well you fucking well get out and have a look then."*

It was pitch-black along the stretch of road, and the area seemed completely deserted. Along the pavement ran a line of trees and the shadows they cast made it even more difficult to make out the figure tied to the railings. Up to that point Tom McShane hadn't even seen the 'body'. He got his torch out and shone it over in the direction of the lead Pig, where he finally picked out the shape of someone dressed in military-style clothing and who had been bound hand and foot. Just at that moment, Tom spotted a drunk staggering down the path towards him and called him over. It was rather obvious to him by then that no-one in the front Pig was prepared to take the risk of leaving the safety of the vehicle and investigate further, so he took it upon himself to send the drunk over to see if the man was still alive.

Gnr Mike Fall, 3 Troop

Tom shone his torch over the 'body' to get a better look, as there were no street lights working, and the night was as black as arseholes. We sat there waiting to get out of the vehicle when Tom called over to a guy who was walking down the road and definitely two sheets to the wind. Tom said to him: *"Go and see if your mate's alright over there."* Seconds passed away when someone, maybe Pete Krasnowski, opened the Pig doors so that we could see what was going on… and then 'BOOOM'; it was a bomb.

From left to right: Mike Fall, Mick 'Titch' Friel and the author. (Courtesy of Mick McHale)

Back in the front Pig, everyone was watching after they heard Tom call the drunk over and begin talking to him. They couldn't hear what was said, but a few moments later the drunk started heading towards the dummy. As he got closer, it suddenly dawned on them that Tom must have assumed the dummy was real and asked the drunk to see if he was alright. Before anyone could stop him, he had almost reached the dummy and there was a blinding flash of light.

Gnr Steve Corbett, 3 Troop

None of us would get out of the Pig to check the 'body', and 'Slug' couldn't decide what to do; then I saw this drunk approaching from the direction of Tom's Pig. The next thing I remember was this bright flash and a rush of air. I didn't hear the bang, but all of a sudden, all this dust entered the Pig. I felt as if I was choking and my ears were ringing like mad; they still do to this day! 'Titch' was thrown to the front of the vehicle and Mick was blinded for a few minutes. The Pig was actually lifted up by the force of the explosion.

I looked at 'Slug' and he was on all fours, which isn't easy to do in the front of a Pig, but he managed it! He kept telling Les to drive on; then he would be telling him to reverse. He was in a right old panic and I thought he looked pathetic the way he was groveling about on the floor; then there were several shots fired at us. I heard them going 'bang-bang-bang'. I don't recall getting out of the Pig, but I must have done because I clearly remember looking down a flight of steps which led to the houses on the estate below – but the gunman had already took off.

Gnr Mike Fall, 3 Troop

There was this brilliant white light and the next thing I remember was silence and me lying in the road that cold night. Sparks were flashing on the tarmac just yards away. I couldn't move and I felt wet down my back; then as I was getting myself together I felt someone running their hands over me. It was Bob Wilson and he was shouting at me. I could see his mouth opening wide and the look of adrenaline running through his face. He told me to get my arse up from the road and back in the Pig. I thought the wet on my back was blood at first, but it turned out to be water from the canister we had in the back of the Pig.

The drunk was found lying in a pool of blood on the pavement with one of his legs pierced by a chunk of railing. At first it was assumed that he had been killed in the explosion, but fortunately for him, as he approached the 'body' he fell against a tree which was between him and the bomb. It was enough to save his life, although he ended up with his leg badly injured.

Gnr Mike Fall, 3 Troop

It had been a stunning few moments. I sat there in the vehicle still trying to get myself together with what seemed like Quasimodo swinging on them bells in Notre Dame Cathedral, when in through the doors of the Pig came this body with Bob Wilson pulling it in. I thought for a moment that the poor bastard was wasted. Bob placed a blanket over him and we set off for Musgrave Park Hospital.

From where Tom was positioned, it would have been impossible for him to tell whether the 'body' tied to the railings was an actual person or a dummy. The only way to find out was to go over to it and check – and no-one in the front Pig seemed prepared to do so. The drunk was approaching the bomb anyway, and it may just be that the short delay caused by Tom calling him over was enough to save his life. When the vehicles reached Musgrave Park Hospital, the attitude of the medical staff towards the injured civilian caused some concern amongst the men.

Gnr Mick McHale, 3 Troop

The Pig I was driving picked the guy up. He had about a yard of one-inch-thick rod stuck through his thigh and into his hip. We picked him up and put him into the back of the Pig, laid flat on the floor. We couldn't get him in a sitting position because of this chunk of metal sticking through his thigh; then we hot-footed it to Musgrave Park Hospital – and when we got there, we gently lifted him out and carried him into emergency. Doctors and nurses came running, and then screeched to a halt when they saw he was a civilian. They didn't want to know and they told us to take him to the Royal Victoria in Belfast, so we loaded him back up and went on our way.

Gnr Mike Fall, 3 Troop

By the time we arrived at the hospital most of us had calmed down a bit, but then it began to sink in what had taken place. As we carried this guy out of the Pig and onto a stretcher, I looked around and noted how busy the medics were. I was asked by the duty doctor if I was OK, and I think I said something like: *"I'll live."* What a bloody night that was.

Gnr Mick 'Titch' Friel, 3 Troop

The drunk was loaded in the back Pig and we set off for Musgrave Park Hospital, but when we got him out of the back of the Pig and carried him inside, the orderlies told us to take him away because he wasn't army. We ended up carrying him back to Tom's vehicle and he was moaning all the time and clutching at his leg. Anyway, we set off for Royal Victoria Hospital and dumped him there for them to sort out.

Gnr Steve Corbett, 3 Troop

I was quite badly shaken by the explosion. I suppose we were all lucky to survive the blast really when you consider how close our vehicle was to it. I don't even remember going to Musgrave Park Hospital or the RVH, but I remember being pretty scared and on edge for the next few days. Even now – after more than 40 years – whenever I hear big bangs, such as at firework displays, I start to think back to that night on the Glen Road.

It had been a very close call. If anyone had left the safety of the vehicles to check the 'body', it is highly likely they would have been killed. Mike Fall and the author both had their hearing badly affected by the force of the blast; it was yet another very close call.

SATURDAY 19th…

VICTIMS OF THE TROUBLES WHO DIED THIS DAY…

David McAuley (14) – A member of the IRA youth wing. He was killed in an accidental shooting, Ardoyne, Belfast.*

* List compiled from *The Troubles* Magazine (Glenravel Publications).

SUNDAY 20th…

At around 2:00 p.m. a patrol left base to carry out car checks around the estates. They toured Riverdale before moving on to Rossnareen, where they met the usual greeting of bricks and bottles laid on by the locals. After a spell on Glen Road, they headed back to base. The vehicles hadn't got that far before they were redirected to Andersonstown Road after reports of a major disturbance. As the patrol made its way up towards the Ulster Bank, they were met by a hostile crowd of about 50 youths who immediately started stoning the Pigs. The bank was blazing away, but the fire brigade couldn't get through because of all the rioting. Eventually, the patrol had no option but to withdraw and return to base. The two vehicles had only been back about 15 minutes before they were sent out yet again to attend the same incident. By now there was a gathering of around 150 people, and the bank was still blazing away. The rioters were strung right across the road and in front of the building – stopping any attempt by the fire brigade to deal with it. The patrol did their best bring the situation under control, but other units were out dealing with various incidents and none could be spared to help them out. Several salvos of rubber bullets were fired, but the situation was getting out of hand and the patrol was forced to withdraw.

That evening, a large search was planned for St Teresa's School up on Glen Road. These operations were always the cause of much resentment to the local population, but unfortunately, the IRA would hide their weapons and explosives anywhere that they thought the troops may not search. Priests and nuns were expected to be neutral in times of conflict, but it was only natural that they would side with their 'flock' and they tended to view the army as an occupying force – and so it was that when carrying out these searches, trouble of some kind was never far away...

Gnr Steve Corbett, 3 Troop

We drew up in the playground of the school and Tom McShane went over to the entrance. This priest came out and started having a go at Tom, calling us all *"Fucking army bastards"* and that kind of thing. I had never heard language like that from a Catholic priest before, and to be honest it was a bit of a shock. I was brought up as a Catholic myself. The priest was comparing us to Oliver Cromwell's troops and that kind of thing – and all the time we were searching, he kept on at Tom. He just reminded me of that firebrand priest, Father Collins, played by Trevor Howard in the film *'Ryan's Daughter.'*

The search continued as the priest followed Tom McShane – and he carried on giving him a hard time. Tom just carried on with the search, smiling at him and apologising for the disruption his men were causing. The search lasted into the early hours of the following day, but nothing was discovered. Another school was once put under surveillance by one of 'Horace's' 'sneaky-beaky' patrols, but unknown to him, there was also a search planned for the same night...

Bdr 'Horace', 2 Troop

During the time I was doing the covert patrols I never – ever – once was compromised, but there was one occasion when I thought I had been, and it was when I had to do a watch on a school after it was suspected that arms or explosives had been hidden in it by the IRA. The BC called me into his office and he told me what he wanted me to do. I was told that a Bdr from 'T' Battery – 'Davey' S******* – who was looking for a bit of action and wanted to come into our area, was going to help out; and me knowing 'Davey', I knew he was a handy lad and it was nice to have him along with me. I got my other two regular lads and I explained to them what I wanted to do, and I also briefed the troop that was taking us out there and told them where I wanted them to drop us off.

We got up to Commedagh Drive and the Pigs slowed down on the bend while we jumped out of the back and made our way over to the waste land in front of the Holy Child School. I waited for a few minutes for the Pigs to disappear and the noise to die down just to make sure we hadn't been spotted. When I was sure everything was alright we moved off and entered the north-east corner of the school-yard through a gap in the fencing. It was nice and dark, fairly late, and all the lights were out and there was plenty of shadow to hide in.

We hadn't been there that long, and all of a sudden the lights started coming on in the buildings. I thought this was a bit unusual, and so I reported it back to base. They didn't seem that bothered and they just told me to keep an eye on it. The next thing is that even more lights came on, and then they started coming on all around the school and not being turned off again. It was starting to get lit up very brightly in the yard where we were, and we had to keep shrinking back into little bits of shadow to stay hidden. The other lads had managed to find a good spot, but I was forced to go forward and I had to take cover under a bicycle shed to stay hidden. There was only about a two-foot gap and it was a bit difficult getting underneath.

I lay there amongst all the rubbish and I watched as it started to get more illuminated as all these lights came on – and then I heard these voices. There were voices in a garden of a house very close to me that backed onto the school, and people were talking rather excitedly. It sounded like the start of Rent-a-Mob getting together, and it started to get noisier as the women started banging their dustbin lids. There was somebody no more than 20 feet away from me, banging a dustbin lid on the concrete, and it was very loud. I started to think that we had been compromised; in fact, I was bloody sure we had been. I decided to pull out, and I got the lads together quickly. We pulled out through the fence and moved back to the waste ground while I radioed through for transport to pick us up.

When I got back to base, I thought I had best go and see the BC and tell him what had happened because he had expected me to be out a long time on this watch. When I walked through the door, he gave me a big smile and said to me: "*Getting too hot for you was it, Bombardier?*" I thought that was a strange comment to make, so I said to him something like: "*Yes, I think I had been compromised Sir,*" and I told him the story – and then he casually said to me: "*Ah yes, one of the other troops was doing a search in the school."* I didn't say anything to him, but I thought: *"Well thank you very much for telling me."*

I would never think anything bad of him – and his decisions *were* absolutely first-class and I had the utmost respect for the man – so whatever he decided to do was good with me.

There is a possibility that the lights which 'Horace' had originally seen coming on was the school janitor doing his rounds – and when he reported the lights, it is possible that another patrol heard their radio message and decided to search the building to check it out. Sometimes there would often be so many patrols out that one patrol may not be aware of the exact location of the others.

MONDAY 21st...

The arrests of Provo volunteers carried on as 9 Battery attempted to round up the last remaining suspects before the end of the tour. Just occasionally, on some lift operations, the patrols would take out a couple of bloodhounds with them along with the dog-handler – and on one operation, two suspects were successfully tracked down to a house and promptly arrested. When they saw the two dogs looming up at them out of the dark they were absolutely terrified, and both seemed to be grateful when they were put in the back of the Pig while the search continued in the house.

The search came to an end, and everyone started to mount up. The two men were made to lay face-down between the benches due to the lack of space – and to the horror of the two suspects, the bloodhounds were put in the back with them. Everyone was packed in like sardines: four soldiers on the bench seats, two suspects on the floor and two great big slobbering bloodhounds stood over their bodies and looking down at them. A look of sheer terror was spreading across their faces as the spittle from the dogs dripped down onto them. For a laugh, someone in the back started grabbing the legs of the suspects – and they thought, for a moment, that they were being attacked by the dogs. Sometimes these operations were almost comical in the way they were carried out. 'Addi' Adamson recalls a search he once took part in while out with 'Sydney Slug':

Gnr Gordon 'Addi' Adamson, 3 Troop

We went out on a search and lift operation one day with 'Sydney Slug' in command. We were looking for a suspected gunman and searched the house we had been sent to, but we couldn't find anything upstairs or down. I was stood there on the landing and 'Slug' looked up at the hatch to the attic, and then he told me to get up and have a look inside. We couldn't find any ladders, so someone lifted me up and I stuck my head inside to have a look around. It was pitch-black up there – there was no light switch – and none of us had a torch either. 'Slug' told me to give my SLR to someone while I climbed up and looked inside, so I got up and I told him again that it was too dark to see anything, so then he told me to move around and use my feet to feel about. I had visions of someone jumping out at me, or me crashing through the ceiling, and it all just seemed so stupid to be searching the attic and not even having a torch. Anyone could have been hiding up there, and I wouldn't even have known about them being there.

Earlier in the day, the Provisional IRA scored an 'own goal' when one of their active service units was transporting a bomb to its target on the outskirts of Belfast. The vehicle used to carry the bomb was completely destroyed when it blew up on the Ballygowan Road. At first it was thought that one of the occupants may have been a woman, but so badly mutilated were the corpses, it was difficult to tell how many people had even been in the car. A pistol was recovered from the side of the road when the wreckage was being removed.

VICTIMS OF THE TROUBLES WHO DIED THIS DAY...

Gerard Steele (27) – Provisional IRA. Blown up in a car while transporting a bomb along the Knockbreda Road, Belfast.

Gerard Bell (20) – Provisional IRA. Killed in the same incident.

Joseph Magee (31) – Provisional IRA. Killed in the same incident.

Robert Dorrian (28) – Provisional IRA. Killed in the same incident.*

* List compiled from *The Troubles* Magazine (Glenravel Publications).

TUESDAY 22nd...

For some time, the Official IRA had been planning a revenge attack on elements of the Parachute Regiment who had taken part in the shooting of 26 civilians at the civil rights march in Derry. The headquarters of 16th Parachute Brigade was at Aldershot Barracks in Hampshire and, despite the security situation in Northern Ireland, it was still very much an 'open' garrison. There were no security checks or access points to try and control who entered or left the camp, and people were free to enter or leave as they saw fit. It was through this total lack of security that the Official IRA were able to launch such a devastating attack. A Ford Cortina packed with an estimated 280lbs of explosives attached to a timer was left parked outside the Officers' Mess. At approximately 12:40 p.m.

it exploded with devastating results. The Officers' Mess building was completely destroyed and several other buildings were badly damaged.

A total of seven people were killed in the explosion, and all of them were civilians. The intended target of the bombers – the Paratroopers – were all stationed abroad at the time; and the remaining staff officers were working from their offices, and so escaped the explosion. Five members of the kitchen staff were just leaving the building as the bomb went off. An elderly gardener and the army chaplain of the regiment also lost their lives. Lieutenant-Colonel Howlett – officer commanding 2nd Battalion, the Parachute Regiment – paid this tribute to Padre Weston, the army chaplain who was killed in the explosion:

> Padre Weston was an absolutely tremendous Roman Catholic priest. He did a tremendous amount to try and bridge the gap between the Catholic community and the Catholic Church and our soldiers, and he was continually going around into Catholic estates to try and achieve this – very often by himself – and obviously completely unarmed and dressed as a priest.[*]

Back in Andersonstown, as in all Nationalist areas, there was much jubilation and celebration as the news of the successful attack reached the Republican community. Those who lost their lives in the bombing were:

Joan Lunn (39)
Cherie Munton (20)
Thelma Bosley (44)
Margaret Grant (32)
Jill Mansfield (34)
John Haslar (58)
Padre Gerry Weston MBE (38) of the Royal Army Chaplains' Department was also killed.[*]

[*] List compiled from *The Troubles* Magazine (Glenravel Publications) and contemporary newspaper reports.

WEDNESDAY 23rd...

Following the explosion at Aldershot the previous day, the Official IRA issued the following statement to the press:

[*] Source taken from the BBC's 'On This Day – 1950-2005' website: http://news.bbc.co.uk/onthisday/hi/dates/stories/february/22/newsid_2519000/2519029.stm

Any civilian casualties would be very much regretted, as our target was the officers responsible for the Derry outrages…

… The bombing would be the first of many such attacks on the headquarters of British Army regiments serving in Northern Ireland.[*]

In the aftermath of the bombing, the Official IRA were subjected to a great deal of criticism because of the large loss of civilian life and by 29 May they decided to call a ceasefire and said that in future they would only attack in self-defence.

The men of 3 Troop had been placed on 10-minute standby for the funeral of four Provos who blew themselves up on Monday 21 February whilst transporting a bomb in a stolen car. One of the four had walked into the Hillfoot Bar near Castlereagh and it appears that as he entered, he recognised someone in the bar and left straight away. He was seen getting into a stolen blue Ford Cortina, which drove off towards the dual carriageway, and shortly afterwards the car was seen to disintegrate in a ball of flame. One of the four men is thought to have been trying to defuse the bomb when it blew up.

The funeral cortege made its way along Leeson Street and paused momentarily while a salvo of shots was fired in a final salute. The military tried to make arrests, which only resulted in angry scenes from the many thousands who were following the procession. Finally, the cortege reached Milltown Cemetery, where the four coffins – draped with the Irish tricolour – were carried through the gates and on to the IRA memorial: the final resting place for many Provo terrorists. The funeral passed off without further incident and 3 Troop stood down. At 9:00 p.m. a mobile took out S/Sgt Burton and his sniper patrol close to the area of the Green Briars Club to drop them off on another of their 'sneaky-beaky' patrols.

Gnr Steve Corbett, 3 Troop

We got them as close as we could to the Green Briars. They weren't going to be out that long as I recall it; all they were doing was monitoring who came and went into the club. Anyway, we left them to it and drove around the estates for a bit to see if anything was going on. At around 10:00 p.m. we were heading back up Shaw's Road on our way to pick up S/Sgt Burton and his patrol, and a single shot was fired at us as we headed towards Glen Road. We didn't bother stopping though, and on the way back I noticed this huge fire at the Catholic Club near Ramoan Gardens. When I got back to camp, I was told that someone had been making bombs and had blown himself up, I remember being really chuffed when I heard that.

---

[*]   Source taken from *The Troubles* Magazine (Glenravel Publications).

DOUBLE EXPLOSION AND FIRE DESTROY CATHOLIC CLUB

A Catholic social club in the Belfast Andersonstown area was destroyed by a double explosion and fire last night, the latest in a series of blasts in the city yesterday.

The premises were known as the Seamus Simpson Club in Gartree Place. Afterwards ambulances stood by as firemen fought the blaze.

Early [sic] today the police reported that no-one had been found in the debris. They were not ruling out the theory that the explosions could have been caused by gas.*

* Sourced from Brian Corser's private collection of newspaper cuttings.

It later transpired that the fire was no accident; it was actually started by a well-known IRA bomb expert, Patrick L********** – also known as 'The Lecturer'. There were rumours that he had fallen out with some other members of the Provisionals who also used the club and he had burned it down in an act of revenge. L********** was linked to many of the bombings and shootings which had happened in Andersonstown, and was high up on the 'wanted' list of 12th Regiment.

THURSDAY 24th...

At around 11:00 a.m. reports started filtering through that an armoured patrol from 9 Battery had just been shot up rather badly in an ambush:

SOLDIER IS SHOT IN THE HEAD BY AMBUSHERS

A soldier was shot in the head today as terrorists ambushed an armoured car patrol in Andersonstown.

Lance-Bombardier John Sutton (28), married, with a four-year-old son, who lives at Middlesborough, was stated to be 'very seriously ill' in the Royal Victoria Hospital.

He was one of a number of soldiers travelling in an armoured car along Bingnian Drive, Andersonstown, when gunmen opened fire from both sides of the road.

The terrorists used a high-velocity weapon and a machine gun. One of the bullets entered the car and hit Lance-Bombardier Sutton on the head.

Three other soldiers in the patrol returned fire but no hits were reported. Later, in a follow-up operation, three youths were detained. They were being questioned by the RUC this afternoon.*

* Source taken from *The Belfast Telegraph*, 24 February 1972.

One of the Pigs was out on a police patrol delivering court summonses when it came under automatic fire from both sides of the road. At first, details were rather sketchy as to exactly what had happened. Initial reports indicated that the ambush had taken place at Kennedy Way roundabout, and then later it was said to have happened on Glen Road near the school. L/Bdr John Sutton was in the back of the Pig with another soldier, acting as guard for the RUC officers who were out delivering court summonses. As the vehicle went down Bingnian Drive, close to Glen Road, they came under heavy automatic fire from both sides of the road. Two of the shots entered the Pig – one of which pierced through the armour plate at the rear of the vehicle – and John was hit in the head. The vehicle immediately set off to Musgrave Park Hospital with the gravely injured Bombardier. At the time, his chances of survival were put at less than 25 percent by the doctors who treated him.

The Padre attached to the battery immediately went to the hospital and sat with L/Bdr Sutton and prayed for him as he lay there in a critical condition, and he stayed by his bedside throughout the night until the following day. The area where the attack took place wasn't even considered to be a dangerous estate, and for the whole of the four-month tour there was only one other incident that took place near there. When the Pig returned to base, it was a terrible mess. The inside of the vehicle was awash with John's blood and a small piece of skull was lying on the bench. The man who had been in the back with L/Bdr Sutton was close to tears and in deep shock by what he had witnessed, and the driver – Joe P**** – was also badly shaken by the experience. John Sutton was his best mate, and he was absolutely distraught by what had happened to him. Joe said that they came under fire and John was looking through the observation slit in the back door. John turned to him and said: "Where's all that blood coming from?" Joe said he looked at John and saw a gaping hole above his right eye – and just at that moment, he collapsed in a heap on the floor of the Pig. The bullet had entered just above the right eye and lodged in the back of his brain. It was all the more tragic as L/Bdr Sutton only had a few weeks to go in the army before he was due to be discharged.

At least 20 to 30 shots had been fired by the gunmen, and one of the bullets had drilled right through the armour plating as though it were made of butter. As word got around about the shooting of L/Bdr Sutton, there was talk of going into the estates and sorting out the locals. The men were determined to have their revenge. This was, by far, the worst injury that anyone from 9 Battery had suffered – and at the time it wasn't even certain if L/Bdr Sutton would survive. Everyone from the battery prepared themselves to go in, but the BC wisely stopped all patrols from leaving the base and gave his men a chance to calm down.

Spare men were drafted in from 58 Battery and 'T' Battery – both from 12th Regiment – while the men of 9 Battery were stood down from all duties. It was a very tense episode and if the men had gone into that area to take it out on the locals, it would have only alienated even more of the community against them. There was less than a month to go to the end of the tour and virtually every day since the men arrived in Andersonstown, they had been subjected to levels of violence on a scale that no-one had ever witnessed before – but their behaviour towards the local population had been exemplary. Even the Provisionals had been forced to acknowledge the unusually good behaviour of the men of 9 Battery in one of their newsletters towards the end of the tour. In the end, commonsense prevailed – and what could have turned into a very serious incident was avoided.

The use of armour-piercing ammunition was, without doubt, a very worrying development for the men who relied on the armoured Pig for their protection while out on patrol. This was the first time that armour-piercing rounds had been used on them, although a quantity had been found in a previous arms search back in January. There had been prior incidents in other units where soldiers had been killed by the use of this ammunition against vehicles, but the military tried to cover up the fact the ammunition was going through the armour by claiming the bullets had entered through open doors or observation slits. The worry was that the Provisionals would use this kind of ammunition even more if they found out it was penetrating the steel plate of the Pigs.

By 6:45 p.m. the situation had calmed down and the men of 9 Battery were allowed back out on patrol. Two Pigs from 3 Troop went out around Rossnareen Estate on the first mobile since the shooting. The locals were still celebrating their latest 'victory' over the soldiers as they entered the estate. As the vehicles made their way around, they were greeted by taunts of: "Sutton's going to die." Details of the shooting had appeared in *The Belfast Telegraph* that evening, and had actually named L/Bdr Sutton – probably because he really wasn't expected to survive. The taunts from the jeering crowds only served to harden the attitude of the soldiers towards the locals even more – and to want to make them pay for what they had done – but mindful of what the BC had said to them, they had to be careful in what they did.

Gnr Steve Corbett, 3 Troop

Despite what the BC had said – and the warnings he had given – most of us were still determined to have a go at the locals for what had happened to Johnny Sutton. We were all really wound up at the way they were celebrating the shooting. As we entered the Rossnareen

Estate, we came under attack from a crowd of youths. We were up near one of the communal car parks, so we drove over and put the two Pigs amongst the other cars and just sat there while they carried on with the bricking and bottling. I had a fag while I was sat there – and we all watched in delight as the cars got wrecked.

After about 15 minutes or so, we decided to move on. The Pigs drove out and we fired a few rubber bullets at some of the youths who had got too close to the back of our Pig and were stoning us. I can still picture the poor bastards scattering as we drove at them with our headlights full-on. Do I feel sorry for our actions that night? Do I hell!

Later in the evening, Clancy Campbell – armed with just a Browning pistol – drove off to Aldergrove Airport in a Mini car accompanied by Sgt Lawson and the Padre to meet L/Bdr Sutton's wife and his mother. His condition was so critical that he couldn't be flown back to England, so his relatives had been flown over to see him at the hospital. At the time it really did look grim for him, and nobody rated his chances of surviving for very long. There had still been no fatalities – and the battery's luck seemed to be holding – but only just. L/Bdr Sutton did eventually pull through, but he was left paralysed down one side of his body.

At 7:50 p.m. several units from the battery headed up to Casement Park after a tip-off about an IRA meeting which was supposed to be taking place. On arrival, there was no sign of any suspicious activity, but four men who arrived at the stadium for training were held for questioning and taken back to the RUC Station.

FOOTBALLERS ARRESTED AT CASEMENT

Four footballers were arrested by the British Army as they arrived at Casement Park, Andersonstown last night to commence a training session. Late last night they were still being held at Andersonstown Police Station.

They included Mr Gilbert McIlhatton, manager of the John Mitchell team.

A club spokesman said the four men had been taken from a Volkswagen car and bundled into a Saracen.

"They were taken away for no reason that anyone could see."

The spokesman added that their legal adviser had been briefed about the arrests.

Earlier, a spokesman for the Association for Legal Justice said that about 12 people had been arrested in the Lower Falls area of Belfast.*

* Sourced from Brian Corser's private collection of newspaper cuttings.

Quite a few 'wanted' cars were pulled in by the cordon set up around the building as the search teams went in. The arrests of the footballers caused further tension between the troops and the locals, and there were minor outbreaks of violence shortly after the men were taken away.

Troops came under fire on several occasions last night, but no-one was injured.

Ten shots were fired at a patrol of The King's Own Scottish Borderers at the junction of the Glen Road and Shaw's Road. Another patrol was fired on at Norglen Drive.[*]

* Taken from the author's collection of newspaper cuttings in his Belfast diaries.

One car failed to stop at the road block, and a Ferret scout car (U42), which was acting as back-up, gave chase down Andersonstown Road. Battery Headquarters (C1) ordered them to turn back, but they ignored the call and carried on with the pursuit. Finally, at Kennedy Way roundabout, the Ferret caught up with the car. They drove into the side of it and forced the driver to swerve off the road. The occupants were dragged out at gunpoint and made to lie down by the side of the Ferret until one of the Pigs could go down and pick them up. Another patrol (Y19) of The King's Own Scottish Borderers got shot up on the edge of 9 Battery's area at the junction of Glen Road and Shaw's Road shortly after the chase, but no-one was hit. While all this activity was going on, 3 Troop continued with the car checks. In the distance could be heard the sound of a gun battle as the Provos fought it out with another army unit somewhere in the city.

FRIDAY 25th…

The ambush of L/Bdr Sutton's vehicle the previous day was a timely reminder to everyone that even the armoured Pigs were no guarantee of their safety. From now on, every time they came under fire, they could never be sure if they too would fall victim to the armour-piercing rounds.

Gnr Gordon 'Addi' Adamson, 3 Troop

I was out on patrol the day after Johnny Sutton got shot with the armour-piercing bullets. I could hear all this shooting going on and I was a bit nervous – and then all of a sudden there was the sound of a machine gun being fired and the bullets were hitting the side of our Pig. I lost my bottle a bit and dropped to the floor because I was worried in case it was armour-piercing bullets again, but when I looked around, everyone else had done the same; we were all on the floor. We got back up, but there was one of us still lying down there. He had completely lost it; his nerve had gone and he wouldn't get back up.

VICTIMS OF THE TROUBLES WHO DIED THIS DAY...

Gerard Doherty (16) – Official IRA. Killed in an accidental shooting, Londonderry.*

* List compiled from *The Troubles* Magazine (Glenravel Publications).

SATURDAY 26th...

The whole of 3 Troop were sent out on a search at 5:00 a.m. in the Rossnareen area after the BC had received a 'hot' tip-off about arms hidden in the vicinity. Again the information turned out to be false, but in one house a large quantity of camouflage-type cloth, which was the same pattern as that used by the army, was found hidden in a room. The search drew to a close and the teams returned to base at around 6:00 a.m. It was around this time that 9 Battery again came in for some criticism over the harsh treatment the locals thought that the soldiers used against 'innocent' youths who were doing nothing more than having a game of football in the street.

ARRESTS – THEN RUBBER BULLET HITS WOMAN

A Belfast woman was struck by a rubber bullet last night after soldiers arrested a group of youths while they were playing football in the street. It happened in Cavanmore Gardens in Andersonstown at about 10pm.

A woman resident said the troops arrived in Saracens. "When I opened the front door I saw the soldiers dragging the youths along the street. They threw them into the Saracens," she said.

"A woman who lives across the street came to her front door to see what was happening. She only came out of hospital about four days ago. She looked after [sic] the Saracens from the door and as she did this a rubber bullet was fired quite deliberately and hit her on the thigh."

Some residents of the street believe that last night's incident may have been in retaliation for a protest local women staged yesterday at La Salle Boys' Intermediate School in Edenmore Drive.

A woman who took part in the protest said: "The army persists in coming to the school just when the boys are leaving twice a day. They have been doing this for months. When the soldiers make finger signs and call the boys 'Fenian Bs' some of the boys throw stones and then the rubber bullets start flying.

"We threatened to keep our children away from school unless the army stayed away. The teachers contacted the army and were told that the soldiers would patrol when and where they wanted."

The woman added: "The BBC sent television people up to cover our demonstration at the school and the army didn't turn up for the first time in months. We'll be back again tomorrow."*

* Sourced from Brian Corser's private collection of newspaper cuttings.

Although it may have appeared to the residents that the soldiers were deliberately antagonising the youths, it simply wasn't the case. Patrols often came under attack during school hours while driving past; it was just some kind of 'game' to them. The claim by the residents that the group of youths were simply out playing a game of football on that particular evening also takes some believing. One only has to look at the time the game supposedly took place to realise it was probably just another attempt to tarnish the reputation of the army.

SUNDAY 27th...

At the top end of the bus depot, Albert Manners was busy pacing around in the Divis Drive sangar as he waited for his sentry duty to finish. His impatience finally got the better of him and he entered the accommodation block of 3 Troop to see if his relief was getting ready to take over from him.

Gnr Steve Corbett, 3 Troop

It was just before 8:00 a.m. and I had dragged myself out of bed to get ready for my stint of guard duty. I was sat on my wooden locker at the foot of my bunk-bed when Albert walked in to make sure I was up to relieve him. I was sat there tying my laces when he walked over and started chatting to me. He had the barrel of his rifle resting on his foot as he spoke to me – and all of a sudden there was a deafening bang as his rifle went off. I sat there stunned. I was convinced that I had been shot. I looked up at Albert and saw the look of horror on his face. By now, other men in the room were jumping out of their bunks – thinking that we had come under attack.

Bob Wilson was in the process of getting dressed when the shot rang out. He picked up his rifle and dashed outside – thinking that was where the shot had come from – but he went sprawling in the shingle outside the building as he tried to get his other leg in his underpants; but Albert just stood there, looking down at his foot.

Gnr Steve Corbett, 3 Troop

I checked myself over to see if I was alright and then looked again at Albert. He was staring intently at his right foot. It gradually dawned on me what had happened, and I got Albert to remove his boot and sock. Just below his big toe was a small purple ring where the bullet had passed through his foot and on the underside was a large jagged hole. After seeing to him I removed the liner of his boot, which was embedded with slithers of bone, and I hung it on our 'trophy wall' with the rest of our souvenirs.

This incident was a timely reminder to all of the need to follow correct safety procedures when handling a weapon. The only time a round of ammunition was supposed to be in the breech of a gun was when the intention was to fire that weapon. At all other times the chamber was to be kept empty and the safety catch on. The punishment for negligent discharge of a weapon was usually a £40 fine – and at that time, it was a considerable amount of money for a soldier to lose. There was another occasion when a patrol had returned to the RUC Station, and when the men dismounted from the Pig, one of the men managed to put a round through his foot while making his weapon safe. There were some soldiers who did it deliberately just so that they would get sent back home to England. It was always a difficult thing to prove, but it certainly did happen.

Later that evening, a patrol led by Sgt 'Punchy' Wilmot entered Falls Park at the back of the bus depot. A long wall ran along one section between a pavilion and a swimming pool, and part of it was in a state of disrepair. Intelligence had advised that there may be an attack launched by Provo gunmen on this particular night, and so it was decided to send out a patrol and monitor the area just in case.

Gnr Steve Corbett, 3 Troop

It was fairly late on when 'Punchy' led us out and into the park. The place was in complete darkness and you could hardly make anything out. We came to this wall which was around six feet high and part of it had fallen down. About 100 yards behind us was the bus yard at the depot, and all you could see was the security lights pointing out towards the park. It was just a wall of light and it made it impossible to see into the compound. 'Punchy' started placing the men from the patrol where he wanted them so that the breach in the wall could be monitored, and we all settled down to watch. The night passed on and then the dawn chorus of birds started up, and then I gradually started to pick out other members of the patrol where they had been placed. I was horrified at what I saw. 'Punchy' had placed us all more or less in a circle around this gap in the wall. If a gunman had stepped through and we had opened up, we would have shot ourselves to pieces!

MONDAY 28th...

The patrols continued probing the estates as the men of 9 Battery pressed on with their searches for weapons. That evening, a foot patrol entered the area around Glassmullin Gardens and started working through the back gardens towards the area of Rossnareen. They hadn't got far before they were spotted; they came under attack from youths and had to beat a hasty retreat.

TUESDAY 29th...

VICTIMS OF THE TROUBLES WHO DIED THIS DAY...

Sgt Henry Dickson (46) – 2nd Battalion, The Ulster Defence Regiment. Shot dead at home by the Provisional IRA, Lawrence Street, Lurgan, County Armagh.*

* List compiled from *The Troubles* Magazine (Glenravel Publications).

7

MARCH
The capture of two top Provos

WEDNESDAY 1st…

At around 2:00 a.m. the Battery were involved in a large search in Rossnareen Avenue. 3 Troop were given two areas to cover, and to aid the search they took along 'Sniffer' the bloodhound. The search continued until about 5:00 a.m. but nothing was found. A little later, 3 Troop were out again on another lift operation in Tullymore Gardens, where they arrested a suspect. The man had only recently started attending IRA meetings and had just joined the Provisionals a few days before he was detained. Speed was the essence when carrying out these operations, and in many cases the soldiers were working from tip-offs. It wasn't unknown for soldiers to be hammering on the front door of a house while the suspects made their escape through the attic into the adjacent property.

Gnr Phil Gallagher, 3 Troop
I remember one lift I went on and when we got to the house, we couldn't get anyone to answer the door. The correct military term for our boots was: *"Boots, ankle-length, DMS,"* but I started to call mine 'the Belfast Boot' because if we got to a house and they wouldn't open the door, I would use the 'spare key': my 'Belfast Boot'. It was a surefire way to wind up the locals, but we really had no choice if they wouldn't open the door. We had to get into the property as quickly as possible, and that was what I did this time; they didn't open up and I kicked the door in and we made the arrest.

At 2:00 p.m. the mobile patrol of C13 went out on one final operation with C12. This was to be a combined mobile / lift operation. The instructions were to drive around the area for an hour and then proceed to 20 Tullymore Gardens, where intelligence claimed there would be four Provos of interest to them. The men of 2 Troop (C12) were to supply the cordon while 3 Troop carried out the lift.

Gnr Steve Corbett, 3 Troop

We got to the house and carried out the lift, but we only found one man. While we were in there, a crowd of around 150 had gathered outside and were giving 2 Troop an absolute pasting. When we came out of the house with the suspect, we ended up getting hammered too. Someone must have sent out a request for help, because a few minutes later Bob Thompson turned up with a couple of Pigs from 1 Troop. They started putting down a barrage of rubber bullets as we all made our way back to the Pig with our prisoner. It was a bit of a scary moment, that one.

Meanwhile, in another part of the area covered by the regiment, one of the patrols had much better luck…

TOP IRA BOMB EXPERT CAUGHT

A Provisional IRA explosives expert who eluded an army raid in Belfast two months ago was captured by troops last night.

Today security chiefs were regarding the capture of the fugitive as an important breakthrough in the fight against terrorism. His name was on the top of the wanted list until last night when soldiers raided a house in Turf lodge.

Men of the 12th Light Air Defence Regiment, Royal Artillery, found him hiding in the attic of the house. The man, described as 'The Lecturer', made off through a garden before troops could get to him – but they detained seven of his 'pupils'.

But last night the vital breakthrough in the hunt came when the army was told he was hiding in a house in the Turf Lodge area. Armed troops surrounded the house as a search party began searching rooms and wardrobes.

It was only when they moved into the attic that they spotted the man cowering in the darkness. The search for the elusive 'Lecturer' was over.*

* Sourced from Brian Corser's private collection of newspaper cuttings.

The search for Patrick L********** had been going on since his escape from the bungalow in Slievegallion Drive on 6 January. He was implicated in many of the incidents which had occurred in Andersonstown, and was also believed by intelligence to have burned down the Catholic Club on 23 February in an act of revenge against some fellow Provo members he had fallen out with. When he was eventually found in the attic, he was hiding underneath a pile of old blankets in the far corner of the roof space. His legs were badly burned – presumably from the fire he started at the Catholic Club. Lieutenant Barry S****** from 1 Troop gave the bomber a 'piggyback' down to the waiting vehicle and laid him face-down between the seats. He was trembling, and had a look of absolute terror on his face.

Gnr Clancy Campbell, 1 Troop
I was there when we found him. He was lay there shaking like a leaf when we grabbed hold of him. I remember dragging him down to the loft access. We grabbed him by his legs and lowered him down. He was screaming because of the burns to his legs, and then Lt S****** carried him out to 'Addi' Adamson's Pig and they laid him face-down. Then the bastard went and shit himself because he was that terrified of what we might do to him.

When the patrol arrived back at the RUC Station there was a reception committee waiting for him – and he was promptly hauled upstairs to the interview room. They made him stand and he complained about his legs being weak because of the burns. He made a sudden move and 'Punchy' Wilmot thought he was trying to have a go at one of the guards, and so he ran his boot down the back of one of his legs to bring him down. He started screaming in pain; then 'The Lecturer' began to talk. It may just be a coincidence, but it was only a few days later that Brendan McNamee was finally captured as well. The search team knew exactly where to go for him.

VICTIMS OF THE TROUBLES WHO DIED THIS DAY...

Pte John Fletcher (43) – 4th Battalion, The Ulster Defence Regiment. Abducted and shot dead in front of his wife outside his home by the Provisional IRA, Frevagh, County Fermanagh.

John Mahon (16) – Shot dead by the RUC while travelling in a stolen car in Belfast city centre. The car was left abandoned outside the Royal Victoria Hospital.

Michael Connors (14) – Killed in the same incident. Both men were found inside the vehicle after it had been abandoned.*

* List compiled from *The Troubles* Magazine (Glenravel Publications).

THURSDAY 2nd...

MYSTERY EXPLOSION ON M1

Several windows in an Ulsterbus bus travelling along the M1 motorway, near Stockmans Lane, have been smashed by a mystery explosion. The RUC and army were waiting until daylight to investigate the incident.*

* Source taken from *The Troubles* Magazine (Glenravel Publications).

A mobile was sent out to check the scene of the explosion. It was suspected that it may have been a trap laid by the Provos to lure the troops into an ambush, but after an initial search of the area, they withdrew. It was around this time that Mick Krasnowski placed one of his biggest bets ever on a horse. Throughout the tour he had this arrangement with one of the Protestant workers at the bus depot: Mick would pick his horse and hand over the money to the engineer, who would place the bet for him. Up to now, the arrangement had worked very well and Mick had amassed over £1,000 in winnings. He decided to have one last big bet before returning to England and placed £1,000 on his horse to win. It came romping home and he won £34,000. That was an absolute fortune at that time and he was unequivocally ecstatic. He waited and waited for his contact to bring his winnings, but he never showed up. A patrol checked his house out in the Shankill area, but it appeared to be deserted. Mick never did get his winnings, and the engineer was never seen again. The temptation to keep the winnings must have been too great for him. It was either that, or he had never placed the bets in the first place. The man knew the regiment was returning to England in a matter of days, so all he had to do was lie low for a while.

Surveillance operations were still being maintained on the Green Briars Club in the hope of catching more suspects, but one night while on patrol at the back of the clubhouse, 'Davey' S******* stumbled upon a milk churn by the edge of the car park...

Bdr 'Davey' S*****, 'T' Battery (Shah Sujah's Troop)**
We were out on patrol one night and we moved to the back of the Green Briars to check it out; then next minute we stumble on this bomb hidden in a milk churn and we had the bomb disposal blokes come out to it. Because we were first on the scene, we had to look after the bomb disposal team when they came, so this bomb disposal bloke turned up – and he only looked about 12 years old – and he says to me: *"Where is it?"* so I walks him down to this milk churn and

he has a look at it – and then he says: *"I've got a problem here, I've never seen one of these like this before"* and I said: *"Well thank you very much"* – and I'm stood right next to the bloody thing and he's telling me he doesn't know how to deal with it! In the end he carried out a controlled explosion on it.

VICTIMS OF THE TROUBLES WHO DIED THIS DAY...

Thomas Morrow (28) – The Royal Ulster Constabulary. He died two days after being shot by the Official IRA while checking a break-in at a factory in Newry, County Down.*

* List compiled from *The Troubles* Magazine (Glenravel Publications).

FRIDAY 3rd...

TROOPS CATCH THREE TOP PROVISIONALS

Three leading IRA Provisionals and a number of volunteers, including some believed to be explosive experts, were detained by troops in Belfast last night.

The three top terrorist suspects detained during raids on a number of homes in the city are thought to be: the Commander of the Ballymurphy Battalion of the Provisionals; a Company Commander from Andersonstown; and a top explosives officer from the Ardoyne Company of the Provisionals.

Soldiers from different regiments raided other homes and detained a number of Provisional IRA volunteers. Two of these are believed to be explosive experts.

Troops and police working on fresh intelligence information searched homes at Ardoyne, Ballymurphy and Andersonstown, but Security Forces did not give any further details.

"This is a really good capture. We have been looking for these men for some time," said a spokesman. No details about the number of men detained has been given by the Security Forces, but it is thought that at least 10 were held.

All the men are now being questioned, but it is not known if charges will be brought against any of them. It is known, however, that the army has been looking for several known IRA men for weeks.

Security chiefs are regarding last night's captures as another important breakthrough in their increasing pressure on terrorists in Belfast following recent fatal bomb blasts. No trouble was reported during the raids.[*]

* Source taken from *The Belfast Telegraph*, 4 March 1972.

One of the men captured in Andersonstown was Brendan McNamee. The men of 9 Battery had been after him since they had arrived last November, and he was widely suspected of involvement in many incidents which had taken place throughout Andersonstown. It was only days since they had captured Patrick _********** and to have McNamee in the bag so close to the end of the tour was an added bonus. McNamee eventually died at the hands of the Official IRA on the 5 June 1975. He was rumoured to be involved in the killing of Billy McMillen - a top man in the Official IRA.

The manner in which the suspects were arrested in Andersonstown over the past days led to talk amongst certain circles about how well behaved the soldiers of 9 Battery were. This led to the publication of an article in one of the Provo papers which was circulated throughout the district. For the Provisionals to be forced into accepting that the men of 9 Battery were behaving in such an exemplary fashion must have been hard for them take, but they could hardly deny the rumours being heard around Andersonstown. In their statement in *The Volunteer*, they tried to put a different slant on the claims being made around the Riverdale Estate:

NOTHING PERSONAL
It is not very often we commend British military personnel for their attitude towards any of our people.

Truth, however, is the best weapon we have and we must comment favourably on the units who were engaged on the raids in the Riverdale Estate on Wednesday night. From what we hear they were almost apologetic and were certainly much better behaved than we have become accustomed to expect from 'our protectors'. Could it be that at least some of them are beginning to realise just how they are being used and for what reason?

Unfortunately we will probably find that they will be injured in the next engagement or the one after that. If they read this we would like to thank them for their concern and to assure them that if they are injured or killed there is nothing personal in it...[*]

* Source taken from *The Volunteer*.

The Battery Commander had always insisted that when dealing with the public, he expected his men to show the utmost courtesy at all times. They had to refer to them as 'Sir' or 'Madam' whatever provocation they may find themselves under. Obviously this approach must have worked, judging by the response from the Provisionals.

Throughout the tour, there were numerous calls made to the RUC Station that the bus depot was going to be bombed or shot up. In the end the men reached the point where they just ignored any warnings as another hoax call. A search would still have to be carried out, but the sense of urgency would be somewhat lower. Security was as tight as it could possibly be, and it seemed inconceivable that anyone would be able to breach it. Early in the evening of 3 March two separate calls were made to the RUC Station. The first one claimed that a bomb would go off between 8:00 p.m. and 9:00 p.m. and the second was a bit more vague and just said that there would be a large bomb explosion in Andersonstown. Everyone made a check of the immediate area to see if anything could be found. The Battery Quartermaster, Joe T*****, had other things on his mind… He had a rather large kit deficiency from the store, and he didn't know how he was going to account for the missing items.

Gnr Steve Corbett, 3 Troop

We got hauled out of our billet and were told to check the engineering workshops for anything suspicious. As far as I remember, we checked to about half-way down while 2 Troop checked from the bottom end. Hoax or not, it was a bit unnerving when you were trying to find a hidden bomb. What if it exploded while you were next to it? All these thoughts went through your head.

Gnr 'Sammy' Symonds, 2 Troop

We were searching the front of the depot for this bomb that was supposed to have been planted, and then one of the 'Thomas twins' spotted a black bus conductor's box hidden underneath a trailer. He went over to it and picked it up to have a closer look. He lifted the lid and looked inside, but someone screamed at him to leave it alone. I was only about two or three yards away from him when he spotted it.

Gnr Pete Roberts, 2 Troop

I spotted the bomb and ran inside the main workshop to get away from it. I had only just got inside when it went up with a huge bang. The roller door ended up all bent and buckled, but it had saved me from the force of the blast.

Gnr 'Snowy' H***, 2 Troop

I was just inside the main building of the depot and we were told to start searching the buses for this bomb that was supposed to have been planted. The other 'Thomas twin' was with us and larking about on a bus. He pressed the bell, and right at that moment the bomb went off.

BUS DEPOT BOMBED

Earlier, another soldier was slightly injured when a bomb exploded inside the Falls Road bus depot where some soldiers are billeted. The bomb was taken into the depot inside a conductor's box, but it was spotted before it went off and the area was evacuated. The injured soldier was cut by flying glass when the bomb shattered windows. Two trailers were also wrecked by the blast, caused by an estimated 10lb charge of gelignite.*

* Taken from the author's collection of newspaper cuttings in his Belfast diaries.

The aftermath of the bomb attack. (Courtesy of Brian Corser)

Outside in the courtyard, it was a scene of absolute devastation. There was a hole in the ground about one foot deep where the trailer had stood. The trailer was completely destroyed, with its contents adorning the branches of the nearby trees like some macabre version of Christmas decorations. All the windows of the old house were blown out. The new showers which had only been fitted a matter of days before were wrecked. Inside the mess room, the colour TV was still blaring away on the shelf. Personal belongings ruined; the flying shards of glass had shredded almost everything. Miraculously, there was only one casualty; the guard in the sangar on the roof of the house received a slight cut to his face.

As for the Quartermaster, he appeared to be the only man happy with the outcome of the bombing. His kit deficiencies were literally wiped out; his worries of how he would be able to cover up the missing items were over. The Provisionals were cock-a-hoop at this rare success on a military base. They had managed to breach the defences of the depot and detonate a bomb, and it was a huge embarrassment to the military. Later that evening a property in nearby Fruithill was raided and the suspected bomber was arrested. Earlier in the day there had been a bomb attack at an office in Kells Avenue, Andersonstown. Four youths turned up in a stolen car. They broke a window and placed a 15lb bomb inside, but fortunately for the owners, the fuse burned out before it had a chance to detonate the device.

VICTIMS OF THE TROUBLES WHO DIED THIS DAY...

Pte Stephen Keating (18) – The Queen's Lancashire Regiment. Shot dead by a Provisional IRA sniper while on foot patrol, Manor Street, Belfast.*

* List compiled from *The Troubles* Magazine (Glenravel Publications).

SATURDAY 4th...

The huge clean-up operation taking place at the bottom end of the depot continued as the men tried to restore some normality after the previous day's bomb attack. The old house was virtually uninhabitable, and the Royal Engineers were brought in to carry out emergency repairs so that 2 Troop would be able to move back into the building as soon as possible. There were now only 11 days to go before the end of the tour, but the attacks on 9 Battery continued as the Provos tried to claim their first 'kill' before the regiment returned to England. Earlier, six people were found tarred and feathered on a patch of ground adjacent to the Busy Bee shops. Patrols were still out in force – trying to round up the last suspects on the 'wanted' list before the tour drew to a close. Two lift ops were undertaken by 3 Troop at 2:45 p.m. but neither produced any results. Shortly after 4:00 p.m. they were out again to pick up the sniper patrol of S/Sgt Burton. There were also reports of an Austin 1100 saloon with four occupants who were acting suspiciously.

The two Pigs toured around Riverdale to see if they could spot the car, and then they entered onto Finaghy Road North and headed up to the Andersonstown Road junction. The lead Pig had just turned left onto Andersonstown Road when there was a burst of automatic fire – possibly from a Bren gun sited on the opposite side of the road towards the bottom end of Tullymore Gardens. There were two more gunmen positioned up on the hill in front of St Joseph's College. Fire poured down on both Pigs as they were caught in the crossfire.

Gnr Steve Corbett, 3 Troop

I was sat in the back of the lead Pig with my mate, 'Scouse' Coulson. We rounded the corner, and then all this shooting broke out. 'Scouse' was sat on the left of the Pig and me on the right near the back doors – and as soon as the shooting started, 'Scouse' sort of threw himself across the Pig and landed on top of me. I ended up with my head stuck against the firing slit for a few moments as 'Scouse' kept leaning back and fiddled with his rifle. I could hear the smack of the bullets hitting the armour plate, but I couldn't see what was going on because of 'Scouse' leaning back on me.

The shooting only lasted a few moments, but in that short time there were an estimated 50 shots fired at the patrol. The crew of the rear vehicle returned fire, but no hits were claimed. After a short search of the area, the two vehicles continued on their way to pick up S/Sgt Burton and his patrol – and by 4:45 p.m. they were back at base.

Gnr Steve Corbett, 3 Troop

After we got back to the depot, I had a look at the side of the Pig to see where the bullets had struck and I was horrified to see that at least one of the bullets had hit the lip of the firing slit. Another fraction lower and it would have probably hit my head.

It was thought that the unit which ambushed the patrol were probably the same ones which shot up the police Pig when L/Bdr Sutton was critically injured on 24 February. In the city centre, another horrific bomb attack had taken place just minutes before the ambush on 3 Troop. The target of the latest outrage was the Abercorn Restaurant, owned by Bill O'Hara, an Irish Catholic. The building comprised of a ground-floor restaurant and upstairs bar, and was situated in Castle Lane in the heart of the Cornmarket area of Belfast. At 4:28 p.m. a 999 phone call was made, warning that a bomb would go off in Castle Lane in five minutes. At the time of the bombing, the area was packed with Saturday shoppers.

At 4:30 p.m. a handbag containing about 5lbs of gelignite exploded under a table in the restaurant – killing Janet Bereen and Anne Owens outright. A further 130 people were badly injured. Two sisters, Rosaleen and Jennifer McNern, were gravely injured in the explosion. Rosaleen, who was due to be married, lost both her legs, her right arm and an eye. Jennifer lost both legs.

No terrorist organisation ever admitted to carrying out the bombing, but both the RUC and British Military Intelligence blamed the Provisional IRA. It is now generally accepted that it was the work of 1st Battalion, Belfast Brigade, and at the time there was much public anger from the Catholic communities following the bombing. The two women killed and the two gravely injured were all Catholic, and so were many of the injured. Some Republican sources later claimed that the restaurant was blown up because off-duty British soldiers were known to use the upstairs bar.

At around 7:45 p.m. back in Andersonstown, two more lift operations were carried out, but again without any success. There was to be one more lift operation that night…

The BC had dreamed up a plan to raid the Green Briars Club just off Glen Road. The idea was to surround the building and then alert the staff that it was about to be raided by the Security Forces. Operation *Cotton Wool* finally swung into action at around 10:30 p.m. Two patrols from 2 and 3 Troop made their way up Glen Road and pulled up some distance away from the turning which led up to the club. The men who were detailed to make up the cordon dismounted and made their way up to the clubhouse and took up their positions and waited. Back at the RUC Station, Paddy Keane from 2 Troop phoned up the club and told the steward at the bar that 'the Brits' were sending troops up to the club to raid it. Paddy was from Southern Ireland, and no-one would doubt the authenticity of his accent.

Gnr Steve Corbett, 3 Troop

We made our way up to the club and took up our positions. It was bloody freezing as well. The frost was coming down like tiny particles of dust and covering everything white. I think we had been lying there for about an hour when suddenly the front door of the club burst open and three men came rushing out.

The men were immediately apprehended and one of the Pigs came roaring up the track to take them away. The ruse had worked a treat.

VICTIMS OF THE TROUBLES WHO DIED THIS DAY...

Marcus McCausland (39) – Former member of the Ulster Defence Regiment. Shot dead by the Official IRA. He was found dead on the Braehead Road, Derry.

Janet Bereen (21) – Killed in the Abercorn Restaurant bombing.

Anne Owens (22) – Killed in the same incident.

Albert Kavanagh (18) – Provisional IRA. Shot dead by the RUC while attempting to blow up the telephone exchange in Boucher Road, Belfast.*

* List compiled from *The Troubles* Magazine (Glenravel Publications).

SUNDAY 5th...

In the early hours of Sunday morning, a phone call was made to the RUC Station claiming that an attack was about to be launched on the base. Everyone was put on a high state of alert and extra guards were posted around the perimeters just in case. As the bomb explosion on 3 March had shown, not every call was a hoax and you could never afford to drop your guard or ignore any warnings issued. By lunchtime nothing had happened and the decision was taken to stand down the extra guards. Life around the base returned to normal and the patrols were resumed. A short time after the all-clear was given, a unit from 3 Troop left the depot and travelled up to Stockmans Lane on a routine mobile patrol. The vehicles turned out of Owenvarragh Park and made the short trip up Andersonstown Road before turning into Riverdale Park. They slowly made their way through and turned into Finaghy Road North and again headed up to the junction with Andersonstown Road. What happened next was a carbon copy of the ambush which happened the day before...

Gnr Steve Corbett, 3 Troop

I was travelling with Dick Rothwell in the rear Pig and Pete Krasnowski was the Vehicle Commander. I had already made my mind up when we left base that if we went anywhere near the Training College that I would cock my rifle and put one up the spout just in case anything happened.

The patrol reached the junction of Finaghy Road North and Andersonstown Road and started to negotiate the corner towards the Shaw's Road junction. Almost unbelievably they were ambushed yet again. Pete Krasnowski recalled the incident at a regimental reunion back in 2008:

L/Bdr Pete Krasnowski, 3 Troop

We had just got around the corner and the shooting started. There was a guy up on the hill firing down at the side of our vehicle. He just kept firing these short bursts at me from a Thompson. He was a short fat guy with thick-rimmed glasses and wearing a beret. I couldn't get my rifle to my shoulder to take aim, so I just stuck the barrel out of the door hatch and pointed it towards where he was and started firing.

Pete used practically a full magazine as he fired back at the gunman, but it didn't seem to have any effect whatsoever. The Provo just carried on firing the Thompson in short bursts at Pete's vehicle. Dick Rothwell had spotted the same gunman and managed to get off two shots before he got a stoppage. On the opposite side of the vehicle, the author returned fire at another gunman situated on the housing estate.

Gnr Steve Corbett, 3 Troop

We left Riverdale and made our way up to the junction – and just as we started turning left, the shooting started. I don't know why I did it, but I was already crouching down low as the Pig made the turn. I suppose I was just expecting to get shot at again. I think we were all a bit jumpy by that time, and when the shooting started I wasn't in the least bit surprised. When the Pig came to a halt I popped up and looked out of the firing slit. There was a girl lying in the road, and at first I thought she had been hit by the bullets fired at our vehicle. Another woman was pushing a pram and started running to get out of the way. All the time there was this noise from the bullets hitting the armour plate; it was like a loud 'splat' sound as they flattened out. I saw evidence of shots being fired from the direction of Tullymore Gardens and I put 12 rounds back at the gunmen. They were behind a low wall in front of the houses just across the green.

The noise inside the Pig from mine and Pete's rifles was incredible. The stench of cordite was quite strong, and all you could hear inside was the 'bang-bang-bang' of our rifles and the clatter of the empty cases as they flew out of the weapons. Dick Rothwell was still busy clearing the stoppage in his gun as me and Pete fired back. The shooting probably only lasted a few moments, but it didn't feel like that at the time; and then the firing stopped, and there seemed to be absolute silence for a few moments. I must admit that at the time I was quite excited; you tend to get caught up in the thrill of it all while it's happening, but when it's all over and you think about it, you realise how lucky you were. We moved off up the Stewartstown Road and came around the roundabout and back down. There was a man being picked up off the road. I thought he was dead at first, but it later turned out that he was suffering from severe shock.

Pete Krasnowski fired 16 rounds at the Provo on the hill, but none of them found their mark. It was estimated that there were three gunmen involved, and they were probably the same men who had launched the attack the day before. A total of 65 rounds were fired at the gunmen by the patrol, but no hits were claimed.

Gunmen fired between 50 and 70 shots at an army patrol yesterday during an ambush in the Andersonstown area.

The army said that four gunmen opened up on a patrol of the 12th Light Air Defence Regiment from the area of St Joseph's Training College and Killeen Park at the corner of Andersonstown Road and Finaghy Road North.

Troops returned the fire, but no hits were reported and no soldiers were injured. The fusillade of shots were heard over a wide area.*

* Taken from the author's collection of newspaper cuttings in his Belfast diaries.

The shooting started to die down and then stopped altogether – and then people started to filter back onto the road. A man was carried towards a house and at first it was thought that he had been shot, but he was only suffering from severe shock. The young girl who had been lying in the road was also found to be unharmed. It was a miracle that no-one was injured or killed by the indiscriminate shooting carried out by some of the gunmen, but that Provo stood on the hill really had some guts to do what he did that day. The ambush had again only lasted just a matter of minutes, but it had been a very intense and very frightening situation to be caught up in. After a quick inspection of the area for empty cases, the patrol returned to base at around 4:00 p.m. In 2014, the author had the opportunity to discuss the incident with a former IRA member who lived in Andersonstown at the time. Although he never claimed to have been involved in the attack, he was able to indicate to the author the locations of the IRA volunteers who took part in the ambush.

Two ambushes in two days were enough to test the nerves of anyone. There were now just less than two weeks to go before the end of the tour and many of the men were beginning to wonder whether they would get to the end of it in one piece. Their luck seemed to be holding out and there had still been no fatalities amongst their ranks. Every single man in the battery had, at some time or other, been either shot at or involved in a life-threatening situation – and this really did make them think that the next patrol could be their last. Earlier in the tour, there had been another shooting incident where a Provo gunman had engaged in an exchange of fire with a mobile patrol near the Busy Bee – and on that occasion the gunman had also shown that he wasn't easily put off by return fire...

Gnr Phil Gallagher, 3 Troop
We were driving up Andersonstown Road and were just approaching the shops at the Busy Bee when Pete Krasnowski spotted someone walking down towards a brick wall at the side of the shops. Pete decided to pull over and check him out, but as soon as we stopped, the next instant this bloke popped up from behind the wall and opened fire on us.

The shops were on the right side of the Pig and this made it impossible for Pete Krasnowski to return fire from the Vehicle Commander's seat, so he dismounted and took up a firing position close to the front of the vehicle. He recalled the incident many years later and said that he did it "so that I could see what the hell I was firing back at." He urged the rest of the men to join him, but no-one was prepared to leave the safety of the vehicle while the shooting was still going on.

Gnr Phil Gallagher, 3 Troop
The gunman fired about six to 10 shots and ducked back behind the wall. We opened up on him and then stopped firing, and then he pops out again and fires some more shots at us. We fired at him again through the slits in the Pig. I myself got off about three shots at him. It's hard to describe how it feels when you can actually see the person who is firing at you. The shooting finally stopped, and so we waited a few minutes and then we all piled out of the back of the Pig and ran down to where the gunman had been. He was gone, but we could see all the spent shell cases on the floor behind the wall. I remember thinking what a pity it was we didn't get him.

The exchange of fire only lasted a few minutes and fortunately no-one was injured in the shooting, but it was a timely reminder that some of the Provisionals were determined and brave fighters. Following the bombing of the Abercorn Restaurant the previous day, the Provisionals came in for heavy criticism from both Protestant and Catholic communities for this latest atrocity they had carried out. The pressure was building up on them to hold a ceasefire and to try and reach a political solution. The bombing was further proof that the Provisionals were not too concerned about the safety of the very people they claimed to be trying to protect: the Catholic community.

In Dublin, the Independent Unionist MP Mr Tom Caldwell held secret talks with high-ranking members of the Provisional IRA and suggested to them that f they were to hold a ceasefire, it may encourage the British Government to hold talks with them. They finally reached an agreement and the Provisional IRA ssued a statement saying that from midnight on 10 March there would be a 72-hour truce.

MONDAY 6th…

Operation *Basset-Hound* was out on the streets again as the hunt continued for the top men of the IRA. By now the deployment of these special patrols was beginning to pay dividends. The Provos out on the streets could never be sure if the Pigs approaching were just another mobile patrol or the snatch teams of *Basset-Hound*. Two Pigs were cruising up Andersonstown Road when the intelligence officer in the lead vehicle spotted a Provo high up on the 'wanted' list. Bdr 'Davey' S******* from 'T' Battery recalls the incident which took place:

Bdr 'Davey' S*******, 'T' Battery (Shah Sujah's Troop)

I was out with Clancy Campbell on *Basset-Hound* somewhere up Andersonstown Road and Corporal Tony W******** from REME was acting as our back-up for when we needed it. A message came through from the lead Pig that the intelligence officer had spotted the Quartermaster for 'A' Coy, PIRA and he wanted him lifting. We had a look through the viewing slit in the back door and picked him out; he only looked a young bloke. Anyway, me and Clancy sprung out of the back of our Pig in our civvy clothes and gave chase. He turned around and saw us coming and tried to make a run for it. There was a bus coming past and he jumped on it to try and get away, so I jumped on after him and then Clancy jumped on as well.

I ran upstairs after this bloke to get him and Clancy pulled out his .32 pistol and said to the bus conductor: "*Stop the bus, I'm in the army.*" Then the bus conductor does no more but kicks Clancy off the bus and I'm left on my own with this bloke upstairs and with everyone staring at me. It was a pretty scary moment for me knowing I was on my own amongst all these people; then I see Clancy running behind trying to get back on the bus and waving his pistol in the air. I wrestled with this bloke and I managed to get him down the stairs and I bundled him off the bus just as Clancy caught up with me. We took him over to a doorway to take cover while the back-up arrived. I can't remember where it was, but I seem to recall that we were still on Andersonstown Road.

All of a sudden, there was Rent-a-Mob around us. There were women and all sorts around us, and there we are stranded and waiting for the back-up to arrive, but Tony W******** managed to get lost; he took a wrong turning somewhere and lost his way, so there's all these people around us and Clancy pulls out his bayonet and starts waving it about and he said: *"If anyone comes near us, I'll cut their fucking throat."* Eventually Tony turned up and then all hell broke loose and we had a big riot on our hands; but anyway, we got him back to the RUC Station, but it was a bit of a scary one that patrol.

Gnr Clancy Campbell, 3 Troop
We jumped on the bus after the Provo and 'Davey' ran upstairs after him while I tried to get the conductor to stop the bus. I was screaming at him that I was in the army and I ordered him to ring the bell and stop the bus, but he refused. All the conductors were Catholics and they hated us, and I suppose that's why he wouldn't stop the bus, so I starts wrestling with him and he pushes me off and I'm lying there dumped in the road. I got up and started running down the road after the bus, and a bit further on it got held up by traffic and I was able to catch it up. I got back on just as 'Davey' was dragging the Provo downstairs, and between us we dragged him off and waited for the back-up to catch us up. We had to take cover in a doorway after the locals spotted us and started to gather around. I pulled out my bayonet and started waving it about to keep them back. At times they seemed more frightened by the sight of that than my .32 pistol.

The day wasn't over for 'Davey' S******* though. That night he was back out on patrol and ended up being caught up in some serious rioting. The risks involved when driving around in the armoured Pigs, with the back doors wide open, once again became evident…

We went back out in uniform that night. I can't remember where we went, but we had to go where they were causing a stink. I was in BSM Don Potter's Pig, and at first they weren't sure if it was a low-velocity bullet or a ball-bearing fired with a catapult that hit me, but I got hit. We had caught this guy on the other patrol when I was out with Clancy, and that was when all this rioting kicked off – and when we went back out, we were caught up in all this rioting again. They took me to Musgrave Park Hospital and I was later told that while I was in hospital my flak jacket was returned to 'T' Battery Quarters and stood against a wall covered in blood. Harry W****** walked in and spotted it and said: *"Whose is that flak jacket?"*

I can't remember who they said it was, but I seem to remember they said it was Dick D*****'s. They told me he said something like: *"That's 'Davey' S*******'s; that'll teach him to go over to 9 Battery looking for a bit of the action."*

Well, Harry W****** went absolutely bananas at that and was going to punch Dick for being so callous about it.

In actual fact 'Davey' had been hit on the back of the head by a rock, or some other missile, which had been thrown in the rioting. He was knocked unconscious and sent sprawling between the seats in the back of the Pig. His injury was considered serious enough for him to be kept in hospital until the following afternoon. Not long after 'Davey' and Clancy made the arrest on the bus, the Provisional IRA were sufficiently concerned about the tactics being used by *Basset-Hound* to issue a veiled warning to those soldiers involved. As was usually the case, they claimed that the patrols were targeting the youths. The reality was that several of their top men had been taken off the streets and it was affecting their ability to carry on with their terror campaign. The following article appeared in issue no.22 of the Provo newspaper *The Volunteer*:

ARMY SENDING OUT 'CLAY PIGEONS'

For the past week Saracens entering the Andersonstown Estate have had on board two men in either track suits or jacket and jeans. The reason? To chase, and catch youths who stone them. These men, who are obviously Privates, are clay pigeons being used by 'Army Brass' to draw IRA fire. We call on the 'TOMMYS' to refuse these suicide missions in future.*

* Source taken from *The Volunteer* (issue no.22).

The front page of *The Volunteer* news sheet which carried the warning. (Taken from *The Volunteer*)

TUESDAY 7th…

Everyone at the bus depot had been put on high alert for the impending funeral of Provo bomber Albert Kavanagh. The main gates of the cemetery had been the scene of scuffles at previous IRA funerals, and this one wasn't expected to be any different. Patrols had gone out and taken up their usual positions in the ditch by the side of the cemetery close to the IRA burial plot. Another patrol was up by the bowling green just inside the park. Army photographers were positioned on the roof of the old house at the bus depot to record those who attended.

1,000 MARCH IN IRA FUNERAL

Nearly 1,000 people marched in military fashion behind an IRA funeral in Belfast this afternoon. It was that of Albert Kavanagh, who was shot dead by police after he had planted a bomb at the Olympia factory near Tates Avenue, Belfast last Saturday morning.

The Security Forces thought the funeral procession would make its way from his home in Cavendish Street and then go straight up the Falls to Milltown Cemetery.

In all surrounding side streets there was a big concentration of army and police. Local people claimed this was the first time that police had been seen inside the Beechmount area for several months.

Kavanagh's coffin was covered with a tricolour and eight members of Fianna Axirann marched on either side of his hearse. They wore dark glasses, green shirts and green berets. Behind the hearse walked about 40 girls carrying wreaths and floral tributes.

In the main body of the funeral, another 30 uniformed members of Fianna Eireann marched, answering marching orders.

Army cameramen were everywhere, in side streets off Oakman Street, Beechmount Avenue, the Falls Road, on top of the Broadway cinema and at the bus depot opposite the gates of Milltown Cemetery.

The funeral had taken an alternative route via Oakman Street and Beechmount Avenue because of heavy army concentration near the Royal Victoria Hospital. Hundreds of women walked alongside the procession.[*]

[*] Sourced from Brian Corser's private collection of newspaper cuttings.

The funeral of Albert Kavanagh. (Courtesy of Brian Corser)

Looking down from the sangar in front of the RUC Station, all that could be seen was two rows of mourners lining the Falls Road. Access to Glen Road was blocked by crowds of Republican sympathisers as the mourners lined up from Divis Drive to the gates of the cemetery. This was, by far, the biggest turnout for a Provo funeral that had ever been witnessed by the men of 9 Battery. The soldiers kept their distance and the funeral passed off without incident.

WEDNESDAY 8th...

At around 3:15 a.m. a Volvo saloon had just turned off the M1 motorway at Stockmans Lane when it was shot at by a lone Provo gunman who may have mistaken it for an RUC patrol car. Fortunately for the driver, the bullets missed their target.

VICTIMS OF THE TROUBLES WHO DIED THIS DAY...

L/Cpl Joseph Jardine (44) – 3rd Battalion, The Ulster Defence Regiment. Shot at his workplace by the Provisional IRA, Middletown, County Armagh.
Eamon Gamble (27) – Unknown Republican terrorist group. Died one month after being injured in a bomb blast at a temporary council office, Keady, County Armagh.*

* List compiled from *The Troubles* Magazine (Glenravel Publications).

THURSDAY 9th…

At around 6:00 a.m. a large search was carried out on the Riverdale Estate as the battery tried to add to their already impressive tally of weapons and explosives found during the tour, but on this occasion all they had to show for their efforts were a few rounds of 9mm and .30 cal ammunition. At 3:15 p.m. a large lift operation was mounted in the Rossnareen area. As the units moved up Glen Road, they were subjected to heavy stoning as they turned into Ramoan Gardens. The youths were lined up and waiting on either side of the road as the Pigs made their way down to Rossnareen Avenue.

Gnr Steve Corbett, 3 Troop
I started firing at them with the riot gun, and I got three hits with my first five shots – I was quite chuffed about that – and then I fired another and it shattered a plate-glass window in someone's house. As we pulled away, I fired two more shots and scored one more hit.

The whole operation from leaving base had lasted a little over 30 minutes.

VICTIMS OF THE TROUBLES WHO DIED THIS DAY…

Gerard Crossen (19) – Provisional IRA. Killed when a bomb he was assembling in a house blew up in Clonard Street, Lower Falls, Belfast.

Anthony Lewis ((16) – Provisional IRA. Killed in the same incident.

Sean Johnson ((19) – Provisional IRA. Killed in the same incident.

Thomas McCann (20) – Provisional IRA. Killed in the same incident.*

* List compiled from *The Troubles* Magazine (Glenravel Publications).

FRIDAY 10th…

As the deadline approached for the IRA truce to be held from midnight, there was an upsurge in violence as the Provos launched attacks against troops, civilians and commercial targets. Hopes were rising that there just may be an end in sight to all the killing. It had been estimated that since January the Provos had used around 2,400lbs of explosives in their bombing campaign since the start of the year.

SATURDAY 11th...

In Belfast, a youth was shot in the hand after being abducted by three armed men who called at his home, and a bomb exploded on waste ground in the Protestant Shankill area. In the city centre, the RUC received a warning that a car bomb had been left in North Street. Army bomb disposal experts blew open the boot of the Ford Corsair, which was found to be empty. Several shoppers scattered at the sound of the explosion – thinking that it was yet another bomb going off. In Newry, a landmine was detonated in front of an army mobile patrol; and in Londonderry, an army patrol came under fire from gunmen. Back in Andersonstown, there were minor disturbances in Bingnian Drive when gangs of youths started stoning a mobile patrol.

The BC had recently given one of his pep talks to the men and he claimed that the battery had given the Provos such a hard time in Andersonstown that they were close to collapse; they were finding it almost impossible to continue with their attacks on the battery. Many of the men found it hard to believe, but some wondered if there was some connection with this and the proposed IRA ceasefire.

At around 8:00 p.m. a ferocious gun battle was heard by several sentries at the bus depot. They reported that it appeared to be in the vicinity of the Royal Victoria Hospital. It started off with a few single shots – probably from snipers – and then the sound of shots from SLRs were heard, followed by long bursts of automatic fire. The shooting lasted for several minutes before it finally died away. At around 9:00 p.m. an arms search was carried out in Rossnareen Avenue by several units from the battery. The women came out and started banging away with their dustbin lids as the search team entered properties in their hunt for weapons. For the whole duration of the search, the rattling of the lids continued and a mighty cheer rang out as the search teams finally pulled out.

SUNDAY 12th...

By now the advance party from 2nd Field Regiment had arrived. The men were divided between the individual troops and they were taken out to be shown the areas they would be expected to patrol for the next four months. The IRA truce was holding, although there had been a few incidents throughout the Province. To the men of 9 Battery, the three-day ceasefire so close to the end of the tour was an absolute godsend. The Roman Catholic Primate of Ireland claimed that the ceasefire was: "A step in the right direction"* but there had still been no reaction from the British and Irish Governments. The Protestant Orange Order issued a statement calling on the army to start claiming back the No-Go areas that had been set up in some Republican areas.

---

*   Source taken from *The Troubles* Magazine (Glenravel Publications).

VICTIMS OF THE TROUBLES WHO DIED THIS DAY...

Bernadette Hyndman (24) – Killed by the Official IRA when they launched an attack on an army foot patrol in Abyssinia Street, Lower Falls, Belfast.*

* List compiled from *The Troubles* Magazine (Glenravel Publications).

MONDAY 13th...

At around 12:00 p.m. 3 Troop were put on five-minute standby in readiness for the funeral of the Provo bombers who had blown themselves to bits on 9 March. Back in Dublin, talks were being held to discuss peace proposals, although the Provisional IRA claimed the terms of the truce were being ignored.

IRA TRUCE TERMS IGNORED BY BRITISH GOVERNMENT

The Opposition Leader, Mr Wilson, has arrived in Dublin for talks with Mr Jack Lynch and other political leaders, as the Provisional IRA was threatening to renew its campaign at the end of its 72-hour truce at midnight. At the same time it is expected that the British Cabinet, now said to be seriously split over the Northern Ireland peace plan, will meet over the next few days to consider the situation.

The IRA's 'truce terms' have been ignored by the British Government and Mr Rory Brady, President of Provisional Sinn Féin, said today that he believed that the campaign would be renewed. He denied that the truce had been called because the Provisionals were running out of explosives.*

* Source taken from *The Troubles* Magazine (Glenravel Publications).

As the politicians tried to reach a solution, those who were tasked with trying to keep the peace were heading out on another lift operation in Andersonstown. Two Pigs made their way up Rossnareen Avenue to arrest another suspect. The lead vehicle of 3 Troop was providing cover for the snatch squad from 2 Troop, whose task it was to make the actual arrest. As they turned into Rossnareen Avenue, both vehicles immediately came under attack from a large mob of rioters.

The crew of the rear Pig dismounted and forced their way into the suspect's house, while 3 Troop did their best to hold the crowd at bay. In a matter of minutes the vehicles were pulling away with their prisoner. As the vehicles turned into Shaw's Road, a bomb was thrown at the rear Pig, but it failed to explode. Coming down Andersonstown Road, they were attacked again when another bomb was thrown at the front Pig. That too failed to explode. The whole operation had lasted just a few minutes.

VICTIMS OF THE TROUBLES WHO DIED THIS DAY...

Patrick McCrory (19) – Shot dead by the Ulster Volunteer Force at his home in Ravenhill Avenue, Belfast.*

* List compiled from *The Troubles* Magazine (Glenravel Publications).

TUESDAY 14th...

Shortly after midnight, the IRA signalled the end of their 72-hour truce by detonating several bombs in the city centre. Three bombs went off between 0010 hrs and 0045 hrs. As preparations continued for the imminent arrival of 2nd Field Regiment, a mobile patrol from 3 Troop went up to Holywood Barracks to bring back a fleet of Macralon-armoured Land Rovers which the new battery would be using in place of the Humber Pigs. As they arrived in the compound, they were viewed with horror by the rest of the men of 9 Battery – the general opinion being that if the Pigs couldn't stop an armour-piercing round, these things would offer no protection at all! There had been a bit of excitement earlier in the day when a man and young girl were driving up Glen Road. A gunman swerved in front of them in his car and opened fire on the occupants – hitting the man in the back. It appears that as soon as he saw the gunman, he swung his car around – and that was how he came to be shot in the back. Despite his injuries, he managed to drive on to Andersonstown RUC Station and was then taken by ambulance to hospital in a very serious condition. Most of the windows in his car had been shot out, so he was very lucky to get hit only once and escape with his life.

VICTIMS OF THE TROUBLES WHO DIED THIS DAY...

Colm Keenan (19) – Provisional IRA. Killed in a gun battle between the IRA and British troops. The IRA later tried to claim that he was not involved in the gun battle. Shot dead in an entry, Dove Gardens, Bogside, Derry. Eugene McGillan (18) – Provisional IRA. Killed in the same incident.*

* List compiled from *The Troubles* Magazine (Glenravel Publications).

WEDNESDAY 15th...

The end of the tour was now only a matter of hours away. The strain on everyone over the past few days had been terrible. Late in the afternoon, a huge bomb had been detonated in Sandy Row, Belfast. The 200lb device caused substantial damage over a wide area. The explosion was so loud that some of the men of 9 Battery actually thought the device had gone off in Falls Park at the back of the depot. The patrols around Andersonstown continued as the men kept the pressure on the Provos to the very end of the tour. That evening, the men of 3 Troop went out on a mobile / foot patrol. The vehicles made their way up to Rossnareen and dropped off the foot patrol, who then set off for their first objective.

Gnr Steve Corbett, 3 Troop

I always remember this incident because it was probably the worst patrol I ever did in the whole of the tour. We had gone out with Lieutenant Smith from 2nd Field. He was part of the advance party for the battery that was taking over from us the next day. Our instructions were to go to this house and lift some bloke of interest to Intelligence. After we had got him, he was to be put in the Pig while we moved in on foot to the next objective.

We got the first house done without any problem, and then we made our way to the next house. Lieutenant Smith decided to send the Pigs up into the estate to have a drive around, while we went into this other house. By the time we got to it, the locals already knew we were in the area and the crowds started to gather. Lieutenant Smith went inside to conduct the search and make the arrest. He left me and another lad at the front of the house, while the rest went inside. By this time, the youths had started throwing all kinds of stuff at us; there was the usual bricks and even iron bars coming our way. I tried to take cover, but there was really nowhere to go, so I knelt down on the path at the side of the house and held my rifle directly in front of me with the butt of the gun on the ground and the barrel pointing in the air and in front of my face.

I have to admit that at that moment, I was absolutely terrified. I really thought this was going to be it for me. The Pigs were nowhere in sight and there was nowhere for us to run. Just then, a house brick hit the barrel of my rifle. It was thrown with such force that the brick broke in two and the pieces went either side of my face. Only for the rifle being in front of me, I'm sure it might have killed me if it had hit me because it was thrown with such force; then the Pigs finally turned up. Lieutenant Smith and the rest of the team came out of the house and we all made a dash for the vehicles. I made my way into the back vehicle with a lad from the RCT. He was only out with us to learn the routes through the estates for 2nd Field and he had been with us for just a few days.

We got in the back and I pulled one door shut and he saw to the other. We were still under attack from the rioters – and they were that close we didn't dare leave the doors open. The RCT lad had his hand through the observation slit in the door as he pulled it shut, and then a brick caught him and took off part of his finger. It was a right bloody mess, but looking on the bright side, it probably kept him out of action for several weeks – and I don't think he would have complained about that too much. As for Lieutenant Smith, I got the impression that he just didn't have a clue what to do, but on reflection, I suppose that was probably how we all were when we first came over. You learn by your mistakes, but unfortunately some soldiers never got the chance to do that.

VICTIMS OF THE TROUBLES WHO DIED THIS DAY...

William Logan (23) – The Royal Ulster Constabulary. Shot dead by the Provisional IRA while on mobile patrol, Brackaville Road, Coalisland, County Tyrone.

S/Sgt Christopher Cracknell (29) – The Royal Army Ordnance Corps. Killed in a bomb explosion in Grosvenor Road, Belfast while trying to make safe a 20lb bomb left on the back seat of a car by the Provisional IRA. He had blown the boot of the car open in a controlled explosion, but it failed to set off the main charge. When he approached the car, it blew up.

Sgt Anthony Butcher (24) – The Royal Army Ordnance Corps. Killed in the same incident.*

* List compiled from *The Troubles* Magazine (Glenravel Publications).

THURSDAY 16th...

The final day of the tour had been reached without anyone from the battery being killed. The men were already starting to relax a little – their ordeal almost over – and knowing that in just a few hours they would be on their way back home. The last four months had been absolute hell, but the regiment – and, in particular, 9 (Plassey) Battery – had much to be proud of. The last operations of the tour were being undertaken just a few hours before the return to England, and then the task of 'keeping the peace' in Andersonstown was handed over to the men of 2nd Field Regiment.

Gnr Steve Corbett, 3 Troop

I cannot begin to describe how it felt to reach the end of the tour in one piece. I took part in the very last operation carried out by 3 Troop in Andersonstown. It was a lift operation on the Riverdale Estate. We got the man without any trouble and were back at base for 6:35 a.m. At 8:00 a.m. I did my last guard duty and then just relaxed and waited until around lunchtime, when we set off for Musgrave Park Hospital to meet up with the men from 2nd Field. I handed over my flak jacket to one of them and a magazine with 10 rounds of ammo. We had to keep some back just in case we needed them on the journey to the docks.

Gnr Pete Hodkinson, HQ Battery

I think, for me, the last few days of the tour felt very uncomfortable; they seemed to drag by ever so slowly... It just became a more nerve-wracking time. It was a hell of a relief to get away from Palace Barracks and down to the docks without incident and on board the ship. When we set sail and I looked at Belfast as it became smaller, I just wanted a quiet corner to collect my own thoughts and thank God for watching over me.

L/Bdr 'Ginger' Robertson, 2 Troop

I remember returning to England on the ship at the end of the tour. Once we were mustered aboard, we all had to partake in a lifeboat drill and identify our respective muster stations. Afterwards there was a group of us playing 'Brag' – including 'Horace'. I raised a bottle and we all gave a toast to absent friends... Renzo Agnello, Johnny Sutton, Brian Kingsnorth and Fred Jeffreys... who were all lying badly injured in hospital. One other thought that I did have when we were sailing back to Liverpool on our return from Belfast was that I don't remember anyone saying that they were glad to be leaving the Troubles... and that they felt safer now. It was clear to me that we all had become inured to the daily grind and, in the best army tradition, just got on and dealt with it.

Gnr Steve Corbett, 3 Troop

At 3:30 p.m. we pulled out of Belfast and were taken down to the docks in a fleet of Bedford 3-tonners. On the way down I heard a huge explosion somewhere in the city centre. I often wondered how many of us would actually get through that tour, and we were very fortunate that none of us were killed. Poor Johnny Sutton was, by far, the worst injured and was very lucky to survive. That last night we spent in Andersonstown was probably the worst. Reports came through that five army posts had been shot up and bombed by the IRA. I had got this far without serious injury and I was worried sick that my luck may run out at the last moment. We got to the docks and boarded the *Sir Galahad* – and a short time later, we pulled out of the dock. A piper played a salute to us as we sailed out, and it was at that point I finally began to relax. I spent a lot of time up on deck as we headed towards Liverpool and thanked God for getting me out of Belfast in one piece. After we got back to England and returned to camp, I can honestly say that I never gave Northern Ireland another thought until I was warned for service again in 1974. Obviously I saw all the reports on TV and in the papers, but as for my own tour over there, I was able to completely switch off and put it all out of my mind for quite a few years.

VICTIMS OF THE TROUBLES WHO DIED THIS DAY...

Carmel Knox (20) – Killed by a Loyalist terrorist group when a bomb exploded in a public toilet. Market Street, Lurgan, County Armagh.*

* List compiled from *The Troubles* Magazine (Glenravel Publications).

Between November 1971 and March 1972, 9 (Plassey) Battery had crippled both the Official and Provisional IRA in Andersonstown. During their four-month tour of operations, they had arrested a record-breaking number of members. Their tally included 30 officers, 46 volunteers and countless members of the youth wing of the IRA, who were actively involved in the movement of weapons; explosives; and the organisation and involvement in rioting and other attacks launched against the Security Forces in Andersonstown. They also found large quantities of arms, ammunition and explosives. This was a testament to their highly effective intelligence network, which they had set up themselves. Although the residents of Andersonstown were glad to see the battery leave at the end of their tour, there were others in the surrounding districts who were full of gratitude for their efforts to keep the peace on the streets of Northern Ireland.

Afterword

The men and women of the terrorist organisations they fought against are now largely free to roam – safe in the knowledge that they will not be prosecuted for their terrible crimes. For the sake of the 'peace process' they were given immunity – and meanwhile, these same people still seek to put on trial British soldiers whose only real crime was to try and keep the peace on the streets of Northern Ireland under extremely difficult and trying circumstances.

This book is intended as a lasting tribute to the men of 9 (Plassey) Battery – and indeed to every member of 12th Regiment, Royal Artillery who served in Northern Ireland at that time – and to give future generations a sense of the hostility and danger that we, and every British soldier, faced while trying to keep the peace in the Province.

The following letter was received by the battery from the grateful residents of Finaghy Baptist Church, Black's Road, Belfast:

A FAREWELL PRESENTATION FROM FINAGHY BAPTIST CHURCH, BLACK'S ROAD, BELFAST

We greatly appreciate all that the army do on behalf of our Province. Many thanks for your share in it. God bless you every one.

And in another letter sent to the battery…

Dear Sir,
There are many groups of praying people all over this Province who would like our troops to know we love them, sympathise with them, admire their magnificent discipline and courage, and are intensely grateful for all they do for our protection. We are so proud of you all.

Some groups meet daily for prayer. All of us believe that our God, in whom we trust, is shortly going to deliver us, and glorify himself.

With heartfelt gratitude.

"Thanks be unto God which giveth us the victory through our Lord Jesus Christ."*

On Regimental Part 1 Orders came the following tributes for the regiment on their return to England, for the exceptional way they had undertaken their

---

* The source of this letter remains anonymous.

peacekeeping duties in Northern Ireland. This tour was considered to be probably the finest ever carried out in the Province:

Lieutenant-General Sir Harry Tuzo KCB OBE MC, General Officer Commanding Northern Ireland

Contrary to my hopes, it looks as if I shall not be able to catch sight of you again before you leave, so this letter must serve to tell you how very greatly I have admired the performance of your regiment during a particularly arduous tour in Belfast. Indeed, as a Colonel Commandant Royal Artillery, I am proud of you and I believe you have set a standard which others will be hard put to follow.

You were certainly confronted with the toughest nut and you have made great progress in cracking it. With any luck we shall get to the kernel very soon indeed thanks to your splendid work.

I hope that you will now all enjoy your leave, which you have so amply earned, and that you will get back refreshed to the important tasks that confront you as part of our very slender Air Defence resources. You will have plenty to do and a mass of interesting techniques to master, but even in the midst of all this activity you may occasionally cast a nostalgic eye towards some of the activities you pursued in Belfast and the peculiar atmosphere in which they were carried out. You can be quite sure that we shall miss you greatly.

Major-General R.C. Ford CBE, Commander Land Forces Northern Ireland

For CO from CLF, I am sorry that I was unable to say farewell to 9, 58, and 'T' Batteries. My deepest gratitude and heartiest congratulations to you and all ranks for your extremely hard work over the past four months. Your area has been probably the most difficult one in Northern Ireland and I have nothing but the highest praise for the extremely efficient manner in which you have handled it. Very well done all ranks. My very best wishes to you all for the future.

Brigadier F.E. Kitson CBE MC, Commander 39 Infantry Brigade

Personal for Commanding Officer from Commander: On your departure I would like to thank you and your regiment for the outstanding contribution you have made towards maintaining the peace during your tour in Belfast and towards destroying the IRA in your area. You are to be congratulated on keeping your casualties to a minimum in spite of a high degree of operational activity – and this, undoubtedly, reflects on the high standard of operational efficiency of all ranks. I have been particularly impressed with the way you have developed your intelligence organisation at regimental and battery level, which frequently led to many of your numerous successes in arresting men and finds of arms and ammunition. Great credit for your success is due to all ranks who have worked so hard and well and have always been noticeably cheerful. The best of luck to you all in the future.

Brigadier C.P. Campbell, Commander 12 Engineer Brigade and Barton Stacey Station

I know that I am expressing the feeling of everyone in Barton Stacey when I say how glad to see you and your regiment back home again.

We have all followed the reports of your tour in Northern Ireland with great interest and we have been full of admiration for the success you have had in unearthing arms caches during search operations.

When I arrived here to take over from Brigadier Len Garret, I heard many reports of the thorough way in which your unit prepared for operating in the infantry role. It is quite obvious that your insistence on 'playing for real' during training has paid handsome dividends.

My sincerest congratulations to you and to everyone in your regiment.

Although these tributes recognise the successful tour of 12th Regiment as a whole, the majority of operational awards went to 9 (Plassey) Battery in recognition of their outstanding achievements. They were given the most difficult task – Andersonstown: 'The toughest nut' – and they gave it their all, as these pages have shown.

The men of 9 (Plassey) Battery after their return from Northern Ireland.
(Courtesy of Steve Corbett)